NO REMORSE

Betty's nightgown clung to her as sweat and Wayne's blood ran down her body, the stench of gunpowder filling her nostrils. Blood poured through the open star-shaped wounds in the back of her husband's head where she'd just fired three shots of her .38-caliber Colt revolver.

Eager to wash the blood from her hands, Betty went into the bathroom, exchanging the sopping nightgown for an old T-shirt. After tucking the sheets of green plastic around Wayne's body, she stuffed the dead weight into a blue canvas sleeping bag. With a healthy push, the body tumbled off the bed and landed with a *thud*.

Little by little, she dragged the gruesome package into the closet and closed the door. The body safely hidden, she scrubbed away every last trace of her husband and his murder before returning to bed.

Without remorse or guilt to trouble her, Betty fell soundly asleep.

Other books by Irene Pence

A CLUE FROM THE GRAVE

TRIANGLE

Published by Pinnacle Books

BURIED
MEMORIES

IRENE PENCE

PINNACLE BOOKS
Kensington Publishing Corp.
http://www.pinnaclebooks.com

PINNACLE BOOKS are published by

Kensington Publishing Corp.
850 Third Avenue
New York, NY 10022

All Kensington Titles, Imprints, and Distributed Lines are available at special quantity discounts for bulk purchases for sales promotions, premiums, fund-raising, and educational or institutional use. Special book excerpts or customized printings can also be created to fit specific needs. For details, write or phone the office of the Kensington special sales manager: Kensington Publishing Corp., 850 Third Avenue, New York, NY 10022, attn: Special Sales Department, Phone: 1-800-221-2647.

Pinnacle and the P logo Reg. U.S. Pat. & TM Off.

First Printing: March 2001
10 9 8 7 6 5 4 3

Printed in the United States of America

For
Mark, Laurie, and Lisa,
who were raised with love,
and are loving adults

ONE

Rick Rose hadn't slept for three days. As the chief criminal investigator for the Henderson County Sheriff, he had spent that time taking statements and searching for evidence. But the dark-haired, ex-Green Beret's job wasn't over yet. In fact, it had just begun.

Shaded by towering oaks in a heavily forested yard, the DA's chief investigator, Michael O'Brien, stood beside Rose as they waited impatiently to see how their hunch played out. The subdivision, called Cherokee Shores, bordered on the twenty-mile-long Cedar Creek Lake in north Texas. The yard sat on an inlet to the lake, and the air was claustrophobic with humidity.

Both men, handsome, tall, muscular, and in their late thirties, had seen action in Vietnam. Now the area in front of them resembled a battlefield with the uniformed men and all the equipment.

"Sure didn't take you long to get the warrant," Rose said.

"You did the groundwork," O'Brien replied. "I just had to convince Judge Holland we had enough probable cause to dig up somebody's yard."

"Digging's a little more intrusive than knocking on someone's door. But we're not exactly doing this with smoke and mirrors. The judge knows by now we'd only take him hearsay we can back up."

"Just the same," O'Brien said, "it's hearsay, and our

informants aren't all that credible. Think about it, we don't have a shot-glassful of physical evidence."

O'Brien glanced at the road running in front of the property. "Look at all those rubberneckers out there. It's going to be embarrassing if we tip over the wishing well and nothing's there."

"If that well's empty, I know a couple lawmen who've stuck their necks out for nothing."

"And there's a district judge who'll think twice before giving us another evidentiary search warrant."

"Let's be positive. I've got that warrant right here," Rose said, patting his shirt pocket. "Nobody can keep us from digging up Betty Lou Beets's yard, and we won't stop 'til we find what we're looking for."

"If it's here."

"Right," Rose replied thoughtfully, "if it's here."

Rose and O'Brien made a good team. Rose had great energy and a dry wit. He acted as the unofficial spokesman for the sheriff's office, and possessed the tenacity to keep trying to solve a case long after others had dropped the ball. O'Brien had a calm demeanor and a quick mind. His photographic memory gave him the ability to remember a crime's minute details, even years later. The legal side of issues was his forte.

While they waited for deputies to unload the backhoe from a flatbed truck, Rose's gaze wandered past the fifty feet of trees, past the inlet, and to the blue waters of Cedar Creek Lake. Sixty miles south of Dallas, the 34,000-acre, man-made lake sat tucked inside the east Texas greenbelt of pine, yaupon holly, and stately oaks. The towns ringing its shores wore colorful names: Enchanted Oaks, Payne Springs, and Star Harbor. But tonight, on June 8, 1985, the action was taking place here in Gun Barrel City.

The wheels of the backhoe touched ground and Rose hurriedly gulped his Coke. Even with his lack of sleep, he didn't need the caffeine, for his knees were already knocking as he went to search for his boss, Sheriff Charlie Fields.

Deputies and investigators clustered around their sheriff, who wore his trademark white Stetson.

Fields looked up at Rose and said, "I understand Mike wants to start with the wishing well?"

Rose nodded.

"I have seven deputies here now," Fields said, "and more are on their way."

For eighteen hours the day before, Rose had Deputy Ron Shields sitting in a car in front of this lot that held a seventy-foot-long trailer. The trailer had mysteriously burst into flames the night before last. Immediately after the fire, fire marshals had taped off the home, but that wasn't enough to keep out anyone bent on getting inside and disrupting evidence. Or removing bodies for that matter.

Now the last rays of the afternoon sun caught the home's front and back decks, which were laden with pots of flowers—some hanging, others clustered on the deck floor. Someone had removed all the weeds from the pots and flower beds, and apparently snipped off any tired blossoms, for only fresh blooms remained. Rose couldn't imagine anyone having that kind of patience with flowers. He brushed by the purple petunias that spilled from a brick-and-wood wishing well in the front yard, and went to talk to police.

"Good, you're about finished stringing the crime-scene tape," he told an officer. "Without that, all those people in the street would be up here as soon as we started digging."

The officer continued taping the entire yard, saying,

"Like the manual says, 'Secure the crime scene.' We've got to keep the curious at bay."

"If we find anything," Rose said, "the curious will want to jump *in* the bay. When we start digging up graves, it won't be pretty."

Any Saturday in June at six P.M. would normally find people racing across the sparkling lake on their motor boats, water skis, or bouncing over waves on their Sea-Dos. Instead, they were watching deputies begin a search. The men had been there an hour, with the temperature still hovering at a sweat-inducing one hundred degrees. They photographed the crime scene and waited for field agent Charles Linch with the Southwestern Institute of Forensic Science. O'Brien had called him before turning over one spadeful of dirt, but it would take Linch more than an hour to drive down from Dallas to lend a scientific hand.

Finally, the young-looking, mustached Charles Linch emerged from his van and went directly to O'Brien and Rose.

"Everything ready to get started?" Linch asked.

"More than ready," O'Brien said, and signaled the driver to climb aboard the bright yellow backhoe. He put the machine in gear and started clawing at the four-foot-square wishing well. Its ladle scraped the redbrick base, then rose to latch on to the four-foot-high top edge of the brown wooden surround. As the backhoe inched forward, nails pulled from the wood and every joint creaked. Then the whole thing fell over, crashing with a thud as dirt and plants splattered everywhere.

Even with the media's widespread use of police scanners, the quick arrival of reporters at this out-of-the-way spot on Red Bluff Loop surprised law enforcement. A helicopter from Channel Eight in Dallas landed two lots down on the street. Reporters had flown in on another helicopter from Tyler's Channel Seven and the *Tyler*

Morning Telegraph. There was also a scattering of corre-
spondents from the *Athens Daily Review,* the *Cedar Creek
Pilot,* and the *Dallas Morning News.* The journalists had
all heard the bizarre rumors, and now waited to see
what would actually unfold.

Rose motioned to three gloved men to bring their
shovels and follow him to the well. "Let's be careful
because we're not sure what we'll find. Just take off a
little dirt at a time. He's probably under the ground,
but we're not positive."

As the men began turning the moist soil, Rose paced
back and forth. All he could see was dirt. Judge Holland
had a record of almost twenty years on the bench, so
he didn't have that much to lose if the search proved
fruitless. But this was Rose's first year here as a homicide
investigator, and he wanted to prove he was no rookie.
He had spent a total of thirteen years in law enforcement, much of it working for the district attorney in
Dallas. Here in Henderson County, he had an opportunity to solve a case that had lain dormant for two years.
In the three years he'd worked for the sheriff, he had
arrested over two hundred drug dealers and had broken
a gun burglary ring that put his reputation on the map.

Reddish-brown dirt flew from the deputies' shovels,
and perspiration dripped from their faces, while their
shirts stuck to their skin. Periodically, they stopped to
wipe off their faces and necks.

After digging a foot, one of the deputy's shovels hit
something hard. He jerked back his shovel, and turned
to Rose. "What's that?"

Rose squatted and brushed away dirt with his gloved
hand. "Looks like wood. Get this thing cleared off and
let's see what we have."

The deputy hurriedly scooped away the soil. Rose
handed him a whisk broom and the man dusted off the
remaining residue.

Irene Pence

Then Rose tapped on a roughly cut piece of plywood, about three-feet square. "Isn't this interesting? Where's Ben? Has anyone seen Deputy Ashley?"

A deputy came running. "Here, sir. I was reloading my camera."

"Good. I want you to get a picture of this. We want to show how premeditated it was. Here, get in close," Rose said, stepping out of the way. "I want that jury to see how someone cut that piece of wood especially for the well."

After Ashley took several photos, Rose bent over and wedged his fingers under the edge of the wood plank and pried it up. A dank, old-house mustiness floated up. Dirt had seeped under the wood and the men began gently digging with claw hammers.

The deputies removed another clump of soil, and a piece of blue canvas came into view. Momentarily, there was awestruck silence.

"Well, I'll be damned," Rose murmured. "He's here. Everyone told me he was buried under the well, but we're still inside the well's foundation."

Rose bent over and examined the fabric. "Two years of dirt hasn't affected its blue color. Take your time, guys, because this is it."

A cheer went up from the men, and the humid night became electric. With high fives and confidence, the men returned to their job, but now they didn't stop to wipe off perspiration.

Following Rose's orders, they tried to stem their enthusiasm, and worked slowly so they wouldn't disturb or damage the evidence. Little by little they dug, then dusted away the loose soil. The piece of blue fabric broadened and lengthened.

Rose again motioned to Deputy Ashley. "Now we need a shot of every step. Let's set up a progression of photos so we can show exactly how this thing looks."

"Yes, sir," Ashley replied, and attempted to move closer to the grave. He gingerly stepped between the other deputies, who were still digging, and steadied his camera.

For half an hour, they carefully bailed out dirt, following the contour of their discovery. Then they uncovered a brass zipper sewn into the cloth, and they realized it was a sleeping bag. The bulk of the material gave every indication that it was not empty, and the way the canvas curved suggested that the body inside had curled into a fetal position.

Now everything happened quickly. Rose remembered his earlier doubt, and it rapidly faded. He dared to believe that he had the evidence to force a jury to find the defendant guilty beyond all reasonable doubt. Then, being a realist, he reminded himself of previous cases where curious neighbors had claimed they saw someone being buried, only to have police come out and dig up a family's beloved German shepherd.

Linch got down on his hands and knees to scrutinize the find. Peering underneath, he found a mud-caked hole. He glanced up at the spilled vines and flowers that still clung to the well's ruptured interior.

"Looks like two years of flower watering rotted the bag," Linch said.

He pointed out the hole to O'Brien and Rose. "Once the bag is removed, we need to get someone over here to sift the soil and check for anything that may have worked its way out."

Meticulously, Linch examined every detail of the sleeping bag and requested more photographs. An hour after his arrival, he nodded to Deputy Rose. "Give me a hand here, Rick, and we'll put the body on a gurney."

Once the dirt-laden sleeping bag was in position, O'Brien paused for a moment to inhale, then held his breath and tugged hard on the zipper. A strong, sick-

ening-sweet odor permeated the night air. Despite all of
their experience and mental preparation, the sight of a
human skull staring at them appalled the investigators.
The skull and the rest of the bones were brown, con-
taminated by the decomposition process. Sparse strands
of dark hair still clung to the top of the skull, and bits
and pieces of tissue remained, especially the nose. Rose
could actually imagine the victim's profile.

More noticeably, he saw pink and white upper den-
tures still tucked into place. In the absence of lips, the
teeth lent the impression of an uninterrupted, macabre
smile.

If Rose's information was correct, it had to be the
skeletal remains of forty-six-year-old Jimmy Don Beets. A
fact that forensics would prove true a few days later.

Linch reached for the skull. He curiously fingered a
hole near its side. "This is a bullet hole," he said calmly.

TWO

The news flew out to the reporters as quickly as a storm could blow across the lake. The investigators had found the remains of Jimmy Don Beets, and he had indeed been murdered.

Suddenly, thousands of residents in the nine chain-linked lake communities remembered that night back on August 5, 1983. Almost two years earlier.

As dusk settled over Cedar Creek Lake, the sky took on canvas-painted pink and coral hues, promising another beautiful sunset. Impressive homes circled the lake, some with as many as eight bedrooms, and just as many baths. Behind those were more modest homes, followed by acceptable trailers on wooded lots, and down the pecking order to rusted trailers that sat anywhere they could find a plot.

The regulars who kept their boats docked at the Redwood Marina had tied up their crafts for the night and were inside the paneled office betting each other on the bass fishing contest planned for the next morning.

Gabby Harrison would have rather stopped at one of the many taverns in Seven Points for a cold draft beer, but fishing had been good so he'd stayed later than usual and now would be late getting home. He had to settle for a can of Miller Lite that swam in melted ice in the bottom of his boat's cooler.

After making some comment about "my old lady will be wondering where I am," he pushed open the door and went out on the dock. He paused a moment and squinted through the gathering darkness; then he turned around and stuck his head back inside the office.

"Hey, y'all," he called, "something looks kinda fishy out here. Pardon the pun."

Tex Beaucamp's curiosity pulled him off a folding chair, and he went outside to investigate. Both men stared at a green-and-white boat bobbing in the dark water about fifty feet from the dock. It appeared empty.

"We better take a look," Gabby suggested, and Tex nodded.

Gabby untied his boat and they climbed aboard. He didn't start the engine because of the short distance, so he rowed to the other boat. By the time they were a stone's throw away, they heard a gathering behind them as their fellow boatmen collected on the dock to watch.

Gabby noticed the motor had been pulled out of the water. "Looks like somebody's had engine problems," he said.

Once they were alongside the nineteen-foot inboard-outboard Glastron, Tex threw his leg over the side and climbed on deck. Then he called back to Gabby, "Nobody's here, but whoever was sure left in a hell of a hurry." He bent over and picked up a card and read, " 'Jimmy Don Beets.' At least that's what his fishing license says."

Gabby frowned. "God, no, not Jimmy Don. He's that Dallas Fire Department captain. Really a nice guy, and he's big enough to swim clear across the lake."

"Maybe he did," Tex replied. Then he reached down to the floorboards and retrieved a small bottle. "On second thought, maybe he didn't. This here's a prescription for nitroglycerin. That's probably what all these pills are around the bottom of the boat. Here's his glasses, too."

Gabby tossed Tex a rope, who threaded it through the boat's towing ring to haul it back to the marina. The waiting cluster of people began examining their find. Many faces darkened when they learned the name of the boat's owner. "He was always the first to offer help if you had a problem," one sailor said. "I went fishing with him just last week," another recalled. Stories flooded back of fishing trips, barbecues, or sitting around Beets' living room, drinking a cold beer while watching the Dallas Cowboys on television.

Another man brushed his hand over the boat's motor. "Must have hit something underwater that sheered off the propeller. Blade's clean missing. He didn't even have a chance to get a wrench out of his toolbox," he said, nodding toward the metal container that also lay in the bottom of the boat.

Nighttime began falling as everyone stood outside, discussing the mystery of the empty boat. Thousands of lacy-winged water flies, twice the size of large mosquitoes, zigzagged back and forth, darting to the lights outlining the dock.

The marina's owner, Lil Smith, sized up the situation and dashed inside for the phone book. She found a listing for a J. D. Beets and dialed the number. Nervously tapping a pencil on her desk, she listened to the phone ring over and over, but no one answered. Periodically, she'd go outside and listen to the men, then trudged back in to make another call. After several unsuccessful tries, it was almost ten before a woman answered.

"Yes, this is Mrs. Beets."

Lil told her of finding the boat and its contents.

"Oh, dear! Jimmy Don went out fishing last night. I've been worried sick about him. I called the sheriff this morning and reported him missing."

"I tried to reach you earlier," Lil said, "but no one answered."

"I went up to Dallas today to do a little shopping with my sons. Got back about eight, but I've been out planting flowers in my yard ever since. Guess that's why I didn't hear the phone. What should I do, come get the boat?"

"I'd suggest you stay by the phone in case he calls. His boat will be fine. We'll tie it up for the night and there won't be any charge."

"I'm a nervous wreck hearing all this. Maybe I'd better come right over."

Ten minutes later, a breathless Betty Beets hurried into the marina's office. "I came as soon as I could."

Lil couldn't help but notice the men eyeing Betty's full bosom, and her Texas-big blond hair. At the same time, Lil took in Betty's perfectly applied makeup, her spotless blouse, and her crisply creased jeans. Very clean looking for a woman who'd been out working in the yard.

Betty asked to see Jimmy Don's boat, so they led her outside to the dock. She gasped when she saw the familiar sight. Then she soberly fingered his eyeglasses, pill bottle, and fishing license. "What on earth could have happened to him?" she said to no one in particular. "He was so good at fixing things. Why, he's fixed dozens of motors for friends, although his own motor had been giving him some trouble lately. 'Course he did have a heart attack five years ago," she said, dropping her head toward her chest.

Lil's husband had drowned a few years before she still remembered the anguish and loss she'd felt. She had screamed and cried and cursed God for taking away the man she loved. She couldn't help but admire the strength Betty showed. Betty wasn't even crying.

A faint noise beckoned from the buoys that had begun sloshing against the waves. Triangular flags on the dock started flapping in concert with flags on boats as the wind continued to build. The thin dark clouds that earlier slithered across the face of the moon had been replaced with thunderheads.

"Don't like the looks of this one bit," Tex complained.

Just then Sheriff Charlie Fields stepped out of his car. The popularly elected sheriff had been around Athens since he was a small boy and could tell stories of horses and buggies kicking up dust on the dirt roads surrounding the Henderson County Courthouse. The sheriff's pointed-toe boots clicked on the concrete parking lot as he made his way to the dock to examine the boat. He shook his head as he checked out the broken motor and spilled medication. Then he eyed the dark clouds rolling in and said, "There'll be no search tonight, boys, not with this storm brewing."

Everyone agreed and promised to be back in the morning. One way or another, they'd find Jimmy Don Beets.

Betty drove herself home while the billowing clouds grew angrier by the second. When she pulled up to her property, she passed the wishing well located near her driveway.

She got out of her truck and fought the wind as it grabbed the door from her grasp. As the storm built with more intensity, she felt the wind blow her hair. Sh watched a flash of lightning crash and disappear into the water.

There was something fresh about a storm; a cleansing that shook all evil out of the air. She hurried to her house, still hearing the storm scream across the water, breaking against barrier walls.

THREE

VALOR

Valor . . . is the fire fighter entering a fire area or burning building to protect life or property. . . . Valor is a nebulous virtue. Sometimes it is observed and recognized; probably more often it is not—but make no mistake, it is the common bond that forms the foundation for the Dallas Fire Department. It is the heart of our emergency organization.

—1980 Medal of Valor Yearbook

At the first crack of daylight, a caravan of cars, pickups, and vans snaked its way down Highway 175 from Dallas. Over fifty fire fighters had learned of Captain Beets's empty boat and were coming to search for him.

The firemen came because they were like family. Having spent twenty-four hours a day eating and sleeping together, they had myriad hours of conversation where they learned about each other's families, the names of their children, and how they got along with their wives. So when one of the firemen died, a brother had died.

The one hundred boats of the bass fishing contest quickly turned into a search party for Jimmy Don. Overhead, wealthy residents in private planes crisscrossed the clear blue sky scanning the lake. Coast Guard and privately owned helicopters slowly hovered over the lake's surface. Never had there been so many people on the lake at one time.

Captain James Blackburn of the Dallas Fire Department lived in Mabank, one of the lake-hugging towns, so he was chosen to set up tactical headquarters at the causeway between Seven Points and Gun Barrel City. Blackburn's commander appointed him, knowing he had been friends with Beets since their rookie days on the fire department switchboard. Using maps of the lake, Blackburn penned a detailed grid—a framework that formed the basis of an organized, complete search. He initially calculated the acres of lake separating Jimmy Don's home from the marina where his boat had been found—an awful lot of water to investigate, but if necessary he'd explore the entire lake.

He glanced from the map to the lake. Water stretched as far as the eye could see. The boundless reservoir was created by damming five creeks into one giant body. The largest, Cedar Creek, ran through terrain overlaid with large stands of cedar trees.

In coordination with the Coast Guard, boats were dispatched hourly to various parts of the lake. And hourly they returned with the same report—no sight of Captain Beets. The Red Cross parked a mobile food center by the search headquarters and busily dispensed cold drinks, sandwiches, and watermelon to the heat-exhausted volunteers throughout the day, a day that saw temperatures climb to over a hundred degrees with rarely a breeze to break the smothering warmth.

While they searched, the throng of local volunteers jabbered to each other about their church activities, and eagerly gloated over their children's and grandchildren's achievements. Family was a priority to these people. And the vast majority of them never doubted for a minute that Jimmy Don's disappearance was anything but an accident. They accepted that one of their own had simply been out night fishing and encountered motor trouble, and the anxiety of trying to make repairs brought on a heart attack. Not even nitroglycerin had helped as Jimmy Don probably stumbled and fell overboard.

The old man sat in his red Chevrolet pickup watching the Coast Guard drag the lake. Every few minutes he'd reach up with a wrinkled handkerchief and blot a tear before it tumbled down his lined cheek. He stared at the dragging mechanism that looked like a big rake attached to a barge. The rake scooped down into the water, rumbled across the bottom, then picked up its findings and dumped them onto another barge. Pieces of old furniture, uprooted tree stumps, and all sorts of rubbish surfaced, but no body.

As the old man observed the Coast Guard's efforts, he glanced toward Captain Blackburn's search headquarters just as a red-and-white Silverado pulled up. His heart leaped when he saw Jimmy Don's truck. He hurriedly sent up a prayer of thanks. Had Jimmy Don gone out of town without telling anyone? How would he explain his absence to all these people?

Then he saw a fluffed-up, perfumed Betty Beets open the driver's door and place her foot on the curb. He doubled up his fist and hit the worn rim of his steering wheel.

"That damn woman," he said aloud to the empty cab of his truck. "Jimmy Don ain't in this lake. No, sir, that bitch of a woman has done something really bad to my son."

As the frantic search continued, everyone had a constant reminder of Jimmy Don's drowning. Motorists coming down Highway 175 from Dallas or Athens, or crossing the bridge on Highway 85 that spanned the blue waters could see the activity. Hordes of boats still cruised the lake while grappling hooks continued dragging the lake's muddy depths.

Shorts- and T-shirt-clad parents loitered outside their houses, wringing their hands and staring at the water's edge. They vowed not to let their children swim in the lake, even in water right by their own docks. Visions of a bloated corpse bobbing up around their offspring was a nightmare too horrible to contemplate.

JoAnn Blackburn wouldn't soon forget the search. She had been planning a party for several friends and relatives to celebrate her twenty-five years of marriage to Captain Blackburn, but because of his role in the search, they had to cancel the party.

Officially, the search lasted thirteen days in the brain-burning heat. Captain Blackburn never missed one of those days, for his supervisor had relieved him of all his other duties to oversee the search personnel. He tried to put aside his personal feelings over the loss of a friend; however, he couldn't help but experience a hollowness every time a boat crew returned with its report of finding nothing. The captain kept stuffing crafts with volunteers and the Red Cross mobile unit kept stuffing volunteers with nourishment.

With firemen working shifts of three days on, three off, Blackburn always had fresh recruits, and those who continued the quest were just as fervent to find Jimmy Don as everyone who had been there earlier.

Every now and then Betty Lou visited the search area to check on progress. Her presence particularly grated the tired, hardworking crews after they had finished probing their section of the lake. They'd drag their sunburned bodies ashore and see a cool-appearing, freshly dressed Betty Lou acting like she didn't have a care in the world. The smile on her lips seemed out of place, and when she said, "I can't thank y'all enough," she sounded insincere.

Serious questions began bobbing to the surface like dead fish.

"This beats the hell out of me," one experienced Coast Guard volunteer said. "The water's not cold, and unless the body's weighted down, the gases expanding the body should have brought it to the surface long before now."

Captain Blackburn admitted that he had questioned the circumstances from the beginning. "I bet if we ever find him, he won't have drowned in the lake," he told fellow rescuers. "He could have been killed somewhere else and dropped here. Just like that boat. Looked like a setup to me. I went over there that first day. Something wasn't right. The broken motor, those spilled pills. I noticed on that prescription that the pills were over two years old. And that business about the motor was just plain peculiar. Jimmy Don could make a motor out of a pile of scrap metal. A missing rotor blade wouldn't give him a heart attack."

As the official search wound down, Captain Blackburn wrote his report from the thorough records he had kept. Two hundred boats had been involved, two helicopters, four airplanes, and hundreds of volunteers. In all, he computed there had been 3,020 man hours logged into looking for Jimmy Don's body.

After thirteen days, the official search ended, but unofficially people continued searching. They couldn't get Beets off their minds. His friends still visited his favorite fishing spots, just in case. Whenever people were out on the lake they couldn't help talking about him or looking for him—just in case.

* * *

Closure for Betty Beets came a little quicker. Two days after she reported her husband missing, she waltzed into a funeral home in Segoville, Texas, chose a white casket lined with blue satin, and picked out a cemetery plot. The next week, she asked that a memorial service be held for her late husband. His family dismissed the idea because they were still looking for his body.

In desperation, people turned to whatever means they could to find Captain Beets. One source was psychics. They more or less appeared, with no one taking credit for calling them. Although the sheriff's office was blamed for hiring at least one, they firmly denied that they had.

One psychic, a four-hundred-pound woman in her sixties, began orchestrating her magic near the site where Jimmy Don's boat had been found. She stood at the water's edge with her eyes closed, inhaling the lake air. Then she asked to be driven to Glen Oaks, where Beets still owned a pretty, frame house painted robin's egg blue. The pleasant three-bedroom, two-bath home had a "great room," which consisted of a combined den, living room, and dining room, all braided together to form a large room where Jimmy Don had loved to entertain.

The home nestled under soaring oaks across the street from the lake, so after visiting the house, the psychic strolled over to neighbors fronting the lake. On the neighbor's dock, she squeezed her massive frame into a chair near a spreading magnolia tree, and tried to sense Beets's presence. After much deliberation, she declared that he was in the water with brown moss on his face. A current siege of Hydrilla, a greenish-brown, moss-type plant held areas of the lake hostage, and the newspapers ran continuous stories about the problem.

Any psychic worth her salt could have learned that from the local press.

A Dallas newspaper reported on another psychic, a short, matronly woman from Georgia who had coal-black hair. To see visions, she also closed her eyes and then gently rocked back and forth as she concentrated. After that, she returned to the lakeside search headquarters and stroked a photograph of Captain Beets. She saw him buried somewhere near a castle, adding that he had sand on his face.

The Coast Guard, eager to try anything to find Beets, slowly cruised the shoreline with her on board looking for a castle. They discovered one house on the lake built of stone with turrets at each end of the roof in castle fashion. The eager men docked their boat and went ashore to investigate the structure and its grounds. The puzzled owner let them examine her yard, but they found no freshly turned earth or any indication of a grave. With their attention directed on dwellings at the water's edge, the Coast Guard overlooked Betty Beets's wishing well that may have symbolized a castle.

Beets's two nieces, Jackie Collins and Diane Hodges, piled into their car and drove to Arlington, Texas, just west of Dallas. They had heard about a psychic there, and found her in a small eerie house that smelled of incense. Her head was wrapped in a silk scarf, turban style.

Without their mentioning their uncle, the psychic said, "I see that you have a relative you're worried about. It's someone who's lost that you're trying to find."

When they heard her accurate description, they immediately hauled the woman back to the lake. There she asked questions and walked through Beets's home in Glen Oaks. She fingered his clothes and touched his comb and sunglasses. Then she walked to the water and for a long time stood staring at the lake.

Finally she revealed, "He's not in the water."

Diane and Jackie, thinking that meant their uncle was still alive, grinned enthusiastically, but their enthusiasm faded as the psychic continued.

"I see a young man in a white shirt. He's in a struggle with a woman." The psychic frowned and placed her fingers to her temple. "He's near the water, but I'm afraid he's in a grave."

Diane and Jackie glanced at each other through tear-fogged eyes. After a few moments of digesting the psychic's words, they swamped her with a stream of questions, but she could give them nothing specific about their uncle's whereabouts. However, she did tell them something that later would send chills through their young bodies: "Mr. Beets will be found on July 8, 1985." She had the day and year right, and only missed the month by one.

FOUR

Roxboro, a village nestled on the green plains of North Carolina, lies in the heart of the tobacco-growing territory. Betty Lou, born there on March 12, 1937, came into the world at a time when the town of 5,000 was trying to pull itself up from the Great Depression. Almost everyone knew poverty, including her young parents, who struggled to make a living as sharecroppers on a tobacco farm. It was a meager beginning for someone who would later be known as Betty Dunevant Branson Lane Threlkeld Barker Beets.

Betty, the second child of James and Louise Dunevant, began life in a small pine cabin that had no electricity, no running water, and no glass in the windows. Rarely did the family have milk or fresh vegetables. They survived on salt pork, flour, and meal—a diet barely capable of nourishing Betty and her older brother, Dewey. Their only source of heat, a black coal stove, could have heated the small home, except that heat escaped through the broken windows, leaving colds and influenza as Betty's constant companions.

When winter came and the tobacco crop had been harvested, Mrs. Dunevant had time to take on another job as a domestic, the occupation she listed on Betty's birth certificate. She cleaned the homes of wealthy people, who had beautiful furnishings, heavily fringed drapes, and thick carpets. She'd return to her little house and describe the mansions to Betty, giving her daughter every glittering detail.

"Life's gonna get better," Betty's mother promised her five-year-old daughter one day. With eager anticipation, Mrs. Dunevant and her husband packed the family's meager belongings and moved twenty miles north to the more-industrial Danville, Virginia, sitting on the border between Virginia and North Carolina. There Betty's parents found work in the cotton mills and placed the children in a communal day-care center. The young couple now happily provided more of life's necessities for their children. They rented a snug little house that stayed warm in the winter, and the general health of the family improved thanks to plenty of fresh fruits, vegetables, and red meat.

However, in that same year, Betty came down with measles. She suffered prolonged sore throats, hacking coughs, and a fever that sometimes reached 105 degrees and lasted for days. Her mother took off from work to care for her, and for hours sat in Betty's small bedroom and sponged her thin body with cold water and placed ice-filled compresses on her forehead. Betty's flaxen hair stuck to her moist scalp and her blue eyes looked dull and lifeless.

With many sleepless nights, and Betty's high fever, her parents' frustration mounted. "You should feel her skin," her mother said to her husband one night. "It's as hot as a frying pan." She sank into a chair and began crying. "She's so sick. I pray to God it doesn't happen, but I'm afraid we're gonna lose her."

Their mood remained somber as Betty endured the long, tedious illness. Ear infections further complicated her convalescence and ultimately left her with a hearing loss. After she recovered and returned to her white clapboard school, she strained to hear her teacher. Learning became more difficult and she felt disconnected from the other students.

By the time she reached fourth grade, her teachers decided it would be best if Betty repeated the grade. Their judgment humiliated Betty, and her embarrassment grew when her former classmates saw her in the halls at school. They taunted her with chants, calling her stupid, and making her feel different. Keeping her head down, she said nothing as she hurried by, believing what they said.

After Betty turned eight, her mother gave birth to a son, Jimmy, and two years later, another daughter, Jackie.

Four years after that, and without any prior symptoms, one day at work her mother suffered what doctors labeled "a psychotic break with reality." The mill summoned an ambulance to rush Mrs. Dunevant to a hospital, where she remained for a week. She came home pale and shaken. The doctor had given her medication, and frequently came by to visit. She suffered hallucinations with strange voices playing in her head. She became hysterical, pushing out her hands to ward off unseen demons.

Betty cowered to see her mother act so suddenly and strangely violent. Watching her mother's strange behavior, she wondered if that condition could be inherited.

The following year, Mrs. Dunevant's mental illness worsened, forcing her to be institutionalized at Eastern State Hospital in Virginia for three months. To combat her serious problem, the barren public psychiatric hospital had to administer shock therapy and seventeen rounds of deep insulin coma therapy.

Her mother's mental state was not lost on Betty's classmates. When they saw Betty, they faked seizures, waving their hands in the air and saying, "Who am I?" The ugliness of her classmates continued and now they made her feel both stupid and crazy. Education for Betty became an excruciating experience that she'd do anything to escape.

Thirteen-year-old Betty Dunevant slammed a kitchen drawer shut as she prepared a dinner of beans and ham. It was the third time that week she had reheated the ham, and the dry meat had begun to taste like sawdust.

Betty found that cooking and cleaning for the family in her mother's absence was sheer drudgery, and her weight dropped to eighty pounds. Frequently too exhausted to attend classes, she missed many days of school.

Adding to her problems, her father drank heavily to overcome depression about his wife's condition. When he was drunk, Betty would cringe every time she saw him remove his belt, knowing she had done something to displease him and he'd soon be beating her with the buckle of that belt. After the beatings, he received obedience from her, but unbeknownst to him, he was creating a tough exterior on his daughter. She came to accept that she would be beaten if she didn't mind him.

Betty dreamed of the day she could escape. That day came when she met a handsome eighteen-year-old, Robert Franklin Branson. Branson's black hair and olive skin contrasted sharply with Betty's fair coloring. He was a quiet youth, who worked in a zipper factory. His prospects seemed limited, but fifteen-year-old Betty didn't mind.

Betty had not yet had her first period and her mother feared that Betty could be pregnant, so she encouraged her young daughter to marry Branson, even though Betty insisted that she had never had sex with anyone. The two married on July 18, 1952, just a month after Betty finished ninth grade.

A year later, their first child, Faye, arrived. Instead of being happy to be married and have a new baby to love, Betty Branson found she had traded one frustrating situation for another. She complained to her husband, "I'm no better off now than when I had to cook and clean for my parents, and having this baby is just like being saddled with my brother and sister."

Thinking more money would make Betty happier, Robert Branson went to the giant Norfolk shipyard looking for a better paying job. When he signed on, he thought his wife would be pleased that he could shower his small family with a few luxuries. Instead, he came home each night to an angry, disillusioned woman who wanted her freedom. "I'm only sixteen," she whimpered. She frequently ran into former classmates who would embellish with enticing detail their proms, football rallies, and all the other high school activities Betty was missing.

The young couple's heated arguments and misunderstandings led to a six-month separation. Betty wasn't sure what she wanted; she only knew what she had missed. But when forced to take Faye and move back with her parents, she slipped into a deep depression. Spiraling down into her dark mood, she tried to commit suicide by swallowing two bottles of aspirin. Betty's parents called her husband with word of the suicide attempt, and he rushed to Betty's bedside and talked her into reconciling.

The next year, Connie came along. With a new baby the Bransons wanted a new start, and Robert found he could make more money with a construction job in Texas. Collecting their two daughters and the few household items they had accumulated, they moved to Mesquite, a small town just southeast of Dallas.

The area looked foreign to them after coming from water-laced Norfolk, Virginia. In Mesquite, trees grew along the sides of creeks that veined the area, but in 1955, few additional trees had been planted, and some residential lots had no trees or shrubbery at all. They rented a plain, unimaginative house no larger than a double-car garage. Frequently, the wood trim became sun damaged, and the paint peeled.

Fortunately, Branson did well in his new profession and Betty could continue as a full-time mother and stay home with her children.

Once in Texas, the family blossomed, and a third daughter, Shirley, arrived in February of 1959. Three years later, Phyllis was born. Finally, their first son, Robert (Robby) Franklin Branson II, entered the family in 1964, and a second son, Bobby, was born in 1966. Now after fourteen years of marriage, they had six children.

Betty was only twenty-nine and still very pretty. She had a knack for choosing clothes that accentuated her figure, a figure that few women would possess after giving birth to six children. Her small waist emphasized her large breasts, and she applied makeup like a professional. She wore four-inch high heels to give the illusion of being taller than five-two.

She bleached her hair to recapture the blond of her childhood, and regular perms gave it an overly fluffy appearance—a look that fit in well at the local bars. She liked to have a good time, and spending all day taking care of six children wasn't her idea of a good time. She began to crave men who reminded her that she was still sexy and desirable.

For her clandestine activities she recruited her older daughters to babysit her young sons, then put on her Sunday-best cotton dress and drove to The Silver Slipper, a bar in East Dallas.

She strolled inside a room lit by the red-and-blue neon-outlined beer signs, and loud jazz pounded from the jukebox. The men stopped sucking on their long-neck beers and glanced admiringly at her, and some invited her to join their table. They laughed at her jokes, and asked why a pretty thing like her hadn't been there before. Betty's charm worked overtime as the men took turns dancing with her, holding her close, and smothering her with compliments. This, she realized, was living.

At last she recaptured the fun she had missed in her teenage years, and her husband made enough money to take her mind off the misery of the poverty she had known as a child.

Gradually, her life away from home became a source of friction at the Branson household. Even the children grew perturbed by her outside interests, and the home she had kept so immaculately fell into disarray.

Branson warned her, "Betty, I'm not going to put up with this. I always thought you were a good wife and I know the kids love you. But I can't handle how you're acting while I'm out trying to support our family."

Her husband had his own romantic options, for he still cut a handsome, lean figure. His full head of black hair complimented his tan, relatively unlined face. In 1969, after seventeen years of marriage, he demanded a divorce and this time there would be no reconciliation. He married a younger woman shortly after the divorce became final.

Betty received full custody of the children and Branson was ordered to pay $350 a month for their support. Now the children suffered through their mother's muffled sobs. "I still love and miss your daddy," she told them. Betty kept an eight-by-ten photograph of her ex-husband on a table in the living room. On the photo he had inscribed: "More than yesterday, but less than tomorrow," a promise that no longer held true. The children thought that their mother never seemed happy with anyone else after that.

Betty's second daughter, Connie, told a friend, "Most of the good things I remember about my mother were before she and my daddy divorced. Mama worked so hard to please him. When Daddy worked nights, she would put on makeup before she went to bed so when he'd get home around two or three in the morning, she'd look nice for him."

In those earlier years, the children had benefitted from Betty wanting to be a good wife and mother, but now after the divorce, all the family customs fell apart. They weren't together for Christmas or Thanksgiving. There were no more big family dinners with turkey and all the trimmings, and no Easter egg hunts at their paternal grandparent's house. Gone were the picnics and the trips to the zoo.

The children were painfully aware how drastically their parents' divorce had changed their lives.

Betty was experiencing life without a man, a life that contained many hardships, especially when Branson went months at a time without paying the court-ordered child support.

To forget her problems, she increased her nights of club hopping and drinking and dancing. Before long, her family began disintegrating and fluttered away like birds from a nest.

First, Faye followed in her mother's footsteps by marrying at fifteen and moving out. Betty sent ten-year-old Phyllis and eight-year-old Robby to live with their father and his new wife. She kissed Robby good-bye, and with tears in his eyes, he asked, "Mama, when can I come home?"

Betty said, "Soon," but five years would pass before

she saw him again and only then for a few minutes. It would be a total of ten years before he moved back with her.

As the family breakup continued, Connie went to live with her sister Faye. Shirley sometimes lived with Betty and sometimes with friends. Bobby, only three at the time of the divorce, had his mother's eyes, and had obviously stolen her heart, for he was the only child she refused to relinquish to other family members.

After Betty's divorce, her vulnerability soared, for she spent hours worrying how she'd pay her bills. The financial woes that had shadowed her childhood now followed her into her adult life.

It was a time of short skirts and big hair, and in spite of her financial situation, Betty kept up with both. Every morning after her shower, she pinned a blond hairpiece of cascading curls into her own hair, working each curl into place. Heads turned wherever she went.

FIVE

A house painter named Billy York Lane came courting a year after Betty's divorce, and he easily swayed her. They both had March birthdays, but he was seven years older. After dating only a few months before deciding to marry, she told her children about her plans.

"Bill is so nice to me," she said. "He's real gentle and kind. I know you're just going to love him."

Had the courtship lasted longer, she might have glimpsed flashes of Bill Lane's hot temper and controlling ways before she married him on July 28, 1970.

Now thirty-three, the once trim and curvaceous Betty couldn't shed the weight she so easily lost after each baby. She began gulping down the diet drug Dexatrim, while still continuing to drink. In her mind, if she took more of the drug than the label suggested, she'd lose weight more rapidly. However, in larger quantities the drug caused insomnia, irritability, restlessness, and headaches.

In addition to the side effects, Betty's personality began to change. Her children noticed that she became two different people. In an instant she flipped from the caring mother they loved, to a woman who used foul language and screamed at them.

Added to those changes, Bill began slapping her around just days following the wedding. In the next few months, his abusive treatment escalated until he was fre-

quently punching and beating her. Her children were
horrified to see Betty covered with bruises.

Lane particularly liked hitting Betty in the face. She
always wanted to look her best, so a swollen and bruised
face caused more than physical damage. She tried to
cover the bruises with makeup, but the dark purplish
injuries refused to hide.

Appalled with her life, Betty mustered the courage to
take out a restraining order against Lane on October
28, 1970, then divorced him two months later. But even
after the divorce, and despite the restraining order, they
continued their love-hate relationship, unable to stay
apart.

Some nights she would drive home from work and
notice a car with its lights out, sitting a half block from
her apartment. From the silhouette of the man inside,
she knew it was Lane. Other nights, she would look in
her rearview mirror and see him following her.

The violence increased, and in May of 1971, he broke
her nose.

"I don't know what's wrong with me," Betty complained to the doctor treating her. "I get so depressed
because I can't pull myself away from this man, and he
keeps hitting me. What can I do?"

The doctor didn't suggest that she leave Lane or report his abuse, even though hospital records provided
sufficient documentation. Instead, he merely prescribed
an antidepressant. A few months later, she took another
trip to the emergency room after Lane doubled up his
fist and hit her left eye. His blow opened a gap that
required several stitches to close.

They continued to frequent the same smoky clubs
where they'd first met. A country song bellowed from
the jukebox, and a neon sign in the window advertised
WOMEN ADMITTED FREE WITHOUT AN ESCORT. They glared
jealously when one or the other danced or talked with

someone else. Betty enjoyed watching a rage build within Lane as she danced closely with other men. When she knew he was watching, she would cuddle tighter and look into the men's eyes until Lane turned crimson. He acted just as vengeful, using other women as she used other men.

Then on January 17, 1972, Lane walked up to her after she had danced with a man he had previously told her to stay away from. He told her to get home or he'd kill her.

"You sorry son of a bitch," Betty screamed at him, then hurried to her car to go home. On the way, she found a policeman, and honked for him to stop. The officer turned around and pulled up beside her. Betty said, "My ex-husband is following me. I'm going right home now, but could you be on the lookout for a '57 white Ford?" The officer assured her that he'd watch for the car and keep an eye out on her apartment.

She now lived in the town of Hutchins, not far from Mesquite where she and Branson first settled. She took pride in her recently built apartment that fronted Franklin Street, close to the open fields and farms of rural Hutchins. The buff brick, two-story structure stood on one of the gently rolling hills of the area, and on the opposite end of town from Hutchins's huge Texas State Jail with its cyclone fences topped with miles of rolled razor wire.

That night, the Dallas County sheriff answered an emergency call from Betty's apartment at 1:45 A.M. When deputies arrived, they found a man lying unconscious in a pool of his own blood outside the apartment's rear door. He had been shot and had fallen from a small concrete stoop, then down three steps.

Two Dallas sheriff's deputies walked into Betty's apartment ready to slap handcuffs on her.

"Okay, who is he and what happened?" a deputy said.

"That's Bill Lane," Betty stammered. "He flew into a jealous rage. Here's what happened. Tonight I was dancing with this man at the Slipper Club." Betty assumed the policeman would know which bar she meant since it sat on a seedy stretch of broken sidewalk on Industrial Boulevard and the manager frequently called police to squelch brawls.

"I was headed toward the ladies' room when Billy grabbed my arm as I passed him. He said, 'You go home and stay away from him, or you're gonna be sorry.'

"I said something like, 'What the hell are you gonna do about it?' and he said, 'Just remember, I know where the fuck you live.' He said that if he couldn't have me, nobody could."

"He ever threaten you before?" a deputy asked.

"Yes. Once with a gun. So when he got that look in his eye and started talking that way, I knew enough to take him seriously. That's when I left the club.

"When I got back here to my apartment, my teenage daughter, Connie—" Betty nodded toward the young woman sitting on the other side of the room, and added, "She's living with me for a while. Connie told me Bill had been calling. Said he was getting to be a real pest."

"Did he call again?"

"Yes. Just shortly after I got home. He told me he was coming to kill me. I begged him not to come, but he was adamant.

"I guess I got hysterical. I told Connie that Bill was coming over. I said whatever she did, she wasn't to answer the door.

"That's when I ran to my bedroom and grabbed my .22 pistol I always keep loaded."

"Where's the gun now?" the deputy asked.

"I keep it in the top drawer of my nightstand."

The deputy nodded toward the bedroom, and Betty

led him there and opened the drawer. When she reached for the gun, he held out his hand to stop her, then wrapped it in a clean white handkerchief to take with him.

"Go on," he said.

"So I pulled out the gun and laid it on the bar by the door. Probably only ten minutes later, I heard knocking at my back door. That's when I screamed for Connie to call the police. At the same time, Bill yelled, 'Open the door, or I'll break it down.' "

"Why did you open the door, lady?"

"I was afraid he'd turn it into kindling. Anyway, I opened it, and Bill rushed in. I was so scared. I remember yelling, 'Leave me alone, you son of a bitch, and get the hell out of my life.'

"He said, 'I'll never leave you alone.' Then he backed me up against the bar, and told me he got crazy when he saw me with other men.

"That's when I reached behind my back and got my gun. He didn't act afraid. Maybe he thought I was bluffing. He took another step toward me, so I fired at him. Can't remember how many times, but I kept firing until I saw him stagger out the back door."

The deputies listened to Betty's story, then read her her rights. They drove her to their office, where she waived her right to an attorney and gave a statement admitting that she had shot Bill Lane. The officers questioned why they found two bullet holes in Lane's back if he were coming toward her as she insisted. When Betty had no answer, they charged her with "Assault with intention to commit murder with malice."

Before Betty had been carted off, a third deputy had arrived, and now stayed at Betty's apartment to take a statement from a tearstained, nervous Connie. The young woman blew her nose and tried to calm herself, but she still sobbed as she told the deputy what she had heard while listening on a bedroom extension when Lane called.

Between sniffles, Connie said, "When Bill called, he told my mother, 'I'm coming over to kill you, and Juvenile will come out and get the kids.' I called the operator and she got the police. Mama told me to get out of the house and she yelled at Bill to leave. That's when I heard some shots and ran to the kitchen. I looked outside and saw Bill on the ground by the porch."

Like a rehearsed drama, Billy Lane's daughter, Barbara, also claimed to have listened on a telephone extension. She told a sheriff's deputy: "Betty called and Dad answered the phone. She was crying and asked Dad to come over and get his things. He asked how many times are you going to shoot me and she told him none. He also asked how many police would be there and she said none. Dad wanted her to meet him at a different location, but she wouldn't do it.

"Dad left at 1:10 A.M. and told me he'd be back in thirty minutes. At the time I begged him not to go, but he went anyway."

After the sheriff's men had arrived at Betty's apartment and called an ambulance, they ordered the driver to take Bill Lane to Parkland Hospital, where the staff pronounced him in critical condition. The doctors had to perform surgery to remove two bullets.

Lane's version differed considerably from Betty's. Because of his injuries, he wasn't strong enough to give a statement until a week later. He finally told deputies, "I was at my daughter's home watching television when

Betty called and asked me to come over 'just to talk.' I thought it was too late and I asked her if it couldn't wait until morning. She said that if I didn't come right then, I could just forget it.

"So I climbed into my car and drove over there, but when I got to the back door of her apartment, everything was dark. I called to her to open the door, but she told me to leave. Guess she had changed her mind about having a conversation. Next thing I know she's at the door holding a gun on me, so I start to leave and she fires the darn thing. I was still able to move, but she fired again and I lost consciousness. Last thing I remember was her saying, 'If you move, I'll shoot again.' "

Lane spent three weeks in the hospital and several weeks afterward enduring painful therapy. One of the bullets badly damaged a nerve leading to his right leg, leaving him unable to walk.

After Parkland released him, Betty immediately went back to him. One of Lane's neighbors told authorities, "I like Billy, but he's jealous of Betty because she's so beautiful. I know Betty loves him. You should have seen those two. After he got out of the hospital his right leg was no good. He had to learn to walk all over again, and Betty spent hours helping him. She'd get him on his feet and they'd put their arms around each other. They'd go back and forth on the sidewalk. Quite a thing to watch. She loved that man. You could tell by the way she'd spend whole afternoons just walking him up and down the street."

The officers didn't know what to make of the case, but they were more puzzled when just days before the hearing, Lane hobbled up to them on crutches and said, "I'm willing to sign an affidavit that I threatened Betty."

Without a plaintiff to press charges, the court had no option but to drop the murder charge to a misdemeanor aggravated assault.

In court, Betty gladly pleaded guilty to the lesser charge, and Lane pulled out his billfold and paid Betty's hundred-dollar fine and fifty-dollar court costs. In addition, she persuaded the judge to return her pistol.

Then, baffling her entire family, Betty and Billy Lane remarried the following month.

The crowd back at the bar where the Lanes usually frequented wondered if Betty had helped Billy learn to walk just to get back in his good graces. They figured she probably promised to remarry him in exchange for his cooperation on her plea reduction.

In any event, their second marriage lasted but one month, and to ensure that the Lane saga had finally ended, thirty-five-year-old Betty packed up Bobby and moved to Little Rock, Arkansas.

SIX

Ronnie Threlkeld saw her through the smoke-filled haze at Stetson's, the country-western bar he frequented most Saturday nights because it had live guitar music decent enough to dance to. He sat on a genuine saddle bolted to a metal pole that served as a bar stool. Enjoying his long-neck beer, he kept glancing at her image through the bar's mirror, squinting as it moved between bottles of bourbon and vodka.

Threlkeld, born and raised in Little Rock, Arkansas, had never run across this woman before. Surely, he'd remember all the blond hair piled high on the head of that sexy body. He watched her sitting alone at a table, nursing a drink, and shaking her head at every man who came by wanting to dance. As the guitarist plunked out the beat, the country-western music pulsated throughout the room. She kept time by tapping her booted foot against the concrete floor. *Look at that. She wants to dance. What a fox, a cute little blond fox.*

She looked authentic in her floral western shirt tucked into a pair of tan, tight-fitting western pants. He particularly liked how the pants hugged her trim figure. A tooled, brown-leather belt matched her boots.

He pulled himself away from the bar and ambled over to Betty's table. Looking directly into her eyes, he said, "I'm only going to ask you to dance with me one time, so you better say yes."

* * *

A smile curled Betty's lips as she peered up at the dark-haired man, and a look of surrender softened her face. When the guitar player began strumming the introductory chords of the *Tennessee Waltz*, Threlkeld extended his hand, and she stood up slowly, placing her small hand in his.

"You've got to be new around here," Threlkeld said.

Betty spun as he twirled her. "Just moved here last week. Don't have any friends."

"You've got one now," he said, and smiled, then drew her closer.

She snuggled her cheek to his chest.

"You a single gal?"

"I'm divorced. I have a little three-year-old boy," she said, not mentioning her other five children, her second marriage or that she had shot Bill Lane.

"Well, I'm divorced, too, but don't have any kids."

"So what do you do?" she asked.

"I've always been in sales, and for the last several years I've been selling automotive parts. Everyone needs replacement parts for their cars."

"I'm working as a cashier at a local Seven-Eleven," Betty volunteered. "Everyone needs last-minute items." They both laughed. "It's just something to do 'til I find a job I really like."

"I can't believe how upbeat you are. You're so much fun, even though you have a job you're not crazy about, and a kid to raise."

"I can pay my bills and I love my son more than anything. Why shouldn't I be happy?"

Around midnight they walked out into the parking lot on a chilly November night in 1973.

"Look at this new Cordova," Therlkeld said. "You are amazing, with your beginning job, as you call it, you do very well. I like the maroon color. Kinda hot and sexy, just like you."

"Don't say sweet things to me," Betty cautioned. "I melt easily." She looked up at him, and he bent down and kissed her lips. She stretched her arms around his neck and kissed him again. "Sure hope you don't think I'm a fast woman if I invite you to come home with me," she said.

"Ma'am, that's an invitation I'll gladly accept."

From that night on he began living in her little house. Betty was thirty-six, and Threlkeld thirty-three.

Over the next four years, they shared many romantic and happy times. Betty was never without her CB radio and she adopted the handle "Tiger."

"That name sure fits," he told her. Whenever Threlkeld came within her CB range, he'd call and ask, "How's the Tiger in that tank?"

But woven into the happy times, any relationship with Betty was bound to be feisty. This one proved no exception. They had heated arguments when Threlkeld treated her roughly. Betty did not act docilely, but took revenge by slashing all of Threlkeld's tires. After another confrontation, she went after him with a tire jack.

Betty complained to Threlkeld, "People take advantage of me, especially my own children. They're always wanting me to do things for them." A month later, she surprised him by saying, "I want to move back to Dallas. I really miss my kids."

He saw Betty as a puzzle of contradictions, and the pieces didn't fit. Within an hour's time, she'd change her mind and deny what she had told him earlier. But she showed great patience with Bobby, and he knew she worshipped the ground he walked on. That made Threlkeld think she was a good mother.

Being able to put aside the highs and lows of Betty's personality, Threlkeld wanted to be with her. But he had a decision to make. He had always lived in Little Rock, and his parents, a host of aunts, uncles, cousins, and many friends lived nearby. Nevertheless, he followed Betty. A salesman's a salesman, he reasoned. He could sell automotive supplies anywhere.

They moved to Dallas and married in February of 1978. Shortly after the wedding, Threlkeld began feeling tied down, and decided he still had wild oats to sow. He drank and shot pool with the boys while Betty stayed home taking care of Bobby.

One time when he came home drunk, he quietly let himself in the back door only to be surprised to find Betty waiting in the kitchen. She stared at him in disgust and said, "There's got to be a good man out there who's looking for a good woman like me."

Betty's family continued to see changes in her. Keeping herself slim, trim, and attractive became an obsession, and she gobbled increasing amounts of Dexatrim. Her mood alterations were obvious. Bobby, now twelve, told a friend, "One moment we got along fine, and the next thing she's a different person. It was like she got hateful all of a sudden, and I mean all of a sudden."

He questioned his mother about these abrupt changes, but when she came out of the distressing moods, she had no recollection of them.

Bobby noticed it didn't matter whether or not she had been drinking, she would change in the middle of a sentence. Her features tightened and her voice grew strangely deep and coarse. She even used harsher words. Betty, not given to cussing freely, now would say "fuck," a word her children had never heard her utter. Two different people lived inside of Betty.

The family had heard stories of Betty's mother who had spent time in mental institutions. They didn't want to think that their own mother had inherited any of their grandmother's psychological problems.

The move to Dallas gave Ronnie Threlkeld the opportunity to know all of Betty's family. He marveled at how Betty's daughters—Faye, Connie, Phyllis, and Shirley—could so easily upset her. Although the young women weren't living with them, Betty complained, "The girls are always getting into trouble, then coming to me asking for money to bail them out of their jams."

Betty also saw her daughters as competition. She became jealous when they were around her husband, so jealous that she accused Threlkeld of sleeping with the girls.

Then one ominous night, he sat at the kitchen table having a drink when one of Betty's daughters sauntered into the room wearing a robe. Whether she intended to tease Threlkeld or to spite her mother, the young woman stood before him making idle chatter, while slowly untying the silken green sash around her tiny waist. The robe dropped to the floor. With timing from hell, Betty came into the room at that moment and saw her daughter standing completely nude in front of her husband.

"You sorry son of a bitch," Betty screamed at the top of her voice. "I knew something like this was going on. You were always giving my girls the eye. But to do something like this right here in my home! Well, that takes it all."

Threlkeld tried to protest, but Betty's screams drowned out his words. Her daughter had grabbed her robe as soon as she spotted her mother, and trying to cover herself, frantically dashed out of the kitchen.

When Betty stopped to inhale, Threlkeld said, "Now wait, Betty, it's not what you think. There's never been anything between me and your daughter. With none of them for that matter."

Betty refused to listen, and as she unleashed her tirade, Threlkeld got the unmistakable message that he'd just been given his walking papers. Dating Betty had been a lot more fun than being married to her. She had changed from the upbeat, happy girl he had first met, to the sullen, negative woman, given frequently to venting her rage. Because of her metamorphosis, he found it easy to leave the hellcat nobody messed with.

Had Threlkeld known that Betty had shot her last husband, he might have been more concerned with what Betty would try doing to him.

The next day, Threlkeld busily loaded his belongings into his car. His mind was occupied with trying to find a place for everything so he would leave nothing behind. When he heard the sound of an engine coming closer, he looked up and saw Betty's car roaring toward him. Quickly, he dashed between two cars in just enough time to avoid being hit as Betty swerved past him, spraying him with gravel.

Moments later, he left for Little Rock, grateful to be alive.

By August of 1979, Betty had pulled herself out of the doldrums and gone to Charlie's Angels Bar, located in the shadow of Dallas skyscrapers, but in a rough neighborhood. She watched a woman on stage shed her clothes. The idea hit her that she possessed all the necessary attributes for the position.

Betty picked up her drink and left to find the manager. The potbellied, balding man listened to Betty's verbal application, all the time eyeing her curvaceous figure.

"Lady, you can't just show up here and go to work," he told her. "You gotta audition. And auditions are held on Thursday nights. Actually we have a pretty good crowd because people like to see amateurs on the stage. Some don't know what the shit they're doing, and it can be pretty funny," he said, and chuckled. "How old are you?"

"Thirty-two," Betty said, shaving off ten years. She held in her stomach and assured him, "I'll know what to do."

On Thursday, August 27, 1979, Betty arrived early to learn the ropes from the professional dancers. A teenage boy directed her backstage to a dressing room. The open cubicle had dirty, peeling paint on the walls. A large room filled with mirrors and lights served as the communal area for dancers to fix their hair and apply makeup.

An experienced stripper, a tall redhead named Candy, gave Betty pointers. "Honey, when you're out there onstage, try not to think about being naked. The first time's always the hardest."

Betty smiled. "Don't you worry about me. This ain't my first rodeo. You think I haven't taken off my clothes in front of men before?"

Everyone laughed, and Betty pulled out the string bikini she brought with her. Candy told her to shave everywhere; then she'd be back to show her how to apply the pasties.

Betty busied herself shaving and smoothing on body makeup, then went back to her new friends. One of the experienced dancers dabbed a bit of rubber cement inside a silver-sequined pasty and told Betty to place it over her nipple. The dancers laughed hysterically as they watched Betty try to cover the large dark areola of her massive breast. She didn't get it right the first time and tried to pull it off to adjust it. She winced.

"Don't worry," Candy said, "the rubber cement will peel right off afterwards."

Betty felt her stomach flutter as she waited backstage for the master of ceremonies to call for "Sexy Tiger," her new stage name derived from her CB handle. She peeked through the curtains to watch other novices strut awkwardly over a stage carpeted in a distracting plum-and-gold floral pattern.

The audience, three-fourths male, looked much like the people she had served in bars. Many wore tired cotton T-shirts and jeans. A few businessmen had come in for quick entertainment and a cold drink. They had removed their suit coats and loosened their ties.

After forty-five minutes, Betty heard: "Ladies and gentlemen, I now give you someone we might find dangerous to play with, 'Sexy Tiger.' " A smattering of applause greeted the recorded bump-and-grind music belting from a tape recorder. Betty pranced on stage, gyrating her hips, and waving her raised arms back and forth over her head. The air conditioning chilled her bare body, despite the hot floodlights ringing the stage. But after a few minutes, she found the coolness refreshing, remembering how sizzling it was outside.

The audience warmed to her with chants of "Take it off, take it off." She reached around for the tie on the back of her bra, but found it knotted and awkward to loosen with one hand. She wanted to look professional, but instead she fumbled as she tried to separate the ribbons. The task became particularly difficult because she tried to keep in step with the music at the same time. Finally, she jerked off the top, only to pull away one of her pasties too. The crowd went into hysterics. Betty couldn't understand their laughter until she looked down at the stage floor and spotted the glitter of silver sequins in the stage lights.

She had to think fast, and she didn't want to appear

like some embarrassed teenager. She twirled around, bent down, and in a flash picked up the pasty and waved it in the air. The crowd roared its approval. Then she slithered up to the microphone and said in her sexiest voice, part Marilyn Monroe and part Mae West, "Is there some nice gentleman in the audience who'd like to assist me in putting this thing back on?"

Seven men rushed the stage. The first one to arrive took the pasty from her, and with his other hand held on to her breast. Half drunk, he awkwardly aimed for her nipple. The audience screamed with laughter.

Suddenly, another man in a black suit shoved him away and approached Betty. He opened a leather wallet that held his identification: "Dallas Police Vice Squad." Betty's shoulders slumped. When she had seen him earlier in the audience, he appeared to be thoroughly enjoying the show.

"Come with me," he said as he escorted the angry woman off the stage. The police arrested Betty and charged her with public lewdness. She gave them her first married name, and her charge read, "Betty Lou Branson knowingly engaged in an act of sexual contact with Archie Phillips by allowing him to touch her breast while said person was in a public place." Later, a judge fined her $250, and unbelievably slapped her in jail for thirty days, and put her on probation for a year.

Six months after Betty's failed dancing attempt, her matrimonial prospects were back on track. She called Ronnie Threlkeld in Little Rock and told him she had filed for divorce. Threlkeld didn't object, even when Betty said, "I've finally found someone who's good to me and treats me right." She further insulted Threlkeld by telling him she had refused to use his name as soon as he left town. It didn't matter, she was going to have a new name before long.

She had been filling her truck with gas at a truck stop in Mesquite one day when Doyle Wayne Barker, a tall, good-looking man, noticed her and struck up a conversation. He worked in construction as a roofer, and lifting heavy tiles kept his body lean and taut. He fit the mold of Betty's other husbands, with his brown hair and eyes, and tan skin. He had a shy but ready smile, and wore a small goatee.

Barker had previously been married for eight years and had two sons from that union. Once Betty invited him to her Dallas apartment, he immediately took to her son Bobby.

Barker worked for Jerry Kuykendall, who owned a roofing company. The company was a forty-five-minute drive from Cedar Creek Lake, but Kuykendall had a farm outside of Mabank within shouting distance of the lake. He considered Barker his lead roofer and his most valuable employee. Barker never minded staying an extra hour or so on a job, not wanting to leave a roof half protected if a storm blew in, and he never complained about hammering down roof tiles when the weather turned glacier cold and made his fingers so numb he could barely feel the hammer in his hand.

Jerry Kuykendall's son, Jerry, Jr., was Bobby's age and the boys became "running buddies." The families frequently visited the lake area, and the boys hunted in the big pasture behind Kuykendall's farmhouse, went fishing at Cedar Creek, and frequently spent nights in each other's homes.

Betty told everyone, "Wayne is just the man I've been looking for," but she said that about each of her husbands. With little fanfare, she and Wayne married in Dallas on October 3, 1979. However, Betty and "just the man she'd been looking for" fought constantly and separated seven weeks after the ceremony. The husband of Betty's oldest daughter, Faye Branson Lane, told Betty that Barker was a big drinker in the Seven Points bars and would intentionally bump into other customers just to start a fight.

They eventually divorced in January 1980.

Shortly afterward, Betty almost died from head injuries received in a serious car accident. She had a basilar skull fracture, lacerations, and a cerebral concussion. Migraine headaches she'd experienced as a child returned and her hearing loss worsened, forcing her to wear hearing aids. She always wore her hair down, so now she fluffed it more fully over her ears for camouflage.

Now even more vulnerable with her physical problems, she listened to Barker when he came to her, saying he was sorry for all their problems. If she'd only give him another chance, he pledged to be a new man.

Betty, wanting desperately to believe the roofer whom she had fought with during their first marriage, remarried him the following year. Her family told her they couldn't understand why she'd remarry someone who had caused her so many problems. She tried to allay their fears by saying, "We've talked over our relationship and we know what our troubles were before. This time it'll be different. We're going to move."

Since Betty and Wayne Barker had frequently been guests of the Kuykendalls at their Cedar Creek home, that was the area where Betty wanted to live. She promised to buy a densely wooded, half-acre lot in the Cherokee Hills section for $8,800 if Barker would match that amount for a new trailer. Betty had her eye on a cream-and-brown, two-bedroom trailer. Barker agreed, and they moved to Cedar Creek Lake at the edge of Gun Barrel City.

Betty had never lived in anything brand new before, and she delighted in decorating the trailer. She bought a matching gray sofa and chair that looked pretty on the fresh-smelling new tweed carpet. She created silk flower arrangements in dainty vases and placed them on tables. In one corner, and perhaps reminiscent of stories her mother had told her of the lovely homes she had cleaned, Betty bought a round table and skirted it with a heavy velvet tablecloth of cut red roses on a black background and fringed with heavy, looping cord.

She enrolled Bobby in Mabank Junior High where he seemed to fit in well. Regardless of his mother's many moves, he always kept up his high grades.

At night, Seven Points was their playground. Seven Points, one of the few "wet," or liquor-allowed regions of the lake, was labeled the honky-tonk of Cedar Creek. The parking lots of the one-story, neon-crested bars were frequently full. Although the majority of the lake's permanent church-centered residents traditionally voted down bars and liquor stores for their areas, they had no hesitation in going to Seven Points to stock up.

Wayne and Betty got along well at first, and they continued a close relationship with the Kuykendalls. Betty drove Wayne to Kuykendall's home each morning at five o'clock for his ride to work with his boss. Each evening, Kuykendall dropped Wayne at his home.

Jerry Kuykendall stood on his porch one morning as Betty drove up. "You know, he said, "this old Wayne of yours is probably as nice a person as you'd want to meet."

Betty smiled at her husband.

"No, really," Kuykendall continued, "my whole family thinks so. Besides, he's an outstanding employee to boot. I can understand why you two get along so well. You both look very happy with each other."

Wayne Barker insisted on seeing his sons from his previous marriage. They were fourteen and sixteen now.

Betty resented the time he spent away from her. The boys had been over to the trailer a few times, but Barker found it lessened tension if he arranged to meet them at the local McDonald's, or a park; anywhere that Betty couldn't interfere. He especially liked having them for an entire weekend, but taking the flak from Betty made him question if it was worth the trouble.

When Betty confided to her children that Barker began slapping her again, they suggested that she divorce him.

She told them, "Not yet. Let me handle this in my own way."

Her children liked Wayne. He was always nice to them, but just as they saw Betty become two different people, they wondered if Wayne Barker had been cut from the same cloth as she.

On a rare, crisp evening in October 1981, Betty collected branches that had dropped from the hundred or so trees covering her large lot.

The year-round residents enjoyed this time of year. Summer crowds were gone, having shied away from the colder lake water. However, with fewer visitors, restaurants and stores were nearly empty.

Betty stacked the branches safely away from her trailer and struck a match.

"Let's hope this takes off the chill and keeps away the bugs. They're the only bad thing about living near the lake."

Her daughter, now Shirley Thompson, nodded in agreement, remembering seeing curtains of webs spun over windows and doorways. She always hated to walk near the outlet to the lake that was at the rear of her mother's property because spiderwebs smothered the area. Lake authorities disallowed insecticide spraying over the water for fear of harming fish, so insects reigned supreme. Shirley watched a fat-bodied spider scamper off a branch as the flames threatened it.

Smoke curled upward and the wood crackled and popped. Shirley stretched out her hands toward the flames. "That feels good. I've always loved a bonfire and the smell of burning wood."

Except for Shirley's voluptuous figure, she looked nothing like her mother. She possessed her father's dark coloring and wore her straight black hair in braids, tied with tiny ribbons. She had driven down from her house in rural Van Zandt County to talk with her mother about Barker, hoping she would listen to her. Finally, she said, "Mama, what are you going to do about Wayne? I just hate to hear how he's treating you."

"I'm going to kill him," Betty said stoically.

Shirley laughed. "No, don't talk silly. I mean, really what are you going to do? You've got to leave him or he could really hurt you."

"So you think I want to take this shit?" Betty asked.

"Mama, you've got to divorce him. That's all there is to it."

Betty remained silent for a moment, then said, "Hell, I can't do that. The trailer's in his name. If I divorce him, he'll get the damn trailer and I'll be stuck with an empty lot. What good would that do me?"

"Then buy a trailer. You told me you made good tips at the Cedar Club. If you start a little nest egg now, in a few months you might have the down payment. In the meantime, you could get a restraining order against him."

"I don't relish getting put out in the damn cold with winter coming."

"Of course not. But you don't mean you're really going to kill him. What if you got caught?"

"I won't get caught. Hell, I've planned every detail enough to see to that. Look over there," Betty said, turning to an open space in the trees behind them. "See that hole?" Betty pointed to a mound of loose soil that had been freshly turned.

"What about it?"

"That's where he's gonna be. No one will ever find him."

"You dug that yourself?"

"No. Of course not. I was talking real nice to one of the construction guys who was fixing the street in the next block. I told him I was building a barbecue pit and needed a hole dug. I said, 'I bet it wouldn't take you but a few minutes to dig something about four feet deep with that big backhoe of yours.' He said he guessed it wouldn't, and offered to come by after work. I told him I'd have a cold one waiting for him. 'Course like most men he said he was hoping I'd have something warm waiting for him." She laughed and gave Shirley a little jab with her elbow. "I couldn't risk a toss in the bed, not with Wayne coming home about the same time. So I thought, what the hell, I'd pay him twenty dollars. I didn't want to get messed up with anyone else right now."

"So somebody knows you had a hole dug?"

"Yes, but he's not the type to put two and two together. If he does, I'll just have something warm waiting for him."

Shirley stood looking out her living room window, awaiting her mother's arrival. She could picture her taking off in her orange-and-white Chevrolet pickup with

Bobby, her youngest brother, in tow. By now they'd be bumping over the two-lane road to Shirley's house.

When Betty and Bobby walked through her front door, Shirley felt disappointed. She'd hoped her mother would have changed her mind. After Betty confirmed that Bobby would be spending the night, she took off for her trailer after staying only an hour.

The rest of the day, Shirley thought of nothing other than her mother's plan. She still wanted to believe it wouldn't happen.

Betty stood outside in the hall, listening to Wayne's quiet snoring. She entered in the dark and went to her nightstand where she kept her loaded .38-caliber Colt revolver. Its antique-ivory handle had darkened with time, making the intricately carved design harder to appreciate.

She plucked her gun from the top drawer, then pulled back the sheet and quietly climbed into bed. The couple belts of Jim Beam she downed earlier helped toughen her resolve.

No houses adjoined her yard, but the Bensons lived two lots away, and she didn't know if they were light sleepers. Hell, she hardly knew them at all.

Betty tried to think how she could stifle the sound of the gunshot. When she plumped her pillow, she had the solution. She picked up the pillow and held it over the gun now aimed at Barker's skull. The gun felt heavier than solid stone. Her hand shook as she took a deep breath and squeezed the trigger. A blaring, ear-splitting eruption exploded into the bedroom. The surrounding metal of the trailer made the noise even louder, making it sound as though she were inside a steel drum. Wayne's body jerked as if in shock, and she realized that the pillow had only thrown off her aim. Barker let out a sharp groan, making Betty afraid she had merely awakened him. Quickly, she recocked the gun and fired again. His body momentarily stiffened, then relaxed on the mattress. She fired a third time, and waited.

After the ricochetting sound of the explosion dissipated, the trailer became as quiet as a tomb. A warm sticky liquid cascaded over Betty's fingers, and the stench of blood and gun powder filled her nose. She touched his blood-soaked neck to check his pulse.

SEVEN

Shirley laid in bed unable to sleep. She didn't dare tell her boyfriend, Larry, about her mother's plans. She wished she had someone she could trust to discuss her mother's intentions. Were her sisters also involved? Had Mama talked to them about killing Wayne? Her curiosity consumed her until she finally decided to find out.

She pulled back the covers, tiptoed out of the bedroom, and headed toward her apartment's small kitchen to call her oldest sister, Faye.

The phone rang several times before Faye's groggy voice answered.

"What's going on?" Faye asked, yawning.

"Have you heard from Mama lately?"

"Gosh no, not for weeks. Three at least. What's wrong?"

"Nothing."

"Then why did you wake me at two in the morning to ask?"

Shirley could visualize her sister's blue eyes widening in disbelief, but she resisted divulging anything about the murder in case her mother had been only bourbon sodden and later changed her mind. "Forget it," she told Faye. "I just had a bad dream about Mama. I dreamt something awful happened to her."

Faye asked, "Since when do you hold any stock in dreams?"

"You're right," Shirley said, "dreams don't mean anything." She hung up, not surprised that her mother hadn't confided in Faye, who was known as the stalwart of the family and had never done drugs. Faye always generously opened her Mesquite home to siblings in need of a bed or a home-cooked meal.

Shirley dialed her other sisters. Connie grumbled because Shirley had called so late, but Phyllis hadn't gone to bed. All three sisters gave identical replies. None of them had talked with their mother in weeks.

The fact that her mother had brought over her brother Bobby, now sleeping in the next bedroom, made Shirley realize that Betty wanted him out of the house so he wouldn't be present when she murdered his stepfather. Her brother Robby lived with their father and Shirley knew better than to involve that household with her problem.

It worried her to realize that her mother had confided to no one but her, and she had to ask herself, "Why?"

Betty Barker's nightgown clung like Saran Wrap as sweat and Wayne's blood ran down her body. She lacked remorse or guilt over Wayne's murder. In fact, she felt relieved to be rid of him. Now, no one could take her trailer.

Crawling out of bed, she turned on the light. The entire room glistened blood red. The sheets were crimson, blood had splashed on the walls, dribbled down the headboard creating ruby stripes, then puddled onto the floor. The back of Wayne's head held matted hair, but blood poured though the open star-shaped wounds of burst skin.

She went to the bathroom, eager to wash the smell of Wayne's blood from her hands. Gun powder smudged her right hand. Hiking up her nightgown, she took it off and stuffed it in the basin of cold water to soak, then threw on an old T-shirt.

Back in her bedroom, she headed for the closet. Pulling out two sheets of green plastic that a new chair had come wrapped in, she tried to tuck the plastic over and under Wayne's body until the blood stopped seeping through onto the sheets. Then she hauled out a blue canvas sleeping bag and fully unzipped it. Little by little she rolled Wayne's body onto it. His weight made everything take much longer than she had anticipated. Once his body lay encased in the bag, she zipped it and slowly rolled him to the edge of the bed. It was like moving a massive chunk of blue granite. She inhaled deeply to give herself strength, then gave him a healthy push. He tumbled off the bed and landed with a thud.

Nervous energy fueled her. She tossed clothes and shoes out of her closet, then inch by inch dragged him inside. She pushed and shoved, sticking him back far enough so she could slide the door shut.

She took another look at the room and groaned, then began spraying Lysol generously on the headboard, walls, and floor. Not wanting the blood to set, she scrubbed all the surfaces quickly and thoroughly. She spent much of the night washing sheets, towels, and night clothes. Repeatedly, she rinsed blood out of towels until the water ran pink, then threw them into the washing machine. With everything finally cleaned, she stood under a steaming hot shower, trying to scrub away every last trace of Barker. Now both mentally and physically exhausted, she went to bed and fell soundly asleep.

After making all the late phone calls, Shirley slept until noon. She awoke to find a note on her pillow from

Larry telling her that on his way to work, he would drop Bobby off at a friend's house to spend the night.

She strolled into the living room and was shocked to see her mother lying on the living room sofa.

Without moving, Betty said, "It's over. I did what I told you I was going to do."

Shirley couldn't believe her mother's nonchalance. They might as well have been exchanging recipes. Shirley stood frozen, and unable to speak.

Betty stoically related every detail of the murder from her problem with the pillow to stuffing his body into her closet.

Shirley's mind dashed back to the recently dug hole in her mother's backyard. She had actually noticed it a week before her mother had told her about it. At the time, she wondered why it had been dug, but wouldn't have imagined Betty's reason for its being there. Somehow an unwritten rule hung over the family that you didn't question Mama. Betty had the knack of giving a look that said, "You better obey." She loved her mother, but she feared asking questions that would make her angry. Lately, it didn't take much to set Betty off into one of her strange moods.

Shirley tried to rationalize Betty's actions by remembering her mother's stories about Wayne Barker abusing her. Maybe a judge would consider killing a wife abuser self-defense. But what if he didn't? What if Betty got arrested and went to prison? Shirley couldn't consider such horror. *If I don't help her bury the body, wouldn't Mama be more apt to get arrested?* she thought.

In a small voice, Shirley asked, "Have you figured out what you're going to do?"

"Somehow I've got to get his body into the barbecue pit," Betty said wryly, with no humor in her voice.

"By yourself?" Shirley asked.

"How else? He'd be awful heavy for me to carry, but

I suppose I can drag him. I'll figure something out. Don't worry about it. It's not your problem."

Shirley already felt tangled in her mother's web and worried how the petite woman would get Wayne's big, heavy body out to the grave by herself.

"Mama, I'll help," she said, suggesting the last thing she wanted to do.

Betty sat up and turned around to look at her. "You don't have to, you know. In fact, I'm not sure I want you to."

"I couldn't stand for anything to happen to you."

Betty smiled affectionately at Shirley and reached out to take her hand. With little hesitation, she said, "Okay, but we have to do it like this. You can never tell a soul. Got that? Not Larry, not your sisters, not anybody."

"I won't," Shirley said. "No one will ever find out. I'd be too afraid for anyone to know. What's next?"

"Tell Larry that Wayne and I got into a big brouhaha and I'm scared shitless of him. Say I don't want to be home alone tonight in case he comes back and wants to hurt me again. Then you come over after dinner and we'll wait 'til dark before we stick him in the ground."

Shirley leaned against the wall and nodded sadly. She wanted the whole matter to disappear. How could her own mother involve her in a murder? Worse yet, what would her mother do to her if she didn't help? She already knew what had happened to Wayne.

For the rest of the day, Betty lingered at Shirley's house and talked. She couldn't stop rambling on about shooting Wayne. While Shirley wanted to forget, her mother continued talking as if needing the discussion as a catharsis.

"If someone saw what looked like a grave it might attract attention," Betty said. "And I don't want any of those damn dogs in the neighborhood comin' over and digging him up. Tomorrow, we'll go to Seven Points and get some cinder blocks. We can build a patio over him and no one will ever know he's there."

A nearly full moon rose in the darkening October sky when Betty unlocked the front door of her trailer and pushed it open. She motioned for Shirley to go inside.

"No, you first," Shirley said, breathing deeply to calm her jitters. Her teeth involuntarily chattered, and she thought she might throw up. Cemeteries scared her silly, let alone walking into a house that hid a dead body.

Betty went directly to the kitchen and opened the pantry where her white poodle lived while she was away from home. As the dog hopped out into the room, Betty picked him up and said, "Hello, sweetkins, have you missed your mommy? You're my good baby aren't you?" She reached into the pantry and retrieved a small dog biscuit. "Here, you deserve a treat. You're such a good little boy."

Then the smile fell from Betty's face, and she said dispassionately, "He's back here."

Hesitantly, Shirley followed her mother down the hall. Betty flipped on the bedroom light, then slid back the closet door. Shirley wanted to shut her eyes, but curiosity made her look. She could see a big blue mound crouched inside. It looked like Wayne was in a sitting position.

"We need to wait until it's so dark that we can't see our hands in front of our faces."

Shirley nodded, knowing it was already dark, but they first needed to bolster their determination to get through this task. "We don't have to stay here in the house, do we?" Shirley asked. "Can't we build a bonfire outside like we did the other night?"

Her mother nodded, and Shirley went into the fastidiously clean compact kitchen and collected milk, vodka, Kahlua, a metal pitcher, and two plastic glasses to take outside.

Once in the yard, both women used flashlights to gather branches that strong winds from the lake had blown from Betty's trees.

Shirley glanced up at the velvety black sky. With fewer city lights to compete with their intensity, the stars glittered brightly and looked close enough to touch.

Betty scooped up several armfuls of leaves and scattered them over the dry wood. Her match ignited the leaves, and they flamed instantly. Now they had a fire that warmed their bodies and distracted their minds from what waited inside the closet.

A car roared by with a loud muffler, and Betty turned to look.

Shirley watched her mother's silhouette against the fire, then shifted her attention to the flickering sparks until they rose above the trees and the wind swept them away. She tried to focus on the fire's glowing red ashes and curling gray smoke, but her mother wanted to talk about Wayne's last five minutes. Shirley had already heard too much, but she let her mother get it off her chest while she slipped into an illusion of listening. She inhaled the smoke and thought of happier family times—going on family vacations, taking off for an afternoon of shopping at one of the Dallas malls, and having Christmas dinners with her big family sitting around a white clothed table.

Shirley mixed the ingredients she brought and made a pitcher of white Russians. The women sipped and talked and soon both of them could feel the intoxicating fumes of the sweet Kahlua. After a couple hours, Betty glanced at her watch. "Almost midnight," she said. "It's time."

Staggering, Shirley slowly stood up, extended a hand to her mother, and looked into her eyes. Betty had that "business as usual" demeanor that Shirley found impossibly hard to accept under the circumstances. It seemed ludicrous to be disposing of a body with the woman who always reminded her to wash her hands before dinner.

They trudged back inside the trailer and swayed down the hall. Once in the bedroom, Betty opened the closet door and tugged on the sleeping bag. Wayne's body felt as heavy as concrete, so they began dragging him. Shirley grabbed what felt like feet while Betty labored with the upper torso. Shirley saw an outline of a head through the heavy canvas as her mother took hold of it. Both women bent over at the waist and panted hard while they slowly slid the body across the carpeted floor. Then they dragged it down the hall and out through the trailer's rear exit.

When they first went outside with the sleeping bag, the moonlight shined impossibly bright. Shirley glanced at the road, worried that someone would come driving down their street, or have Ray Price come by, the security officer who made routine drive-throughs of the area. All noises seemed magnified. Cicadas buzzed loudly and waves from Cedar Creek Lake slapped against brick and stone retaining walls as the women bounced Wayne Barker down the three back steps. Then they jostled him over ground that held thin, sparse grass because of the ever-present shade. While he lay by the side of the grave, the women cleared out the loosely crumbled soil with shovels Betty had hidden under the trailer. They rolled him into the four-foot-deep opening and tried to flatten him as best they could. Then unceremoniously, they picked up their shovels and blanketed him with dirt, one spadeful at a time. As Barker became more concealed, moonlight shined on the mound that grew disturbingly high, forcing them to scoop the rest of the soil into flower beds and pots—anywhere to camouflage the existence of a grave.

"Cinder blocks will hide all that," Betty said, slurring her words.

After they finished their chore, they went back into the house and got very drunk.

Shirley lay awake all night in the spare bedroom at her mother's. With Bobby at a friend's house for the night, she had access to the trailer's only other bedroom. Every time she thought of her mother sleeping in the next room, the room where she'd killed Wayne Barker the night before, chills bounced up and down her spine.

The next morning, Shirley sluggishly pulled herself out of bed and went over to the window. Sunshine walked across the lawn, mottled by trees, but enhanced the mound of dirt she had hoped was only a bad dream. She rubbed her pounding head, feeling much older than her twenty-four years. Then she jumped as music blared from her mother's room.

In no time her mother stood at Shirley's bedroom door. Shirley squinted in disbelief. Betty looked pretty. She wore a pair of freshly pressed jeans, a soft turquoise sweater, and perennially perfect makeup. "Time to rise and shine," Betty said pertly. "I'll go put on the coffee and make some toast. We've got to get to Seven Points and pick up those blocks we talked about."

EIGHT

At five in the morning, Betty called Jerry Kuykendall. It was the time he'd be expecting her to deliver her husband for his ride to work, as she had five mornings every week.

When Kuykendall answered the phone, Betty said, "Wayne's run off."

The man gasped. "Run off?"

"Unh-huh. We had a little fight last night and he stomped out. Said he needed to buy some cigarettes, but I haven't seen him since."

"This is so hard to believe," Kuykendall said. "Guys like Wayne don't just leave. I've got him in charge of a big crew we have going this morning. Talked to him just last night and he sounded fine. He even asked my boy to spend the night."

"Well he's gone. It doesn't make any sense to me either."

"Did he say where he was going? There must be some way I can get hold of him."

"I have no idea. If he knew where he'd be, he didn't tell me."

Kuykendall pondered Wayne's disappearance for three days. How could a man be such a contradiction—dependable at work and a flake at home?

After finishing his third day of work without his best employee, he drove by the Barker home to see if he could learn any more about Wayne's abrupt departure.

Kuykendall remembered all the good times he and his wife had with Wayne and Betty—spending the day fishing, or going to McClain's and eating fried catfish. He pulled up to the trailer and relief flooded through him when he saw Barker's truck parked in the driveway. "Thank God," he said as he turned into the driveway and pulled behind the truck.

He strolled to the familiar porch, swathed in flowers, and rang the doorbell. But something about the blond woman who answered the door wasn't familiar at all.

"Sure glad Wayne's changed his mind," he said, nodding toward the truck.

"What the hell you talking about?"

"Well, obviously Wayne's come back. You said he'd run off."

"He did leave," Betty replied, acting more antagonistic than emotional over Wayne's sudden departure. She secured the lock on the screen door.

"I never heard of a man leaving without taking his truck," Kuykendall said.

Betty flashed him a hostile stare. She didn't invite him in, nor did she appear interested in talking. "I've told you all I know. Wayne got mad and left. He hasn't called me or anything since."

"Well, shoot. I sure need him back on the job. If you hear from him, please let him know his job's waiting."

"All right," Betty replied, almost shutting the door in Kuykendall's face.

He stood staring at the closed door knowing something was wrong. What happened to the friendly Betty who had spent so much time with him and his wife? Where was the woman who frequently invited his son to spend the night with Bobby, then fixed pancakes for the boys the next morning?

As he went back to his car, he looked again at Wayne's truck. A man just doesn't leave his new pickup and go away willingly.

Kuykendall was still questioning Wayne's disappearance when Betty showed up the following Friday at his office to collect Wayne's paycheck.

Betty needed a man like people need air to breathe. Her job at the Cedar Club fulfilled that need perfectly, as it allowed her to meet dozens of men.

Located on Seven Points's Highway 274, the club could easily be found as the highway crossed the only intersection in town that had traffic lights. The wheels of customers' cars had to crunch over a gravel parking lot that separated the club from the highway. Housed in a sterile-looking, concrete-block structure that had been painted numerous times, the club's current color was gray. The window glass, also coated with gray paint, kept out sunshine and prying eyes.

Inside the place, a customer had to take a moment for his eyes to adjust to the cave-dark interior. Once adapted, customers could see a U-shaped bar in the middle of the large room, with dozens of glasses hanging upside down from an overhead wooden rack. Four pool tables sat to the left of the bar, and several dart boards were bolted on walls to the right.

By the time people stepped onto the charcoal-color tile floors, no one sensed they were drinking in the middle of the day. Nor in the early morning for that matter. Like other bars in Seven Points, it opened early for business and Happy Hour ran from seven to eleven in the morning. For some, drinking their breakfast was a way of life.

The selection of men varied. Hard-working cowboys breathed the same smoky air as retired oldsters, and having a full set of teeth was not a customer requirement. But every now and then someone attractive with a decent job dropped by. Betty kept her antennae up for them. Her caustic wit and salty tongue fit in perfectly with the bar crowd, and the majority of patrons loved her.

Tonight she dressed in a conservative gray blouse tucked into a gathered gray-and-coral print skirt. The hem of her skirt flared out as she spun away from the bar with a tray of four draft Coors, taking them to a table where one of her customers had just sneezed. "Whew, I've got a cold," the man drawled in his slow colloquial twang.

"No shit. Now we all have a cold," Betty said, not looking up as she placed a beer in front of each patron.

"I covered my mouth with my hand," her customer protested.

"That's a hell of a big job for one hand," Betty said, and turned on her heel.

Waves of laughter erupted behind her, but she ignored those people when she caught the eye of a handsome new customer. He sat watching her, and also laughed. She stepped over to his table, and said, "What would you like, sir?"

"You," he said. "Why don't you come sit down here?" He patted the Naugahyde seat of the chair next to him.

"As much as I'd like to, I'm afraid fraternizing is against the rules. Besides, you look like you wouldn't have any trouble finding company," she said with a wink.

"This place has rules?" he asked, sincerely surprised. "What's your name?"

"My friends call me Jimmy Don."

"Nice to meet you, Mr. Don."

He smiled. "Do you have an answer for everything?"

"I wish."

"When do you get off work?"

"Late. Those big brown eyes of yours would be pretty sleepy if you waited for me. I go home sometime between one-thirty and two."

"That's past my bedtime. I'll need to catch you when I don't have an early shift the next day."

"Shift?"

"I'm with the Dallas Fire Department."

"What did you do before that?"

"I was in the army during the Korean War."

"Korean War? That was a hundred years ago," Betty said.

"I've been with the fire department for twenty-six years. Four more and I get to retire."

"Lucky you. Then what are you going to do, sit on your dock and fish?"

"Or in my boat."

"I wish they'd give barmaids retirement benefits. I wouldn't mind doing some fishing myself." Betty gave him a long, lingering smile.

A native Texan, Jimmy Don Beets had one child, James Donald Beets III, born on December 24, 1957, who went by the nickname Jamie. That Christmas Eve was the only time that Jimmy Don ever missed a shift at the fire department. He had rushed his pregnant wife, Charlene, to the hospital only an hour before the baby's birth. Three years after that, another son came along, but lived just five heartbreaking hours. Two years later, a daughter was stillborn. The deaths of their children left both parents depressed. Jimmy Don sought solace in alcohol. Charlene understandably objected to all the time he spent drinking after work. She didn't like the taverns he visited nor his absence from the family. His new lifestyle proved to be the dismantling of their marriage, and he and Charlene divorced after Jamie turned nine. The divorce devastated the young child, who somehow felt responsible. He went to live with his mother until his twelfth birthday. By then Jimmy Don had remarried.

A few months after his divorce, he met Suzy Robertson through mutual friends in Dallas. He frequently ran into the tall, attractive brunette at various clubs, but at the time they both had other love interests.

Then one night after dancing and partying at one of the clubs, Suzy left and walked out to her car in the parking lot, but she couldn't get it started. The gears were frozen.

As she tugged on the gearshift, Jimmy Don just happened to leave the club and saw her struggling. Anyone needing help was his specialty. He went to her car and made a circular motion with his hand for Suzy to put down the window.

"You look like a lady with a problem," he said.

"I can't get the gears to move. Otherwise, I think it would start."

Jimmy Don opened the door and sat down, turned the steering wheel a couple of times, and after a click, shifted the gears and the engine roared to life.

Suzy's red face showed in the lights from the dashboard. "I'm really embarrassed. You're going to think I set that up."

"If you did, I'm flattered. Gives us a chance to get to know each other better." They talked for over an hour. He enjoyed her robust personality and she was taken by his sincere interest in people.

The next morning he came over for coffee, and after that they began seeing each other on a regular basis. Suzy had been married once before, but never had children. She thoroughly enjoyed the times Jimmy Don brought his son along. Suzy doted on the boy, who appeared to love all the attention.

In six months, Suzy and Jimmy Don married, and soon afterward built a home in Kemp, a small rural community north of Cedar Creek Lake. No stranger to commuting, Jimmy Don drove to the fire department each day, and Suzy willingly motored to Dallas and her job at Western Auto.

Later, they bought the blue house in Glen Oaks where Jimmy Don and Suzy were the favorites of the neighborhood. There was always a group ready to go out boating with them. They'd navigate far out into the water, tie their boats together, then have a picnic in the middle of the lake. Jimmy Don partied on his free days—either with fishing, swimming, barbecuing, or watching football.

To Jamie, life with Dad and Suzie was fun and exciting; something he would like on a more permanent basis. When Jamie turned twelve, his mother consented to let him live full-time with Jimmy Don. Jamie became close to Suzy, enjoying her frequent hugs and patient willingness to listen to him. But there were times when Jamie would pout and say, "If you don't let me have that I'll just go back to Mama."

After Jamie used that threat twice, they gave him an ultimatum. He chose his father and Suzy.

Those years proved happy for Jamie as he stood on the threshold of young adulthood. He was wavy haired and handsome, in addition to being an outstanding student. He whipped off high school in three years. When he graduated ahead of time, his father and Suzy were very proud of him.

"Here's what we do for brilliant people in our family," his father told him. "We're going to buy you a car; then you get to take the summer off. You won't have to work for any spending money since you've worked so hard in school. What do you think of that?"

Jamie thought it was wonderful, but it proved to be his undoing. With time on his hands, he began running with a crowd that frequently used marijuana. He became enthralled with their lazy, hazy lifestyle and, as he used drugs, he mimicked his friends' long hair and unkempt appearance, much to the chagrin of his neatly groomed father.

That summer created a chasm between father and son. Jimmy Don had no use for someone on drugs, who had no desire for either college or a job.

Like tumbling dominoes, the upheaval with Jimmy Don's son crushed the marriage. Because of the many heated arguments over how to handle the boy, Suzy subsequently divorced Jimmy Don after fourteen years of matrimony. Once the divorce was final, it still hurt her to see him with other women.

Jimmy Don's desire for companionship rushed him into a third marriage—only months after divorcing Suzy. Unfortunately, that rapid decision caused an even quicker divorce three months later.

But still attracted to Suzy, Jimmy Don met with her several times and began talking seriously of getting back together and possibly remarrying.

However, those conversations were permanently interrupted the night he strode into the Cedar Club and met Betty Lou Barker.

"Mama? It's Faye. What the hell's going on down there? I was talking to Bobby the other night and he tells me Wayne's run off."

"And thank God he has," Betty said.

"I guess I agree with that," Faye said. "You told us how badly he treated you."

"I should have kicked him out a long time ago. But here's what happened, honey. We had this really bad argument. Worse than any we ever had before. And he just huffed out the front door, saying he was going to get some cigarettes. Ever since, I've been expecting that door to open and see him come walking back in, but he never has."

"Just like that? He drove off and you haven't seen him since?"

"Actually, he walked away. That's how mad he was. Even left his new truck parked in the driveway. Guess I can sell it so he won't be a total loss."

"Sure sounds strange that he left without his truck," Faye said.

Betty knew it sounded strange, but she had no other explanation, so she stuck with her story.

After a brief silence, Faye said, "Well, good riddance."

"That's what I say," Betty replied.

Betty sparkled when she saw Jimmy Don walk into the Cedar Club the following weekend. She stood at the bar, sliding clean stemware into the overhead glass racks as he approached.

"I'm not one to drag things out," he said. "I've got the weekend off, so we can spend some time Saturday unless you're already busy."

"I don't have plans."

"I assume you just work here at night." He pointed to the spigot for Coors draft beer. "I'll take one of those, please."

Betty nodded, then pulled down a mug and began filling it with the frothy brew. "I'm off until six P.M. every day. You know, Mr. Don, I've never heard of a last name like that before."

He laughed. "I'm Jimmy Don Beets."

"Like the vegetable?"

"Oh, great, you'll think of me as a vegetable. Just don't call me a fruit."

They both laughed, and Betty enjoyed how sincere and friendly he seemed. He also appeared laid back. She liked that.

"The weather's supposed to be good," he said. "How about going boating? I keep my boat near my house."

"Where's that?"

"Over at Glen Oaks," he said, taking a gulp of his cold beer. "It's just a three bedroom, but it's all paid for."

"Well, I'm impressed. Did you win the lottery or something?"

"It wasn't easy. Had to double up on my payments, but I saved a lot in interest."

"Hmmm, a smart businessman," she said, leaning toward him, letting him smell her perfume and giving him an opportunity to look deeply into her blue eyes, and other parts of her anatomy.

At that moment, three customers approached the bar, interrupting their conversation. Jimmy Don went over to shoot darts. One of the printed signs above a target read: MY WIFE TOLD ME TO CHOOSE BETWEEN HER AND DARTS. I'M SURE GONNA MISS THAT WOMAN.

Beets stayed another hour, then made arrangements to pick up Betty at ten the next morning.

It was before ten when Jimmy Don stood at the front door of Betty's trailer. She came to the door with a smile and a wicker basket. He walked her outside and opened the door of his car for her. It took about ten minutes to drive to his house, and as soon as they arrived, two sets of neighbors who lived across the street came over to inspect the latest woman their favorite bachelor had brought home.

Jimmy Don introduced Betty to everyone.

The two couples, the Burtons and the Leonards, had known Jimmy Don through his three marriages, and had told him how they wished he'd find someone to settle down with who would make him happy. Had they been polled, they'd probably want him to still be married to Suzy, someone they felt comfortable to be around. Now they took long, lingering glances at Betty, who wore tight-fitting clothes and had hair much lighter than anything they had seen outside of their youngest grandchildren. They appeared fascinated with the little woman they would soon take to calling "Blondie."

"This is some man here," Russ Leonard said, nodding toward Jimmy Don.

"Now careful," Jimmy Don replied. "Don't give out any secrets."

"I'm not going to tell her the racy stuff until I know her better," Leonard said, laughing. "I just want to tell her about Dub. He lives over there," he said, pointing to a house across the street. "Been blind since the Second World War. Jimmy Don had a little heart attack a while back after laying a concrete driveway for him. Then while he was recovering, he went back over and fixed Dub's screen door. That's the kind of man this is," he said, clapping an embarrassed Jimmy Don on the back.

"Shall we see about getting your boat?" Betty asked him. "I brought us a picnic lunch."

The couples took the hint and turned to go back to their houses. Betty overheard one woman say, "Did you see that figure? It's just not normal for a woman her age to be so trim. Why she can still wear her blouses tucked in."

Betty was glad to see them go for she had tired of

the small talk. Besides, she didn't need anyone to sell her on Jimmy Don. He was just the man she had been looking for.

Jimmy Don's house didn't front on the lake, but his friends' houses across the street did and everyone had a long dock and a boathouse. Since many of his neighbors were beholden to him for his many favors over the years, he had several invitations to tie his boat at any one of their docks.

He carried the picnic basket and ushered Betty across the street to his boat. Once there, he frowned and retrieved a soft cloth from the boat's cabin to remove a smudge from its side. "Someone must have stepped aboard with a dirty foot." He stood back a moment to admire the shine of his nineteen-foot Glastron. He had traded a smaller boat for it, and even though the Glastron had been used, it appeared brand new and Jimmy Don kept it looking that way. He enjoyed puttering with mechanical things too, and took pleasure in spending his leisure time maintaining the motor in perfect condition.

Once on the water, Betty stood behind Jimmy Don's leather captain's chair and spoke in his ear over the roar of the motor. She frequently massaged his shoulders. When he shut down the boat so they could eat lunch, she sat close to him, laughing at his jokes. She affectionately patted his hand. "You know the best stories," she said. "You are so much fun to be with."

"I've never known anyone more positive than you," Jimmy Don told her. "Here you are supporting yourself and you never complain about how hard you have to work. Carrying all those heavy trays. Having to clean up trashed-out tables after people leave."

"I like my job. I like being with people. What's there to complain about?"

He reached up and took her hand. She followed his cue by pulling herself onto his lap. Then she placed her hands on his face and kissed him passionately. After a lingering stare, she told him, "I get all cozy inside when I'm with you."

That day, Jimmy Don Beets fell in love. He adored the way Betty smothered him with affection—frequently sitting on his lap, or at least being close enough to stroke his back or kiss his cheek. She behaved the same way whether they were alone or with his friends and neighbors.

At first the neighbors appeared uncomfortable with her public displays of affection. Then the displays became a source of humor.

"You better watch out, Jimmy Don. No woman can keep that up forever," J. R. Burton said. "Just wait till the other shoe drops." The neighbors laughed heartily, but Betty only smiled.

She seemed bored when the neighbors bragged about their grandchildren. Jimmy Don glanced around his family oriented neighborhood and realized Betty was as out of place as a brass band at a funeral.

After a month, Jimmy Don had partially moved in with her, spending a week at a time in the trailer. Since he wasn't living full time in his blue frame house in Glen Oaks, Betty was able to nudge him away from his friends and more into the crowd she liked.

He knew he had found the woman who would keep him company during his retirement years. For a man who loved people, being alone was anathema to him. In fact, he blamed rushing into his brief third marriage on the fear of being alone, especially as he faced retirement.

Then when he repeatedly heard Betty say, "Jimmy

Don's the man I've been looking for all my life," it seemed only natural to ask her to marry him, and she enthusiastically accepted.

Even though Jimmy Don rarely saw his son, Jamie, he felt obligated to tell him that he was about to acquire a new stepmother.

Twenty-five-year-old Jamie Beets had married a pretty little blonde with wavy hair, perfect skin, and eyes spaced wide apart that turned up at the outer edges with a laughing, elfin tilt. She liked wearing snug-fitting blue jeans that complimented her petite figure.

Much to his father's chagrin, Jamie's hair flowed around his handsome face and well past his collar. His mustache connected to a goatee. The couple had given Jimmy Don two grandchildren, whom he loved very much. He would admit to anyone that they were the main reasons he stayed in contact with his son. During the times his son had experimented with drugs, he had trouble keeping a job. Jimmy Don worried that during those times, his grandchildren would go without life's necessities, so he provided them with money to tide them over.

Betty accompanied Jimmy Don to his son's apartment. Immediately Jamie's posture straightened and he eyed Betty suspiciously. The more Betty and Jimmy Don talked about their life together, the more distant Jamie became.

However, Jamie saved his words for the next visit when his father came alone. At that time, Jamie stiffened again and said, "I can't stand her, Dad. She a manipulative, self-centered bitch."

Jamie's words shocked Jimmy Don. "But I love her, Jamie. And I'm going to marry her."

* * *

After Jimmy Don heard the tale of Betty's previous husband, Wayne Barker, running off one night, he said, "Betty, I just can't understand why any man would do that to you. Especially you. It'd be the last of my thoughts."

"He drank an awful lot," Betty replied. "So there were many arguments. After he stayed gone a while, I filed for divorce and charged him with desertion. He didn't contest."

On August 19, 1982, Betty Lou Barker and Jimmy Don Beets went to the courthouse in Kaufman, Texas, a small town north of the lake, and said their vows to become husband and wife.

Jimmy Don happily moved into Betty's trailer. He particularly liked the fact that the back of her property had an inlet connected to the lake. Now he no longer had to count on someone else's dock, and eagerly tied his boat to a post in his own backyard.

His fire department schedule of three days on, three off gave him a span of days he happily considered a vacation with his new bride.

The ink had scarcely dried on the wedding license when Betty Beets began criticizing Jimmy Don's generosity toward his son. Once she learned that a couple thousand dollars a year poured into the young man's pockets, she was determined to stop it.

She convinced her husband to have Jamie visit them in the trailer, and had practically written the script for their meeting.

That night, Jamie walked in, appearing apprehensive and dispirited, as if expecting bad news. Betty knew that he didn't like her, but she was no friend of his either because he represented competition for Jimmy Don's resources.

"Son," Jimmy Don began, "Betty's convinced me that it's high time you grew up. You're twenty-five now and you need to be more responsible, especially since you have a wife and two children to support. I don't want to hear anymore, 'Dad, can you loan me a few bucks 'til I can find another job?' With all your family responsibilities, you need to see to it that you stay employed. No more of this job-hopping."

Jimmy Don softened his voice. "Betty and I agree that you can live in my lake house, but you'll have to pay rent and utilities. Understand?"

Jamie nodded numbly, all the time squinting hateful glances at Betty.

"I've got to be honest with you, Jamie. The only thing I really want from you is to see my two grandchildren."

Jimmy Don and Betty became well known in the party circuit at the lake. Much to Betty's delight, they frequented the clubs in Seven Points as opposed to doing things with his neighbors. Jimmy Don had almost permanently severed that connection when he let his son move into his Glen Oaks house.

One night at the Frontier Club, Betty and Jimmy Don encountered his ex-wife, Suzy, enjoying a night out with her new husband. They pranced over to Suzy's table and she invited them to sit down. The awkwardness of her ex-husband joining her table melted as the evening progressed. The four of them talked of their lives at the lake as Betty continued sipping several Cokes laced heavily with bourbon. Before long she became very drunk. Betty and Jimmy Don got up to dance and Betty was so dizzy he had to hold her up. Jimmy Don only teased Betty about her condition.

Betty continued drinking and began slurring her words. When her new husband tried to hush her, she said, "Don't you tell me what to do."

Jimmy Don's forehead beaded with perspiration and his faced reddened; obviously embarrassed by the situation. "I've got to take my bride home," he said. "She's having a little too much fun."

Suzy watched as he half carried, half dragged Betty out through the doorway. She thought back to when she had been married to Jimmy Don and the times she had drunk too much. He would be disgusted with her and would tell her so. After thinking over the evening, she realized Jimmy Don treated Betty differently because he loved her so much more.

In 1982, Betty and Jimmy Don celebrated their first Christmas together as husband and wife. Jamie avoided them by taking his family to Celina, Texas, where his wife's mother lived. Everything went smoothly and both families enjoyed the holidays until December 28. On that day, Jamie was still in Celina, and Jimmy Don was in Dallas, manning his shift at the fire station.

Russ and Peggy Leonard saw flames coming from the blue house across the street right before J. R. and Marion Burton did. The ex-neighbors of Jimmy Don called the fire department, then raced across the street. They coughed in the billowing smoke as they looked for a hose. When they found it, they grabbed the hose and turned on the water spigot. To their dismay, they found that someone had shut off the water.

NINE

A little past eight on a spring night in 1983, Freddie Gilbert drove up to Robby Branson's house in his beat-up green Ford that had one blue fender. He laid on his horn until Betty Beets came to the door.

"You crazy or something making all that noise out there?" Betty hollered from her front porch.

"Sorry, ma'am, I'm just lookin' for Robby. Is he home?"

Betty frowned, and saying nothing, turned away, but kept the door ajar. Moments later, eighteen-year-old Robby appeared. He had his father's dark good looks and thick brown wavy hair. He had lived with his father for ten years, and had recently moved back to his mother's.

"Mom says to quit making that racket. What do you want anyway?"

"How about going for a ride? The swimmin' pool might be open. We could check it out. Might be some girls there."

"Then what?"

"What do you think? Do you want me to draw you a fuckin' picture? We'll pick up a couple chicks and go get some beer. I don't know. We'll do something."

Robby shrugged and ambled toward Freddie's car. "Guess so," he said and opened the door, sitting down on the worn, dirty front seat.

Freddie floored his ancient vehicle until it jumped forward; the tires squealed as he bumped across Robby's front yard. They drove past the Cherokee Shores swimming pool, but only saw a basin of dirty concrete that contained the muddy remnant of last summer's water. Ropes still blocked access to the pool. Freddie stopped when he saw a heavy-set young woman strolling past the pool. He rolled down his window and snorted like a pig. Then in a loud, high voice he called, "Sowie, sowie, sooowie!

"Get the hell out of here," Robby said. "You're acting like a jerk."

Freddie put the car in gear and drove on.

Robby asked, "What now?"

"Wish I had a beer," Freddie said, "but I don't have any ID. Do you?"

"Not on me. Got a couple cards back at the house."

"Nah. There's a faster way."

"What?" Robbie asked, getting bored and frustrated with the evening.

Freddie cruised down a street that had small lake homes on one side. "I'm looking for one that's dark." He drove slowly, then paused in front of a small frame house painted yellow. No lights shined from the windows. "Look there. A boat out on the dock and nobody inside."

"If you wanted to go for a boat ride, Jimmy Don's got a boat."

"I don't want no boat ride." He shut off the engine and looked around. "If someone likes boats, he probably likes beer. Don't you get it?" He gazed up and down the street. "I don't see anybody, let's go."

"Where?"

"Inside, where in the hell else? You wanted some beer, didn't you?"

"You're fuckin' out of your mind. You're going to break in?"

"Do you want beer or don't you? I thought you had balls. Guess you're just a wuss."

"I ain't no wuss. I just think it's stupid to break in. What if we get caught?"

"Only dummies get caught. I never have."

"You've done this before?"

"Sure. And no cop's ever nabbed me. Come on, I'll show you how." Freddie grabbed a flashlight from his glove compartment.

It didn't feel right to Robby, but curious about Freddie's confidence, he followed him around to the back of the house.

Freddie's scrawny body was a contrast to Robby's stocky build, but Freddie had a few inches in height over his friend. He shined his light on the sliding-glass and screen-door combination, then pulled a knife from his pocket and cut a hole in the screen. He slipped his knife into the flimsy lock and snapped it open. They quietly walked into the kitchen. Freddie stuck out his arm to stop Robby for a couple minutes to listen for an alarm system; then they headed toward the refrigerator.

Freddie opened the door and the light lit up the room. They found milk and orange juice, but no beer. They searched through other cabinets, but found no liquor anywhere.

"Damn fucking Baptists," Freddie murmured. "Let's look around and see what they have."

"This is taking too long," Robby complained. "Let's get the hell out of here."

"Hold on a sec. Look over there. Bet those are worth something." Freddie went to two crossed, silver-sheathed swords that hung above the mantel over the brick fireplace. He reached up and removed them. Handing one

to Robby, he raised his sword high in the air, and yelled.
"Zorro!"

"That's it," Robby said and gave back the sword. "I'll
meet you in the car."

Freddie followed him out with the swords tucked under his arm. They climbed in the car and drove away.
When Freddie dropped Robby off at his house, both
swords remained in his car.

The next day, police were at Robby Branson's front
door with an arrest warrant for burglary of a habitation.

"What are you talking about?" Robby asked the officer, trying to buy time to absorb the situation.

"When the owners returned last night," the officer
explained, "they found some expensive swords missing.
That's when they called us. Just happened that the next-
door neighbor jotted down your friend's license plate,
and said he saw two suspicious-looking youths leave with
the swords."

"You talked to Freddie?" Robby asked, thinking the
police had worked so fast.

"Oh sure. Told us everything. Said it was all your idea
and he just drove the car."

Betty Beets paced back and forth in her small living
room.

"Now sit down and tell me again what happened,"
Jimmy Don said.

"I've explained what the police said a hundred
times," Betty replied. "I don't know about Freddie. He
might have to do some jail time because police found
him with the loot. But the hell with Freddie. The police
told me if we could make Robby's bail, he'll get out
until his hearing. Since they found he didn't take anything and has no prior record, they'll probably give him
probation."

"Then let's go get him," Jimmy Don said.

Betty looked longingly at her husband. "You don't understand. We'd have to come up with a cool grand just to get him out of jail. I couldn't ask you to do that."

Jimmy Don stood up and put his arms around her. "Whatever I have is yours. If we have to spend a thousand dollars to get Robby out of jail, we will. He's never done anything wrong before. He'll just need to stay away from Freddie what's-his-name."

Later that day, Betty and Jimmy Don bailed a contrite Robby out of the Henderson County Jail, and hired an attorney, E. Ray Andrews, to represent him. Betty had frequently run into E. Ray when she worked in the bars.

Betty and Jimmy Don attended Robby's hearing a month later where the judge gave him six years probation. Legally, Robby now had a criminal record.

Jimmy Don, fastidious and organized, appreciated Betty's penchant for neatness as well. He wanted to encourage that, so when she suggested he build a storage shed, he listened.

"Sweetie," she said, "we really could use a place to keep all our stuff. We don't have anywhere to put your tools. All those things you need for your boat. Just sticking them behind the trailer looks so tacky."

Jimmy Don caught a glimpse of his fishing gear and boat-repair equipment leaning against the trailer and had to agree.

"Yeah. We could use a storage shed." He looked around the large lot. "Let's see. How about over there?" he said, gesturing toward the rear of the backyard.

"That wouldn't be convenient. No sense in going all the way back there when we need something. Just build it here over the patio."

"Over those old cinder blocks?"

"They can be moved."

"That's a bad place. Just look at the center. It's all sunken in. May have a water problem or something."

"I really want the shed here."

"No, Betty, there's another problem. I'd have to get the gas company out to move the butane tank so we'd have enough room."

"So move the tank."

"Betty, you're not being reasonable. On a half-acre lot we have dozens of places. There's no need to put it there."

Her bottom lip protruded. "Why are you acting that way? All I asked was for a storage shed so our place would look nicer, and now you're arguing with me."

Betty went to him and spread her arms around his broad shoulders. "Please, Jimmy Don. Please do it for me?"

A few days later, Jimmy Don was piling all the cinder blocks in several stacks and busily adding dirt to the sunken spot when Phyllis's husband, William Coleman, drove over.

"What's going on?" William asked.

"This is known as 'Betty's Shed,' " Jimmy Don joked. "She wanted this built, but for some reason she had her heart set on it being right here. Couldn't talk her out of it. We had to do without fuel for the water heater and stove all day yesterday while the gas company moved the butane tank."

"Sounds like a hell of a lot of trouble," Coleman said.

"It was. But when my wife makes up her mind, there's no changing it."

* * *

Thirty-one-year-old Jackie Collins idolized her Uncle Jimmy Don Beets. When his name flashed on her computer at J.C. Penney Insurance where she worked in the Dallas suburb of Plano, she took particular care to read the new life insurance policy. She was stripping the policy—taking the policy information from her computer and verifying that it perfectly matched the insurance application.

The policy had been in force for a month because the first premium had already been paid. Initially, Jackie saw nothing unusual about the $10,000 policy, until she checked the address. The address given on the application differed from her uncle's and even the address of his new wife. An attached note indicated all correspondence regarding the policy be directed to an address on Park Street in Mesquite, Texas. She had no idea who lived there.

Jackie sat back in her chair and analyzed the situation. Without his address being used, her uncle may not know about the policy. A sense of uncertainty grew in her stomach. She decided to give him a call.

After catching up on his new marriage, she asked, "Did you take out a life insurance policy recently?"

"Life insurance? No, why?"

"One just came across my desk with your name on it."

"You're kidding me. I never applied for any insurance. How much is it for?"

"Ten thousand." She heard her uncle's low whistle.

"There's another thing," she said, "we're supposed to send all correspondence to a Mesquite address. Doesn't that sound strange?"

"Sounds more than strange. I've got over $100,000 in insurance already with Betty's name as the beneficiary. I sure don't need any more. How about sending that to me, honey, so I can get to the bottom of this?"

Jackie agreed, then hung up the receiver, but she couldn't get the policy off her mind. Who lived at that Mesquite address? A person needed an insurable right before they could purchase a policy on someone else. Who knew Jimmy Don well enough to get a policy without his knowledge?

She searched the application and found a phone number for that address. After punching in the number, she waited through several rings. No one answered.

Clutching the papers, Jackie decided to talk with her supervisor. Jackie's office was in the large Penney's headquarters building, and it took a few moments to walk the long carpeted corridor and into the spacious, well-appointed office of her boss.

She explained the situation to him, and he listened patiently.

"Actually this sounds rather serious, Jackie. If someone's buying insurance that the insured doesn't know about, there may be, well there could be something sinister about it." Then he chuckled. "I don't know. Maybe I've been watching too many mysteries on TV. But my gut tells me we should check this out."

Jackie's eyes widened as she listened. "You mean someone could be planning to kill him to collect the proceeds?"

"Let's not get carried away, but that's a possibility. It could be someone he feels safe to be around, but he's in danger since he hasn't been told about the policy."

"This is terrible. My poor uncle."

"Tell you what. Take those papers and leave work right now. Hand carry the policy to your uncle, and we won't have to worry about it any longer. If Mr. Beets doesn't want that policy, he needs to cancel it immediately. Just precautionary, of course."

As Jackie drove to the Number Nine fire station in

southeast Dallas that her uncle commanded, she couldn't get her boss's concerned expression off her mind.

Once she arrived at the big, open fire station, Jimmy Don gave her a hug. He pulled up a chair for her, then reached for the policy and glanced at it. A shocked expression lined his handsome face.

"I have no idea what this is about." He drew a diagonal line across the face of the policy and wrote "Please Cancel, Jimmy Don Beets" in large letters.

After reading more of the policy, he said, "Hmmm. Betty's the beneficiary. I'm going to have a little talk with her when I get home.

"Now that I see it, this Mesquite address looks familiar. I think it belongs to Betty's daughter, Faye Lane. This *is* strange. Faye doesn't get any of our other mail."

Late the next afternoon, Jimmy Don returned to the lake from his shift. He walked through the pristine house and found Betty in the laundry room sorting his socks.

After he gave her cheek a peck, he said, "What's with this insurance policy?" He waved the copy his niece had left for him.

Betty looked mystified. "I've no idea. I certainly didn't buy one."

He frowned as he told her about his niece who discovered the J.C. Penney policy.

"All I remember about Penney's is getting something in the mail to open a charge account. Isn't that all right?"

"This isn't a charge account, Betty. It's a $10,000 policy on my life. And *you're* the beneficiary."

"Let me see." She placed her hand on her chin. "There was something about insurance, but I thought they were just insuring the charge account in case I missed a payment or something."

Jimmy Don shook his head. "Betty, promise me. Leave the business affairs to me, okay? You obviously don't understand them."

Betty knew enough of Jimmy Don's finances to know that Jamie Beets hadn't paid his father rent for living in his lake house all those months before the fire. In addition, Jimmy Don paid his son's utilities.

Betty goaded her husband into another meeting with Jamie. "A Come-to-Jesus" meeting she called it. "It's high time that that boy of yours learns to be responsible."

Since Betty had already coached her husband, she felt confident enough to let him handle it. She'd go shopping.

Jimmy Don's insurance company had promptly paid him several thousand for the fire damage to his house, but his handyman skills had saved him money. When Betty learned about the windfall, she had no intention of letting it go to Jamie Beets, even if Jamie's property did burn along with the house.

Jamie strolled up to the trailer door to meet with his father. But once he stood at the door, the scene felt all too familiar. Every conversation with his father would be uncomfortable since his father knew how much Jamie detested Betty.

Jimmy Don opened the door and Jamie came in with a hat-in-hand demeanor. He looked into the eyes of his father, the father he always seemed to fail. With all that his father had given him, what Jamie wanted most was his father's approval.

Jimmy Don motioned for his son to sit at the kitchen table where he had placed a few sheets of papers with numbers on them.

"Okay, here's what I figure you owe me from the rent you didn't pay, in addition to the utilities."

Jamie looked at "$3,000" scribbled on the paper and gulped. He had no savings.

"Here's what I plan to do. I'll keep that much from the insurance settlement and consider your debt paid."

Relief swept over Jamie, and he smiled.

Jimmy Don handed him a check for $850. "Here, this should cover any clothes and personal belongings your family lost in the blaze."

Fortunately for Jamie, he and his family had packed many of their clothes for their Christmas trip to his wife's mother's, and that's where they had lived during the lake house's construction.

Jamie took the check, relieved and excited at the same time. He reached out to hug his father, but Jimmy Don pushed him away.

"The only thing I want from you is to see my grandchildren."

Both relief and anger struggled inside Jamie. He would have been more upset had he known that this would be the last time he'd ever see his father alive.

A year before Jimmy Don married Betty, her brother Dewey had died and Jimmy Don had driven her back to Virginia for the funeral. Betty was grateful to have Jimmy Don there, for he was comforting and understanding. The unexpected death of Betty's brother, only two years older than she, had shocked her. She cried at the funeral home when she first saw him in his casket and cried again through the entire service the next day.

Her mother, Louise Dunevant, suggested Betty and

Jimmy Don return this year. It would be a happier time, and she could get to know the nice man Betty had brought with her. They left on July 3, 1983, and took Bobby with them for the two-week trip. Robby, the oldest son, stayed home by himself because he had a summer job pumping gas at a station in Seven Points.

Betty was eager to get reacquainted with her younger brother and sister, who were still small when she left home at fifteen to marry Robert Branson.

Once in Virginia, Betty's mother exclaimed how delighted she was to see her with a man like Jimmy Don Beets because Betty had never looked so happy in her life.

Home alone, Robby took advantage of the situation and played with his parents' toys.

First he took in the glittering lake and envied people out there racing their boats. It was always hot in mid-July and today seemed hotter than most. He glanced at Jimmy Don's boat, then back at the water. Jimmy Don always kept the boat's ignition key on the key chain for his car, so there'd be no point looking for it in the house. Robby disconnected the ignition wires, spliced them together, and soon the boat's engine roared to life. He raced across the lake, smiling as the breeze cooled his skin and blew his thick hair.

A few days later, he decided to try out his brother's new motorcycle. It was small compared to his, but Robby wanted to air it out.

Only two years older than Bobby, Robby had a man's body compared to his 120-pound kid brother, who always rode his motorcycle cautiously. He knew that his brother kept the key in his top dresser drawer.

Jumping on the cycle, he started it, gunned the engine until it screamed, and took off down the narrow

road in front of his house, racing the cycle to higher
and faster speeds. He found it fun to push the cycle at
speeds his wimpy brother refused to try.

He turned sharply on a narrow road, but his speed
proved too fast for the machine. The cycle's tires slipped
on the oil-slick road and skidded. He lost control. Barely
holding on, he stayed with the cycle as it spun off into
the woods. Finally, crunching into a tree, it came to a
halt with one wheel spinning and Robby underneath.

After a few moments, Robby collected himself and
painfully unwound from the broken cycle. He surveyed
the damage and winced at the sight of the front fender
that had accordion-pleated over the flat front tire. Shaking his head, he limped home to get his mother's truck.

He returned to the motorcycle, but because of the
distance he had ventured into the trees, he couldn't
avoid driving through deep mud to reach the cycle. At
the time, he was just glad the truck didn't get stuck in
the mud. Heaving the mangled motorcycle into the
truck bed, he closed the tailgate, and went home.

His mother always kept their house in perfect order.
Every magazine was put away, no dirty dish ever sat out,
and she daily whisked away every speck of dust. Robby
took the immaculate home for granted, but he never
thought of cleaning it himself. And he especially didn't
clean anything for the two weeks Betty and Jimmy Don
were gone.

His favorite nighttime snack consisted of a peanut
butter and jelly sandwich with a can of Coke. He took
it into the living room, where his mother never allowed
him to eat. After flipping on the TV, he set his Coke
on the polished coffee table, put up his feet, and took
a big bite of his sandwich. The nights he enjoyed this
ritual could be counted by the number of Coke rings
imprinted on the table's wood surface.

One night he became curious about a large glass jar

of coins Jimmy Don kept on his dresser. Robby didn't want the money, but he wondered why Jimmy Don saved them. He poured the jar's contents onto the dresser, then scattered the coins about. He studied them for a few minutes, but saw nothing that made them look special, so he left them strewn on the dresser and went to the kitchen to make his nightly peanut butter sandwich.

Having tired of pumping gas, he quit his job, so with nothing to do day or night, he found it lonely in the empty trailer. It would be great to see his family when they returned the next afternoon.

"Robby Branson, get your butt in here right this minute!"

From his bedroom, Robby heard the unmistakable voice of his incensed mother greeting him from the other end of the trailer.

He clambered off his bed where he had been enjoying an afternoon nap, and went to talk with her.

"What the hell have you been doing while we were gone?" Betty asked.

"What do you mean?" Robby asked.

"For an opener, you drove my truck through the mud. It's just caked all over. But that's not the worst of it. For God's sake come look at Bobby's new motorcycle." She grabbed him by his shirtsleeve and dragged him outside. "Do you have any idea what it's gonna cost to get that fixed?" she said, pointing angrily.

"I had an accident," Robby stammered.

Just then Jimmy Don came from the back slip where he kept his boat. "What's with the loose wires, Robby? Did you take out my boat?"

Robby didn't want to answer. His world was falling down all around him.

"Let me tell you one thing, young man," Betty said.

"You're gonna pay every last damn cent for all the damage you've caused. You go down to that filling station right now and tell them you want more hours."

Robby hung his head. "I quit my job. I got tired of having grease under my nails and smelling like gasoline."

Two weeks slipped by before Betty or Jimmy Don would speak to Robby. He tried to be absent if they were home and spent most of his time riding on his motorcycle or dirt bike.

His younger brother, Bobby, enjoyed all of Robby's misery, for if the bigger and stronger Robby ever wanted something, he bullied Bobby until he finally gave in.

By the first week in August 1983, Robby tired of his ostracized life and decided to make peace with his family. One morning he woke up, threw back his sheet, then sat up and rubbed his tired eyes from a late night of watching television. Then he glanced out his bedroom window and saw Jimmy Don in the front yard with lumber and bricks.

After breakfast, he sheepishly strolled outside. "Need some help?" he asked, hoping his stepfather wouldn't hold a grudge.

Jimmy Don looked up, eyed him suspiciously for a moment, then said, "Yeah. You can finish unloading those bricks for me. They're over in the truck."

Relieved, Robby went to Jimmy Don's new red-and-white Silverado truck, lowered its tailgate, then reached for the bricks. He stacked four red bricks at a time and carried them back to Jimmy Don.

"What's all this for?" Robby asked.

"Your mother wants a wishing well. I had these bricks left over after I rebuilt my house in Glen Oaks. I used them for the fireplace over there. Chimney's made out of them too."

Jimmy Don showed Robby a cleared patch of ground and told him to measure an area four feet square. Then he instructed him to hammer wooden pegs at each corner. Jimmy Don followed by tying string from peg to peg as a guideline for the brick foundation. He handed Robby a shovel.

"Here, get some calluses on your hands."

Both men dug until they dripped with sweat and had gone down a good foot in the soil.

Jimmy Don eyed their project and said, "This won't work. Any water we put here, like a real well is supposed to have, will drain out to the lake unless we line it with concrete."

"Won't the water just stagnate and breed mosquitoes?" Robby asked.

Jimmy Don scratched his head. "Darn if it wouldn't. Good idea. Let's put the dirt back and just make it a planter."

Jimmy Don opened a bag of concrete mortar mix, added water, and stirred vigorously. After the mortar became the right consistency, he began laying brick while Robby served as his apprentice helper.

The project turned out to be bigger than Robby could ever have dreamed. After three days, they had erected four brick side walls, each two feet high. In the meantime, Jimmy Don cut two-foot-long strips of wood to place on top of the brick, so in all, the brick and wood sides would be four feet tall.

All the while Robby complained that his mother couldn't have chosen a hotter time for the project. It took another day to hammer the wood in place. Then they attached two vertical two-by-fours reaching up another four feet above the base. The upward stretching arms were connected by a strip of wood for hanging plants.

After Jimmy Don painted the wood brown, both men stood back to admire the completed well.

"I can't believe we did this just because Mom wanted it," Robby groaned.

"You haven't figured it out by now?" Jimmy Don asked with a smile. "Whatever Betty wants, Betty gets."

TEN

On Friday night, Robby Branson stood in the trailer's small kitchen, leaning against a metal cabinet his mother had bought at a garage sale. He stared at her in fright and disbelief, thinking he hadn't heard her correctly. He asked again, "You're what?"

"I'm going to kill Jimmy Don," Betty repeated.

Robby dropped to a chair by the pale green Formica table and put his hands in his lap. At nineteen, he reasoned he was too old to let anyone see his hands shake. "Why, Mom?"

"For one thing, he's got a bunch of insurance."

"So?"

"I've spent my entire life worrying about how I'm gonna pay the bills. I'm tired of it. Who knows when he'll start slapping me around like the others?"

Robby remembered hearing of fights his mother had with other husbands, but for God's sake, she was talking about Jimmy Don. He had never hit her once and was always so nice to her. They had never come close to having a serious argument.

Robby said hesitantly, "All's I ever heard was something about an insurance policy from J.C. Penney."

"I'm not talking about Penney's. He's bound to have some with the fire department."

The kitchen whirled around Robby. Could Betty be in another of her moods? She looked sober. She wasn't screaming profanities or acting strange. Her brow knitted in concern like it always did when she said something serious. But she appeared calm. Her voice sounded very matter-of-fact.

Robby didn't know what to do. He had only moved back home last year, and he didn't want her to send him away again. He recalled his misery when he was eight years old and had been sent to live with his father.

His memory kept drifting to Jimmy Don. Even when he messed up the boat and motorcycle when the rest of the family went to Virginia, Jimmy Don had treated him decently. For a brief moment, he wondered if he should warn Jimmy Don, then discarded the thought, fearing what his mother would do to him.

Robby's mind flashed back to that morning. The family had said good-bye to Jimmy Don in the trailer, then spent the entire day shopping in Dallas. On the way back, they stopped to see Robby's sister, Shirley Thompson. He had heard his mother arguing with her, but didn't ask her about it.

Now around nine P.M., if Jimmy Don had an early shift tomorrow, he'd probably be in bed, asleep. His room wasn't that far down the hall from where Betty now discussed killing him.

"But, Mom, what if you get caught?"

"Don't worry. Got it all figured out. All I'll need is your help."

Betty didn't ask Robby to cooperate, she seemed to expect it. He remained silent, but continued worrying over his mother's plans.

She's never killed anyone before. With no experience, she could get caught. He couldn't think about his mother being sent to a penitentiary.

"I want you to leave now and go find Bobby," Betty said. "But come back here in a couple hours. And come alone. Get going now. I don't want you around when I shoot him."

Robby headed toward the door over a kitchen floor that seemed to tilt under his feet. He climbed onto his dirt bike and pedaled down the road alongside the woods. Less than a mile farther, he spotted his younger brother.

"Hey, wait up," he called to Bobby.

His brother slowed his bike and waited. They often hung out together and his sudden appearance tonight wouldn't appear peculiar to Bobby. They rode together, with Robby remaining uncharacteristically quiet. His mind kept churning with the freshness of his mother's words. Her emphasis on his returning alone made him not want to mention her intentions to his brother.

After two hours of tracing the roads that snaked through their subdivision, he told his brother he wanted to go home to watch television.

"What's on?" Bobby asked. "Maybe it's something I want to see."

"I don't know. I may just go to bed."

"It's only eleven. Why so early?"

Robby had to think quickly since he had to return home alone. "I'm not feeling too great. I had a greasy cheeseburger. I gotta go. See ya." He turned around and pedaled away, praying that Bobby wouldn't follow. He finally took a deep breath when he heard Bobby's wheels crunching over gravel as he disappeared into the darkness behind him.

Now Robby wondered what his mother wanted him to do. She had said nothing specific, but whatever it was, he wanted no part of it. Conflict and fear built inside him, for he didn't want to disappoint her.

On the way home, his hands shook on the handle

bars as thoughts tumbled in his mind. *Why is Mama doing this?*

Betty quietly slipped into her bedroom. Not wanting to turn on the light, she kept on the one in the hall. Through the open door, a sliver of light filtered into the room, and shot a strange wedge of brightness across Jimmy Don's body. She stood over the bed, watching him sleep.

He looked exceptionally peaceful and content. But this man's death could solve every problem she ever had. With his insurance, in addition to his lifelong pension, she'd never have a financial worry. And she'd never again have to put up with any man slapping her or bitching at her.

Calmly, she opened the drawer to fetch her ivory-handled pistol. It felt cold in her hand. Hard and cold. She would do it quickly. No need for him to suffer, and more important, she wanted to do it fast before he woke up. Quietly, she put one knee on the bed and held her breath as the mattress sagged. She exhaled and let the full weight of her body rest on the mattress. The night had been too hot for even a sheet and Jimmy Don slept in the nude. She concentrated on her purpose instead of his body. If she touched his bare body, it would surely deter her from her plan.

Betty raised the pistol and aimed at him. At that incredible moment, he rolled over to face her. His eyes remained closed and he appeared to be asleep. Just an unconscious nocturnal turn, but it had unnerved her, making her hand waver. When he had moved, Betty instinctively hid the gun behind her back. Now she brought the weapon out again. She didn't dare give him a chance to awaken. Taking quick aim, she shot his chest, hoping to hit his heart. Then hurriedly recocking the gun, she fired at his head.

Blood spurted everywhere. Experience taught her that head wounds did that, but because the room had been dark when she shot Wayne, she hadn't seen it gush as it did now. The graphic scene before her made her queasy.

Turning on the bedroom light revealed a scene worse than when she killed Wayne because she had also shot Jimmy Don's chest. Now blood poured from Jimmy Don's head, nose, and mouth, in addition to his chest. Again, blood covered the bed and walls. She needed to contain the flow before it soaked her mattress. Ignoring her red-splattered nightgown, she reached for the closest item she could find and grabbed her blue-and-white bedspread. With great effort, she rolled Jimmy Don on it, then tucked the spread securely around his body, hoping most of the blood would seep into that.

From the closet she pulled a blue sleeping bag, and a flash of déjà vu hit her when she unzipped it and spotted the same red lining. Opening the bag on the bed, she discovered that Jimmy Don's heavy muscular body weighed every bit as much as Wayne's and proved just as difficult to move. She tried to keep the bedspread around him while she rolled him onto the bag. She zipped it and continued to roll him toward the edge of the bed, and waited for the familiar thud.

She knew she needed to hurry and clean the room before the blood set into everything. A flood of memories rushed to her. She thought of Shirley helping dispose of Wayne two years ago. Reaching for the phone, she punched in her daughter's number. She told Shirley earlier that she planned to kill Jimmy Don, and Shirley became furious, saying she understood Betty's killing someone she claimed abused her, but not Jimmy Don.

"You promised you'd never kill anyone again," Shirley had screamed.

Maybe Betty wanted Shirley's forgiveness, but in any

regard, she had to talk with her. Soon Shirley's voice came on the line.

"Well, I did it," Betty said.

Silence greeted her for a moment, then Shirley said, "You sound upset."

"I am. I need to see you. Please come down."

"Mama, I said I wouldn't help. You know I told you explicitly that I didn't want anything to do with this."

"Please come," Betty pleaded.

"It's late," Shirley said. "What will my husband think?"

"Tell him that Jimmy Don and I've been fighting and he took off for Dallas."

Robby quietly opened the trailer's front door and peered inside. He heard the washer and dryer running, and assumed that blood must have spilled onto linens and things from the shooting. He saw his mother busily folding towels as she stood in front of the dryer.

She glanced at him. "You alone?"

Robby nodded.

"Come with me," she said, and led him down the hall toward her bedroom.

As they neared the back door, he saw a large blue mound leaning against the wall. He swallowed hard. His heart almost burst, it was so filled with anxiety. Now that his mother had actually killed someone, she could be in serious trouble. Had she changed that much since he lived with her as a boy? He remembered her as kind and loving then.

"Don't just stand there gawking, Robby, we've got to get this out to the wishing well."

"The well?"

"Sure. Why'd you think I had Jimmy Don build it? Now grab that end and I'll take his feet."

They bumped the body down the same back steps and managed to carry it to the front of the trailer.

"Shit," Robby said. "He's still limber. Makes him heavier to lift."

"Hush up," Betty whispered. "Do you want someone to hear us?"

Now, at almost midnight, the neighborhood appeared calm. With no wind, the lake too remained relatively quiet, but a dog barked incessantly a few lots away.

"Hold on a sec," Betty said as she ventured near the street in front of her property. "Okay, doesn't look like anyone's around. All the houses are pretty dark." She returned to the sleeping bag and picked up her end.

"Let's pull him over here on the grass. It'll make a lot less noise than the gravel driveway. Good thing we're dragging him," Betty said. "This thing's about to break my back."

They stopped in front of the well and Betty wiped her forehead on her sleeve.

Robby glanced at the well for a second, and couldn't help but remember working on it with Jimmy Don. The man had been so diligent, so caring to build it the best he knew how.

"Ready?" Betty asked, and snapped Robby from his thoughts. "It's not going to be a picnic getting him over the side of this thing," she said.

Robby knew the task would basically be his, although his petite mother had surprised him numerous times with her strength.

Robby searched the exterior of the sleeping bag with his hands; he found Jimmy Don's upper torso in the roughness of the canvas and took hold. At five foot nine and 195 pounds, the young man strained as he picked up the body and threw it into the well.

At almost two in the morning, Jody Thompson drove

Shirley to her mother's house. She asked him to stay in the car while she ran in and talked with her mother.

All during their hour drive from Dallas, Shirley had seemed agitated. She talked about how upset her mother had been on the telephone. At times, Shirley dabbed at the corners of her eyes and continued ruminating about her mother.

All married people have arguments, Jody mused. He didn't see this as any big deal. But hearing Shirley say that Jimmy Don had left for Dallas surprised him. He had known him for a year and had spent many leisurely hours drinking beer with him and cruising the lake in his boat. He'd been a heck of a nice guy, so his running off like this didn't fit the picture.

Then Jody squinted through the darkness at Jimmy Don's truck. If he had gone to Dallas, how'd he get there? And if he was still home, why wouldn't he come out and talk with Jody? Nothing made sense.

Fifteen minutes later, Shirley and Betty came out arm in arm, laughing and talking. Shirley showed none of the edginess that had clouded their trip down.

On the way back, Shirley never mentioned anything her mother had told her. She talked of other things, happier times, and plans for the future. Jody found such a complete reversal of her personality as strange. Women. Go figure.

The morning sun streamed into Robby's bedroom, awakening him. He hadn't slept well. The image of that blue mound kept creeping back every time he closed his eyes. He'd listened for hours to the whirl of the washer and dryer before he finally fell asleep.

Now, he peered at the beginning of another hot August day. He saw his mother busy planting flowers in the wishing well. A large bag of peat moss and several containers of red begonias rested beside her. Other containers of white begonias sat on the ground waiting their turn to be planted. He figured she had hidden the peat moss in the shed. How else could it so magically appear this early in the morning?

He pulled himself out of bed, put on clean blue jeans and a T-shirt, then went outside.

Betty didn't stop working as he approached.

"You doing okay?" she asked.

Robby shrugged.

"I need an alibi," Betty said. "Got to make sure Jimmy Don's disappearance looks like a drowning.

"How?"

"I can do it with your help."

Those words made him cringe, yet he felt obligated to protect his mother. If she had some idea to cover up what she'd done, he'd go along with it. Maybe then this entire nightmare would disappear.

"What do you want?"

"Go get the boat," she said, nodding over to Jimmy Don's craft that bobbed in the narrow slip behind their property. "Take it by water to Highway 85. You know, the one that runs between Gun Barrel and Seven Points. Then get yourself over to the bridge by Big Chief's Landing and I'll pick you up there."

"How's it gonna look like Jimmy Don drowned?"

"I put his fishing license in the boat. That way whoever finds it will know it's Jimmy Don's. Then I tossed in his glasses and scattered some of his heart pills in the bottom. You know, like he had another heart attack. I want you to take the prop off the motor so it'll look like he had motor trouble. He always kept his toolbox in the boat, so you can find something in that to use."

Robby stood looking at her, having trouble believing how carefully she had planned everything.

"Get going. I'm going to report him missing. That boat's got to be in the water before I do."

Robby nodded and went into the house for the boat's ignition key. When he came out, he headed directly for the boat. The sooner he got this over, the better.

When Robby approached the bridge by Big Chief's Landing, he cut the engine and let the boat bob in the waves as he searched the toolbox for a wrench. With a flick of the wrench he loosened the nut and stuffed it into his pocket, then removed the prop.

Using an oar, he maneuvered the boat to the base of the bridge, and grabbed for a large granite rock at the water's edge. He scrambled onto the accumulation of dark rocks, some almost boulder sized, and was thankful his new tennis shoes grabbed the slippery stones. He leaned over and shoved the boat off with an oar, then tossed the oar back into the craft.

Once on the bridge, he only waited a few minutes before seeing Jimmy Don's Chevy Silverado pickup with his mother at the wheel. He climbed in beside her. As he thought over his actions of the last several hours, actions his mother had forced on him, he visualized his world spiraling down into a dark void. The one person who should teach him morality had asked him to assist in a murder. Everything became crazier by the moment. He had to get away. He couldn't go back to the slaughterhouse that now sat on a cemetery.

Robby turned to his mother and said, "I need to leave for a few days. I'm going to see Dad."

Betty pivoted toward him. Her eyes squinted, and she said evenly, "Don't you ever in your life breathe a word of this to anyone. Got that? Especially not to your father!"

ELEVEN

The next morning, Saturday, August 6, 1983, the doorbell rang at 8:30. It surprised Betty to see two men standing there. She had only called the sheriff thirty minutes earlier to register her missing person report.

One man wore a white cowboy hat, black western-cut jeans, and boots. The gold star pinned to his chest immediately identified him as a sheriff's deputy. The other man was casually dressed in blue jeans and a sports shirt.

The deputy introduced himself as Johnny Marr, and the man with him as Hugh DeWoody, the fire chief of Payne Springs.

"Ma'am, we both know Jimmy Don," DeWoody said, "and sure hope we find him safely."

Betty nodded, wondering why a fire department chief would be involved.

"Come in," she said, stepping aside.

"We need to get a statement from you," Marr said as Betty motioned them over to the gray upholstered sofa; she took the nearby matching chair.

Marr had carried in a clipboard with forms and now balanced it on his knee. He pulled a pen from his shirt pocket and filled in the top of the form. "Okay," he said as if beginning a task he didn't relish. "Tell me the last time you saw your husband."

"Around nine-thirty last night," Betty said softly. "He

went out fishing. Should have been back by midnight. But I haven't seen hide nor hair of him since."

"He does this night fishing often?" Marr asked.

"About once a month. He loves to fish every day when the weather's good. If he's not up in Dallas at the fire station, he's out there in his boat."

"He went alone?"

"He did last night, but first he was supposed to go over to our friends, the Swansons. They live just around the cove here. Kyle Swanson promised to help him with his motor. Jimmy Don's been having a little trouble lately."

"You've talked to the Swansons?" Marr asked.

"Sure. Called them first thing. They never saw him. He never did get there," she said, looking away from him.

Marr frowned as he wrote. He asked for more biographical details about Jimmy Don and requested a recent photograph. He promised to let the Parks and Wildlife Service know.

"We'll get this information out as soon as we can. Everybody will be on the lookout. Now don't you worry. He probably spent the night in a cove somewhere. There's boat races goin' on today. If he's had trouble, it'll be pretty tough getting across the lake with a lame boat."

"This just isn't like him," Betty said, shaking her head. "He's real responsible. Always lets me know where he is."

"That sounds like Jimmy Don. I'll give you a call as soon as we know something," Marr added as he passed the form to Betty to sign.

Betty wondered how long it would be before someone called about finding Jimmy Don's boat.

Bobby had decided to accompany Robby to their father's house in Corsicana. She felt a sense of relief knowing neither boy knew how Wayne Barker had disappeared; now Robby had better keep his mouth shut about Jimmy Don.

Apprehensively, she glanced around her empty trailer and out to the wishing well. She shivered. Now she lived between two graves.

When the phone rang at nine that evening, Betty jumped. It had to be the call she'd expected all day, but somehow she didn't feel ready for it. Instead, she decided to take a shower and wash her hair. She'd have to put on some kind of performance when they told her about the boat, and looking her best would bolster her confidence.

An hour later, after she backcombed and fluffed her blond hair into her favorite bouffant style, she applied makeup and felt prepared. When the phone rang again at ten, she took a deep breath and reached for the receiver.

After separating from Jimmy Don, Suzy had remarried and moved a mile away from the blue frame house. Her new home, coincidentally, sat across the street from his parents in Timber Oaks, another oak-endowed lake community. Early in the morning before Jimmy Don had been reported missing, and before Suzy or his parents knew about it, she bicycled through her neighborhood and stopped at his parents' house. As was Suzy's custom, she knocked on the door and walked in. Mrs. Beets was hanging up the phone when Suzy came through the door.

"That was Betty," Mrs. Beets said. "She called to say

if we see Jimmy Don, to let him know she went to Dallas to buy Bobby some school clothes."

"That's weird," Mr. Beets said. "You'd think she'd have told him that herself when they got up this morning."

Suzy agreed.

Later that day when Suzy learned the dreadful details of Jimmy Don's abandoned boat, and after she collected herself from the heaving sobs she could not prevent, she found the story strange.

She went back to the senior Beets's home. She cried with Jimmy Don's devastated parents and told them how sorry she was. Then she said, "You know that story about his boat doesn't make sense. For one thing, whenever we went boating, he always emptied his pockets. There's a little Plexiglas ledge above the glove compartment on the passenger side where he kept his CB radio. He'd dig out his loose change and put it there with his waterproof watch. I didn't hear anything about those items being in his boat."

Late that day, the mood around the lake changed from cautious optimism that Jimmy Don Beets could be alive, to wondering how long before a boat captain or a dredging hook discovered his body.

The hundreds of people who turned out to search for Betty's husband excited Betty. She enjoyed being the center of the frenzied attention and the tender sympathy. She visited the search site both morning and afternoon to show her interest, but she also had visitors in her home as well.

On that Sunday morning with the search in full sway, one of the first to arrive at Betty's house was fire department chaplain Denny Burris. Experienced in dealing with grief-stricken survivors, the six-foot-two, soft-spoken chaplain came with the intention of comforting Betty.

He was accustomed to relatives wailing over their loved ones while others remained in shock over the tragedy, so he walked a fine line between the reality of what happened and the survivors' inability to accept their loss. However, nothing prepared him for Betty Beets.

After his initial introduction and offering of condolences, he expected her to be anxious and concerned, but she wasn't. She and four friends were sitting in her living room, having an everyday talk about the weather.

His visit the following day proved more interesting. Almost immediately she asked, "If they don't find Jimmy Don, what kind of benefits will I be eligible for?"

Her question caught him off guard. He would have anticipated, "Do you think the Lord will spare my husband?" But no, this woman wanted to know about life insurance.

He had just come from visiting James and Aleen Beets, Jimmy Don's parents, who were overcome with grief. His mother had to leave the room, for her constant crying made it difficult to speak. On the other hand, his father appeared madder than hell. He ranted and raved about someone being responsible for his son's death, and without naming names, he swore he'd get the culprit. Burris considered the man's reactions as expressions of grief. The chaplain ran into all types of emotional displays.

After Chaplain Burris collected his thoughts, he said to Betty, "You would get life insurance and the pension."

"How much insurance?"

"I'd have to check into that. But I'm sure there'd be some."

"What about the pension? How much would that be?"

"I'll check into that too."

Betty smiled warmly at him.

When Deputy Fire Chief Jim Blackburn pulled his car up to Betty's property that Sunday, he found her in her front yard, watering flowers. He stepped out, his posture straight with confidence.

"Mornin', ma'am," he said, with a touch of sympathy in his voice. He introduced himself. "They've got me in charge of this search for your husband. I sure am sorry, ma'am. I thought a lot of Jimmy Don. We were good, long-time friends."

Betty nodded, but showed no emotion. Instead, she continued dragging the hose around, watering the hanging pots above her front porch.

"I hate to bother you," he said, "but I came to get a little information. We need to know what Jimmy Don was wearing that night he went out fishing. It would help us since we're dragging the lake. We might find some of the clothing."

Blackburn found himself staring at her face. Her eyes lacked the redness from shedding tears and she seemed too calm under the circumstances. He saw no evidence of grieving.

"He'd have on shorts," Betty said. "That night probably didn't get much under eighty. He might have had on his blue-plaid shirt. It's hard to remember. When he went out the door that night I didn't think to pay attention to his clothes. Had no idea I wouldn't see him again."

"Yes, ma'am. I know this is hard. Would he have worn a hat?"

She thought for a moment. "He might have out of

habit. On the other hand, maybe not since it was night." Betty moved to the wishing well and began watering the flowers there.

Chaplain Burris returned for his third visit with Betty. He had still not seen her cry over the loss of her husband and that puzzled him.

Betty eagerly greeted him at her door that morning, and asked what he had found out.

"Jimmy Don had a fair amount of insurance," Burris told her. Over $110,000. There's also a double-indemnity clause in some. His insurance is doubled because his death was accidental. And, of course, Mr. Beets's pension plan pays survivor benefits, so you'd receive those too. They'd probably be in the neighborhood of roughly $900 a month for the rest of your life."

Betty's smile lit up the room. "When would I get the insurance and the pension?"

Burris cleared his throat. "The pension is governed by the Dallas Fire and Police Pension Board, and they'll have to meet to decide about paying that."

A frown quickly replaced Betty's smile. "And the insurance?" she asked.

"Texas law is pretty strict about paying death benefits when there's no body. If a body isn't found, no payment is made for seven years."

Betty unconsciously stepped backward and her hand flew to her opened mouth. *"Seven years?* What do they expect me to do in the meantime?"

Churches announced the discovery of Jimmy Don's empty boat. Local television and radio stations also aired the information. His neighbors in Glen Oaks were in shock, for they'd just seen Jimmy Don the day before when he came by to help his ex-wife and her husband with their boat.

That Sunday, Betty visited the Glen Oaks house and Russ Leonard spotted her. He rushed to offer his condolences.

She looked at him with clear blue eyes and pleaded, "Russ, I know something really bad's happened to Jimmy Don. I know it has and you've got to help us find him. Please, Russ."

Her emotional pleadings touched Leonard, and he agreed to look for him. He went to the dock behind his house to untie his boat, all the time musing that up until today he had only had a few scattered conversations with Betty. Now she treated him as her long-lost friend.

Her words continued to ring in his ears. *You've got to help me. You've got to help me.*

He felt sorry for her and worried that Jimmy Don could be out there somewhere still alive. He spent the rest of the day cruising the lake and found himself only one of an army of searchers. Later that night, he secured his boat and stepped with heavy feet onto his dock, all the while pondering his earlier conversation with Betty and the information he had gleaned about Jimmy Don's boat. He heard about the glasses and heart pills, but he'd never seen Jimmy Don with those.

The more he thought about the search, the more confused he became. Jimmy Don would never go out on the lake alone—he always had someone around. Something was wrong. The facts weren't adding up.

Jamie Beets's aunt woke him on the morning after authorities found his father's empty boat. Jamie immediately rushed to Cedar Creek to search. But first the

Coast Guard took him to see his father's boat. The sight of his father's pride and joy shocked Jamie.

"My dad wasn't on this boat," Jamie insisted to the Coast Guard. "None of my dad's habits had been followed. See that Plexiglas shelf?" he said, pointing. "That's where he always put his CB for safety's sake. Said he wouldn't leave a dock without it."

He glanced at the nitroglycerin tablets. "Dad had a heart attack five years ago, but he hadn't used those in two years.

"He's somewhere else and I bet Betty knows where he is. You just go round up Betty and make her tell you what happened to Dad."

"Now calm down," one of the searchers said. "You're covered up with grief and getting carried away with your imagination."

That only made Jamie angrier.

Then a couple of days later, he heard Betty had gone to the fire department to collect Jimmy Don's final paycheck. Jamie felt he needed to do something about her, so he made an appointment with Reed Canton, a lawyer in Gun Barrel City, who coincidentally had used his own airplane to search for Jimmy Don. He wanted the lawyer to tie up his father's assets to keep them out of Betty's hands until they found out what had actually happened.

"Take a deep breath, Jamie, and try to relax," Canton said. "I think a lot of your fears are springing from emotion and grief."

Jamie realized Canton knew of his previous drug use and his dislike of Betty, and wondered if the lawyer thought he had hallucinated the story.

Later, Jamie discussed his concerns with law enforcement, his wife, and other members of his family. Not one person took him seriously.

* * *

Devastated by the news that seven years would elapse before she could gain anything from murdering Jimmy Don, Betty started laying claim to his property and prepared for an all-out war with his son. Within a week of Jimmy Don's disappearance, Betty bought two Doberman pinschers and tied them up in the backyard of the pretty blue house on Oak Street. They would act as sentries, her first line of defense in her war with Jamie.

Then Jimmy Don's father began driving by his son's Glen Oaks neighborhood. The old red Ford pickup drove slowly down Oak Street, never over twenty-five miles an hour. Jimmy Don's father was a familiar sight in Glen Oaks and he had many friends there. Friends he'd met through his son. He stopped if he saw any of them in their yards.

J. R. Burton busily sawed branches from a limb that the wind had blown off one of his oak trees when "Beets" came by, the name everyone called the old man.

Burton immediately went to Beets's open window. The old man had lived by the lake for four decades and never understood why people needed air conditioning.

"I haven't cried in years," Burton told him, "but I cried when I heard about Jimmy Don. This has gotta be the worst thing that's ever happened to you. Just against nature to lose a son. Marion and I sure want you to know how sorry we are."

"Hurump!" the man said in disgust. "It's the way I lost him that bothers me most. That no-good woman of his had something to do with this. Betty always tried to keep my son away from me, and she sure as hell wouldn't come over to see me and the missus. You just mark my words," he said, pointing a weathered, crooked finger at Burton. "My boy ain't in that lake. She's killed him and put him somewhere."

Because of all the questionable circumstances of Jimmy Don's disappearance, Burton wanted to say that he held that same thought, but Beets didn't look like he needed encouragement.

"He was the best son a man could ever ask for," Beets continued. "Yes, sir. Even with Betty trying to keep him to herself, he called every day to check up on us, and like clockwork he'd be there each week to cut our grass. And that's not 'cause he didn't have other things to do. No way. That boy had a million friends. Could have been out with his buds every minute, but he always looked after his old parents." Beets turned in the direction of his son's house.

"What's with those dogs at Jimmy Don's?"

"Looks like Betty's trying to establish her territory," Burton offered. "Maybe if her dogs are peeing on Jimmy Don's property it makes it hers."

"Look at those things," Beets said. "Digging up the yard. Trashing out all of Jimmy Don's hard work."

"Betty or her boys come over a few times a week to water and feed them," Burton said.

Both men watched the dogs nose through the grass and paw at the dirt.

"Probably trying to dig up a body," Beets said. Then without waiting for a reply, he slowly drove on to spread his message to the next neighbor, or anyone else who would listen.

TWELVE

At the time Jamie heard the news of his father's drowning, he was living in an apartment in Dallas with his wife and two small children to be near his heating and air-conditioning repair job. While he lived there, he couldn't help but worry that Betty would be spinning her web over everything his father owned. Since he couldn't get law enforcement or even his own attorney to act, he decided to strike out on his own and protect what he considered rightfully his.

In order to make it appear that he lived in his father's lake house, six weeks after his father disappeared, Jamie began spending each weekend at the Glen Oaks home. He'd leave after work on Friday and return late Sunday night. Jamie had heard about Betty's dogs, but she had apparently tired of caring for them, for they were no longer there.

His plan worked well until late October, when his wife became annoyed with the arrangement. One Sunday night, Jamie returned to his empty apartment, save for a note on the kitchen countertop. His wife had penned a message saying she had taken his children, all the furniture, and wanted a divorce.

Four months after Jimmy Don's disappearance, a deputy listened to an excited Betty Henderson, who had called the sheriff's office. She identified herself as Jimmy Don's sister from Dallas.

"My daughter, Kathy, saw Jimmy Don last night," she told the deputy. "I couldn't believe it was true."

The deputy pulled out a report form. "Where did she see him?"

"In the Denny's Restaurant in Duncanville, just south of Dallas. I think it was around one in the morning."

"Did she talk to him?"

"She couldn't bring herself to because she thought she was seeing a ghost. Can't you imagine how she felt? But she saw him plain as day. That restaurant's always so brightly lit. It really flustered her, beings we're all looking for him and so worried about him. She ran to the phone and called me, but by the time I got over there, he had left."

"If she didn't talk to him, how can she be sure it was Mr. Beets?" the deputy asked, his voice embracing skepticism that had to be noticed by Mrs. Henderson.

"When I got over there, we talked to the same waitress that had waited on him. We showed her Jimmy Don's picture and she said, 'Yes, that's the man who was here.' She remembered him coming in at the same time as a couple did, and he told her to go ahead and wait on them first. To me, that sure sounded like Jimmy Don."

Everyone held a theory of what had happened to Jimmy Don. Even months after his disappearance, his name still came up in lake area cafés and bars.

A good friend of Jimmy Don's from the fire department, Craig Hollander, shared his theory with Sheriff Charlie Fields.

As anxious to solve the crime as anyone, the sheriff patiently listened to all ideas about the mystery. Fields had followed his father's footsteps into law enforcement. His father's goal was to be Henderson County's sheriff, but as a deputy, his father had been shot and killed while serving a warrant. Inspired to fulfill his father's ambition, Fields worked as a deputy until his election to sheriff. Under his tutelage, what little crime Henderson County had, decreased even more. And when time came for his second term, he ran unopposed.

Hollander entered the sheriff's office, which had walls covered with sports and law enforcement awards, as well as plaques of appreciation from the Rotary to the local Girl Scout troops. He sat in front of the sheriff's desk and began his theory.

"We all know Jimmy Don's not in that lake."

Fields nodded. "Yep. Covered every square inch of it."

"And I don't buy that heart attack angle either. Right before he disappeared, he had a physical and passed with flying colors. I also know that he needed glasses only for reading. Certainly not for fishing in the dark. Besides, if they were in his pocket, they'd gone overboard with him."

"I agree with all that, so what's your read on this?"

"I've heard talk in the bars that Betty Beets's former husband deserted her."

"We heard that too, but couldn't trace him down."

"What if the guy changed his mind, decides he wants her back, and shoots Jimmy Don when he's out on the lake? Say he puts a couple bullets in him, doesn't want him discovered like that, and drags him off somewhere?"

"That's interesting, Craig, but it's only speculation. How you gonna prove any of that?"

"You could start by calling Betty."

"I'll be glad to do that." The sheriff promised Craig

a full report, but a month lapsed before a deputy could pin Betty down. The sheriff called Hollander.

"We finally talked with Betty," the sheriff told him. "She tells me she has never heard from her former husband. Wayne Barker was his name. She also said that none of her male friends would be jealous enough to kill Beets and she's just as puzzled by this as anyone. Got any more theories?"

Betty spent time at both her trailer and the blue frame house. She frequently had her two boys with her. Robby worked on his car in front of the house, gunning his motor as he tested his engine. The loud roar blasted through the neighborhood.

The young men wore army fatigues, and didn't speak to neighbors. The friendly lake community deemed that mysterious. In return, the neighbors kept their distance. All they could do was grit their teeth at the disturbing noises and a yard cluttered with automotive parts.

After the shock of his pending divorce, Jamie had stopped his routine weekend lake visits, which allowed Betty to virtually take over his father's house. The next time he returned to the Glen Oaks house, he found his belongings in the backyard, and saw Betty had been there, for some of her things sat neatly packed in closets. He decided to put a stop to that and had the locks changed.

The Glen Oaks neighbors had banded together against Betty, and called Jamie to report on Betty's activities regarding the house. A week after Jamie changed the locks, neighbors greeted him with news that Betty had people over looking at the house and it appeared she was trying to sell it.

Furious with Betty's attempt to get rid of his father's home, Jamie called around and learned the name of her Realtor, who divulged that Betty had listed the house for $42,000. Finally, Jamie had concrete evidence to take to an attorney.

Now, his attorney took Jamie seriously and filed a restraining order against Betty Beets. The order legally bound her from selling any property belonging to Jimmy Don. The house promptly came off the market.

In the following months, no truce loomed in the fight for Jimmy Don's lake house. Betty stayed determined to hold on to the place and Jamie remained just as resolute to keep the property. Jamie was still bent on proving that Betty had been the culprit in his father's disappearance, but by January 1984, he became disheartened because he couldn't find any new information to link her to his father's death.

In hopes of hearing tidbits about Betty to take to his lawyer, Jamie hired on as a bartender at a huge new country-western club. One patron told him that Betty's fourth husband had also mysteriously disappeared. Thinking he had heard news no one else knew, Jamie reported the fact to his attorney the next morning.

Ironically, Betty came into the bar that night and Jamie confronted her. Pointing his finger in her face, he said, "I know damn well that you had something to do with my father's death. You just wait. I don't care how long it takes, but some day I'm gonna find out what really happened."

Betty ignored him like a bottle of stale beer.

However, the next night when Jamie showed up for work, the owner was waiting for him. "You don't work here anymore," the man told him. "I won't have the help talking to my friends like you talked to Betty Beets."

Old Beets still kept his daily vigil. He continued driving his red truck down Oak Street, cutting his speed even lower when he came to the blue house. Then he'd go up a nearby hill near the woods and watch Betty on those days he was lucky enough to catch her there.

His anger boiled every time he saw her. As his health diminished, the neighbors urged him not to bother with the woman, for his concern about her made his life a living hell. But he continued, and only moved when police came by, obviously alerted by Betty.

Undaunted by Jamie's restraining order not to sell any of Jimmy Don's property, and almost one year to the date of Jimmy Don's disappearance, Betty faked a power-of-attorney form and inscribed her name on it as having full power over all of Jimmy Don's possessions. She put an ad in the *Cedar Creek Pilot*. With the fabricated document, she sold his boat for $3,250. She also signed over the boat's title to the new owners, a nice couple from Garland, Texas, who were impressed by the little widow who had described how hard she worked to keep the Glastron in tip-top condition.

Robby Branson fell in love with Jennifer Cook. He'd known her from high school, and every time he visited the local Dairy Queen where she worked, he'd stay and talk with her until the manager ran him off. Robby spent his days earning minimum wage working as an apprentice carpenter for a construction company.

Jennifer lived by herself in a small, sparsely furnished efficiency apartment, but Robby liked how peaceful and serene it was compared to his living conditions with his mother and her wide assortment of friends.

After dating Jennifer for two months, twenty-year-old Robby moved in with his girlfriend. They had lived together for six happy months, before Betty decided the relationship might be serious and invited them for dinner.

Betty had promised roast beef and all the trimmings, an offer too delicious for two people on a limited budget to pass up.

Once Robby walked into Betty's house after driving past the well, he couldn't forget his dreaded recollections. Old memories flooded back—his mother fighting with her husbands and boyfriends, and all the other twisted turmoil he had witnessed. But above all, he still suffered from the guilt of having helped with a murder.

In the weeks following the killing, Betty frequently tried to talk with him about Jimmy Don, but he refused. When he told her how badly he felt, she tried to assuage his guilt by saying, "Don't worry about it. You're no worse than Shirley."

"What's that supposed to mean?" Robby had asked.

"Shirley helped me bury Wayne."

Until that moment Robby hadn't suspected that his mother had also killed Wayne Barker. His stomach heaved at the thought.

Now he watched Jennifer glance at the vase of flowers sitting in the middle of Betty's table.

"Your flowers are beautiful, Mrs. Beets," she said.

"Why don't you show Jennifer the flowers outside?" Betty suggested. "The lazy Susans are still blooming. Pretty good for October."

Robby marched his girlfriend outside and she immediately went to the wishing well.

"Not there," Robby said. "Those aren't the flowers my mom meant."

Jennifer shot Robby an "I'll go where I want" look and continued toward the well.

He grabbed her arm and jerked her away. "I said not there."

She shook her arm free from his grasp. "What's gotten into you? All of a sudden you're acting like an ass."

Robby ushered her away from the well and walked her to the backyard.

"What's in that?" she asked, pointing to the shed.

Robby kicked at a tuft of grass. His red face glowed with frustration.

"Let's go inside," he said. "Dinner's probably ready by now."

Seeing the well and shed washed Robby with depression, a rare mood for him. Now he regretted having to sit with his mother, who was the core of his nightmares.

"How's your job going, Robby?" Betty asked.

"Okay."

"Did you get that raise you expected?"

"No."

"Robby tells me you work at Dairy Queen," Betty said to Jennifer."

"Uh-huh."

Conversation subsided and the rest of the meal continued in silence. Right after they helped with the dishes, Robby and Jennifer left.

"That was a fun evening," Jennifer said sarcastically as they drove home.

Robby remained quiet.

It wasn't until Robby and Jennifer climbed into bed that night that he realized his girlfriend needed an explanation. One that would entail telling her something he never intended to breathe to another living soul.

"If you knew all I've been through in my life, you'd understand," he whispered.

"You haven't been through any more than the rest of us," she retorted, and turned her back to him.

"Oh no? Why didn't I want you by that well tonight?"

"You were being a control freak."

"Hell I was. Try this. You don't know my stepfather is buried in that well."

"Liar. How'd you expect me to believe that?"

"Not only is he buried there, Mom shot him, and I helped bury him."

Jennifer turned over and raised up on her elbows. "Get a grip, Robby. You're dreaming."

"Remember that shed out back?"

"What about it?" Her voice now cautious and apprehensive.

"That's over the grave of another of my mother's husbands."

"Stop. You're freaking me out. Will you just shut up!"

"You don't believe me?"

"Robby, if what you're saying's true, you're an accomplice to murder!"

Jennifer couldn't sleep. She lay awake waiting for the alarm to ring. The next morning, she eagerly called her grandmother, a woman she could always confide in. Her own mother lived in California and they seldom talked, so she had grown close to her grandmother in Dallas.

Jennifer waited impatiently for her grandmother to answer. When she picked up, Jennifer said, "You won't believe what Robby told me last night."

"I bet you're gonna tell me," her grandmother said, chuckling.

"He said there are two bodies buried out by his mother's trailer. They used to be her husbands, and his mother killed both of them!"

THIRTEEN

Ray Bone ran into Betty Beets one night at the Cedar Club. He would be one of the roughest characters she had ever met. His documented entrance into the world of crime was October 9, 1970, when police charged him with felony theft and gave him two years probation. Undeterred, on June 23, 1977, he murdered a man and received twenty years in the state penitentiary.

Now out on parole after serving less than eight years of that sentence, Ray, a muscular, good-looking blond, proved a departure from Betty's dark-haired lovers. His unusual hazel eyes appeared almost yellow, a strange yellow like that of stained glass, illuminating through to the evil inside. Around the bars, common knowledge held that Ray Bone was meaner than hell.

Bobby didn't like Ray from the first night his mother brought him home. Now, a few weeks later, all three were sitting outside in metal yard chairs that Betty had given several coats of white enamel. A huge white pelican lumbered onto their property, having strayed from one of the lake's islands that served as a natural bird refuge. They watched the bird, laughing as he walked because the big pouch under his bill jiggled. After a few minutes, Ray picked up rocks from a nearby planter and began pelting the pelican. The frightened bird turned quickly and stumbled back toward the safety of the lake.

Bobby resented Ray's cruelty and later told his mother, "I don't know why you had to tie up with him. We don't need a jerk like that around here."

Betty ignored the hostility between the two, because for her, having a man was as important as having a roof over her head.

Jimmy Don's former neighbor, J. R. Burton, hated Betty, but at the same time was fascinated with her. Although he called her the battle-ax, he couldn't help but watch from his front window whenever she visited the house across the street.

One early fall day in 1984, he looked out his window and saw Betty drive up, but today he was more concerned about the blanket of fog beginning to drape over everything. The lake phenomenon occurred when the warm lake water met the chilly fall air, causing fog to billow up and move with ghostly fingers over houses, streets, and trees. Through the wet mist, he caught another glimpse of Betty, and squinted, watching her bend down by the large outdoor mounted air-conditioning unit. She appeared to be doing something with the bolts that secured the unit to its concrete base. Then she threw her tools into a box, and to his amazement, she single-handedly picked up the unit and loaded it onto her truck.

The next day, the weather had cleared when Betty returned. Burton watched her walk quickly to the house, carrying a large box from her truck. She stayed inside for almost fifteen minutes. Coming out empty handed, she promptly returned to her truck and drove away. After reaching the top of the hill, she pulled over by a clump of trees and parked.

Burton stood there, puzzled by the scene. Then in minutes, black smoke filtered up from the rear of the house. It took him a moment to realize what was happening, and when he did, he called the fire department, then hollered to his wife to summon the Leonards.

All four neighbors rushed across the street with a sense of déjà vu. The fire took off with the speed of an explosion. When Jimmy Don had rebuilt the house from the last fire, he had used a polyurethane insulation that now boiled like a cauldron and sent flames and black smoke high in the afternoon sky.

The sirens of approaching fire engines came as a relief until J. R. looked up the hill and noticed Betty still there, watching. He couldn't help but think that the woman was plum out of her mind.

After the officers extinguished the fire, J. R. turned to one of the firemen. "I never saw a blaze take off so fast."

"You'd burn fast too if you had diesel oil poured all over you. Come back here," the fireman said.

The four, now joined by other neighbors, followed him to the rear of the house where the back wall had been eaten away by flames. Near the patio door they found an oil can sitting in a rocking chair. Spent matches lay strewn on the charred patio concrete.

"The fire started in this back bedroom," the fireman explained. "Someone stacked papers and documents on the bed, then poured diesel over it. It's a hell of a mess."

Burton knew he needed to report what he'd seen. He glanced up the hill again to substantiate his story.

Betty had vanished.

Gerald Albright was married, had two children, a pretty wife, a beautiful home, and an appetite for other women. He liked to hang out and drink at the Cedar Club in the afternoon after spending the morning at his real-estate business. He found Betty Beets good company, and whenever she'd laugh at his jokes, she had a way of falling into him, teasing him with her generous breasts.

"That's some body, girl. What I wouldn't do for a roll in the hay with that."

Betty laughed. "I'm used to your kind. All whiskey talk and no action."

"You're right. If I have any more whiskey, there'll be no action."

They both laughed a bawdy laugh and then quietly stared at each other.

"Don't look at me that way, Gerald. You know I've got Ray at home. It would be kinda crowded."

"Place ain't important. There's a motel up the street called County Line or Country Lane, something like that."

"Yeah, I know where you mean."

"What say I leave now and you follow me over there in about ten minutes? I'll be ready and waiting."

Betty had had a verbal blowout with Ray the night before and she still smarted from it. Running off for the afternoon with Gerald would do Ray good, if only to let him know other men were still interested.

"I'd need more time," she said. "Got to come up with some excuse to take off early. I'll work on that and see you in about a half hour."

Gerald chugged his drink. "You got yourself a date, lady. See you in thirty minutes."

Betty saw Gerald's sport coupe parked outside Room 8 at the motel. The motel's exterior sported yellow peeling paint, revealing its previous white coat. With the noise of cars and trucks from the nearby highway, it looked anything but romantic.

She knocked softly on the door, and whispered, "It's Betty."

In a split second, the door opened and Gerald grinned a lopsided smile. "Thought you weren't comin'."

"And miss a chance like this?" Betty said.

"I brought your favorite vodka," Gerald said.

"Anything's my favorite. What do you have to go with it?"

"You need something?"

Betty thought for a moment, then shrugged. She grabbed the bottle, unscrewed the cap, and raised it to her lips, taking a generous slug. "Mmm. Makes me warm all over."

"I'm hot all over," Gerald said, roughly pulling her closer and smashing her breasts against his chest as he kissed her lips.

"Let me have a little more of this," Betty said, raising the vodka to her lips again.

This time Gerald held her close and unzipped her dress. Then his hands found the back of her bra and unhooked the clasp. His fingers worked their way to her chest.

"God, a guy could get lost in all this flesh," he said, kissing Betty's neck. He peeled off her dress and bra, then his lips found the hard centers of her breasts.

She briefly interrupted him to reach for the bottle of vodka and guzzled down several more gulps.

He kissed off the remaining vodka from her lips and took her hand, placing it on his extended fly. "Feel what's waiting for you?"

Betty stumbled to her knees and unzipped his pants. When her lips took hold of him, he groaned with pleasure.

"Lady," he said hoarsely, "why haven't we gotten together before now?"

An hour later, the empty bottle lay on the floor. They sprawled nude on the bed with their arms wrapped around each other. Everything seemed warm, happy, and funny. The vodka unhinged Betty's mouth, evaporating any control over her words.

Gerald giggled at something she said and started to mount her again. Betty pushed him away.

"Here we are fuckin' and having so much fun. You wouldn't think it was so funny if you knew that one guy I fucked is buried in my front yard."

FOURTEEN

"Someone burned down my house, for God's sake," Betty bellowed into the phone. "It's been months ago. What do you mean your company won't pay?"

"There's still questions that have to be answered," the woman from Southern Casualty Insurance told her. "Our investigator's pretty sure the fire was arson, and until that's cleared up, we can't make any payment."

Betty paced back and forth over her living room floor. Jimmy Don had paid those fire insurance premiums for years, and she had continued paying after he died. This wasn't right. She needed a lawyer. She thought of E. Ray Andrews, the counselor she used when her son Robby had been accused of stealing the swords. E. Ray had two personalities. She had seen him in the clubs falling-down drunk, but when he defended Robby, he was sober and did a fair job. She phoned him.

E. Ray Andrews had a law practice and a cult following. He didn't need a last name. Everyone in Henderson County knew him as "E. Ray." His clients proved easily recycled. He'd represent them and they'd go to jail. Then they'd get out, get into more trouble, and land back in E. Ray's office. He also received many referred clients—brothers and cousins of previous clients. He had more than his fair share of success because of his ability to create sheer havoc in the courtroom. Asking bizarre questions that caused a mishmash of justice, he could confuse jurors until they knew no better than to let his client off scot-free.

He liked to brag that he had received the highest grade of anyone who ever took the bar exam in the state of Texas, but some wondered whom he had sent to take the exam for him. For trials, the articulate man spoke a hillbilly type of English, sounding like a good ole country boy, or just someone incapable of constructing a proper sentence.

Nineteen months after her husband disappeared, Betty traipsed over to E. Ray Andrews's office, ostensibly to force the insurance company to pay for fire damage on the Oak Street home. If she were only after collecting on the fire, she received more than she bargained for. Betty entered his small, unimpressive office and closed the door.

E. Ray insisted that whatever transpired in his office that day was his doing, and Betty Beets was only a willing but innocent participant. He remained emphatic that Betty had never questioned him about the insurance carried by Jimmy Don or the pension that would give her a lifetime of security.

Once she was seated in front of his desk, he asked if Jimmy Don Beets had any life insurance she would inherit. He said that Betty didn't know, so out of the goodness of his heart, he investigated the matter for her, almost pushing her to go after the benefits he considered hers for the asking.

He first suggested she seek a "Determination of Death" for Jimmy Don Beets. That way they could fast forward the seven-year waiting period and Betty could inherit over $153,000 in insurance and the widow's pension.

* * *

Andrews, a criminal defense attorney, had little practice in civil law, so he suggested the firm of Roberts and Roberts from Tyler, Texas, to represent her in her bid to have Jimmy Don declared legally dead.

Betty filed for the death certificate on a cold winter day in February 1985. Outside the Henderson County courtroom, the oak trees stood bare as icy waves of air rushed across the lake causing everyone to secure their crafts and hover inside their warm homes. However, Betty didn't feel the chill. Heated with excitement, she stood beside Harry Loftis, one of Roberts and Roberts's attorneys.

Before the judge, Betty reiterated every painful memory of Jimmy Don's disappearance, and included the fact that he died without a will. She testified that the people closest to him, she and his parents, would normally see him daily, but after August 6, 1983, no one had had any contact. She asserted that she was his legal spouse and entitled to inherit his entire estate.

She told the judge, "I really need to get this declaration because there's at least two debts against the estate that need to be paid." Betty didn't elaborate on what debts existed. She also asked to be appointed the administrator. Lastly, she waived the appointment of an appraiser. She knew what Jimmy Don had.

The judge took her request under advisement.

Now three weeks later, March showed more promise as white blossoms began flowering on the Bradford pear trees, and the Carolina jasmine vines were covered with yellow blooms. Amid the reassurance of spring, Betty happily went back to court and signed the papers to become the administrator of Jimmy Don's estate. The court officially decided that Jimmy Don Beets died on August 6, 1983. Betty could now inherit thousands of dollars in insurance, pensions, and everything else Jimmy Don had ever owned.

FIFTEEN

Seven Points enhanced its honky-tonk reputation with the opening of Plowboys, a bar and dance hall that attracted local residents, in addition to summer visitors looking for local color. The cement-block structure had previously been known as Jokers, just one in a line of rehashed and refurbished bars. Instead of Jokers' white exterior, Plowboys now sported a coat of happy coral paint, and sat near Highway 274, competing for business amid the string of bars on the highway.

After Jamie Beets's divorce, he picked himself up and began dating Kay Ruthledge, a pretty divorcée with two small children. On Saturday night, February 23, 1985, Jamie invited her to Plowboys. They were out on the dance floor, talking and laughing, and for once he forgot about how he could connect Betty with his father's disappearance. That would soon change.

The music ended and Jamie escorted Kay back to their table.

"I'm going to order another beer, do you want one?" he asked.

"That'd be great. I'll run off to the ladies' room."

Kay reached for her purse. "That's strange, I don't remember leaving my purse open like this." She picked it up from the floor and gasped. "My billfold's gone. Damn. I had at least forty dollars in it, and worst of all, the pictures of my kids."

"Maybe it fell out in the car," Jamie said.

"No. Remember, I had to show my ID when we came in?"

"That's right."

Jamie searched under their table. Nothing. He scanned the people around them, wondering if the culprit sat nearby. No one seemed to be paying them any attention and, besides, all the surrounding couples looked more interested in each other than filching a billfold.

"Let's tell the manager. See if anyone's turned it in in case it just fell out of your purse."

They went to the manager, who listened to their predicament and told them nobody had turned in a billfold. He suggested they report the theft to the police.

Four days later, on the following Wednesday, Jamie's apartment's phone rang. He picked up the receiver and heard a tough-sounding male voice on the other end.

"Jamie? This is a warning. If you go out tonight, we're going to get you!"

He heard a click; then the line went dead. He wrote it off as a prank and went out anyway, returning around midnight. Again, the phone rang.

"Listen up," the same male voice said. "Your dad is gone. You had better stop looking for him."

Jamie knew this was no random nuisance call.

Twenty minutes later, the phone rang for the third time. The man identified himself as Sam Dickerson and asked Jamie to meet him at the Cherokee Shores entrance at 1:15 A.M. Jamie knew Sam Dickerson had a cousin, Bud Wilson, and both men were friends of Ray Bone's.

* * *

At the same time, Kay had her own problems. On that Wednesday, she drove to Seven Points with her children. A brown-and-beige long-bed pickup closed in behind her, and stayed there for a few minutes before it began repeatedly pushing her car. Hysterical, she knew she couldn't deal with the two big men inside, so she pushed down on the accelerator and hurried to find more traffic. Once surrounded by other drivers, the men backed off, turned the corner, and were gone.

Shaken, Kay stopped in front of a grocery store. She helped her children out of the car and hurried in to buy the few items she had come to get. When she returned, she found a note inside her car. Written in true cloak-and-dagger style, someone had cut words and letters out of the newspaper and glued them onto a piece of paper. It read: "You love the wrong man. Your [sic] in it now. Did you lose a handbag Kay?" "Handbag" was not the right word, but apparently the note's author couldn't find "billfold" in the newspaper. Most chilling of all, someone had attached the pictures of her children to the note.

At nine P.M., her phone rang and a man told her if she wanted her billfold back, she had to meet him at the entrance to Cherokee Shores. Her head told her not to go, but she had already reported the theft to the police, and they had done nothing, so this was her only chance. Forgetting about her safety, she drove to the entrance and discovered the same two men in the brown-and-beige Chevy pickup waiting for her. She got out and walked over to them.

"Where's my billfold?" she asked.

They got out of the truck. One man was heavy, had a mustache, and dressed in nicely tailored slacks and a shirt. The other man, skinny and at least six feet tall, wore jeans and a western shirt.

"What does Jamie know about Jimmy Don's disappearance?" the mustache asked.

"What does that have to do with anything?"

"Bitch," the man said, and slapped Kay across the face. "Answer us. What does he know?"

Kay fingered her stinging cheek. "I have no idea."

"You're holding out," he said, and slapped her harder.

Kay backed up as tears rolled down her face. "All I know is that he drowned."

Both men came after her, slapping her, and knocking her to the ground. They laughed as she lay in the dirt alongside the road. Then they climbed in their truck and drove away.

Sheriff's Deputy Rick Rose owned a gift for gab in addition to being blessed with nonstop energy for both work and play. His office held fishing and golf trophies, as well as sharpshooting plaques. Four prized deer heads shared wall space with a stuffed fish.

But work was his highest priority and he became known for his thoroughness. He checked out any phone number given him to see if that person could shed any light on a case. He ran down all tips he heard. His work sometimes went into the wee hours of the morning, but he had the support of his wife, who was an emergency room nurse and understood difficult hours. Besides, the pretty brunette was his confidante, his lover, and his best friend.

Rose was accustomed to working on cases others couldn't crack, for he believed that no amount of effort was too much if it brought someone to justice. But he did things his own way. Sometimes he didn't arrest a petty lawbreaker if that person might prove more valuable down the road for information against someone else who had committed a more serious crime.

That very situation came up in the spring of 1985 when a deputy arrested Ron Becker.

Rose looked up to see two men standing in the doorway of his office. One was another deputy, who had a tight hold on a handcuffed Ron Becker.

"This guy wants to see you," the deputy announced. "Okay?"

"Sure. Come in, Ron. Looks like you've gotten yourself into a little trouble."

"Possession," the other deputy interjected. "Had four marijuana cigarettes on him when we stopped him for speeding."

"Ron," Rose said in mock disgust. "Fast cars, fast drugs. What's next, fast women?"

"I wish," Becker said, and dropped into the chair in front of Rose's desk.

"Thanks," Rose said to the other deputy. "I'll handle this from here."

After the deputy left, Rose asked, "So what's up?"

"Got some info you might be interested in," Becker said.

Rose tolerated the familiar petty criminal. Twice before, Becker had given Rose information that solved a couple of cases. Becker always told the truth, and Rose would cut anybody slack who had that trait.

"What do you know?" Rose asked.

"Remember Jimmy Don Beets?"

"Has anyone forgotten him?"

"That's what my info's about. I know who offed him."

Rose sat up straighter. "Who's your source?"

"Some guy Betty Beets been screwing. When she told him all this stuff, she was three sheets to the wind. She let it all hang out."

"What'd she say?"

"What do I get for telling?"

"If we wire you to the lie detector and you're a hundred percent, we'll take away your cigarettes and slap your wrists."

"Betty did it," he said abruptly. "Shot Jimmy and stuffed him in a wishing well she has in her yard."

Rose flinched. "In a wishing well?"

"Yeah. Guess she had Jimmy build it first. Woman's got ice water in her veins."

"She buried him all by her little self?"

"Got her kid to help. Sweet mom, huh?"

"Sweet information, if it's true."

Rose loved the chase. He had an inquisitive mind and a background in law enforcement. His granddaddy was a cop, as well as his dad. His grandfather had a heart attack and died on the job, while his father later switched to fire fighting and retired a fireman.

Rose immediately called the DA's chief investigator, Michael O'Brien, his good friend and counterpart in the DA's office, who would be very interested to hear Becker's information. Rose thought about one of the courses he took for his degree in criminal justice. He learned that a female killer remained undetected for a longer period of time than the male, for she tended to be painstakingly methodical and just as lethal. The problem was more with the male-dominated law community that just didn't think a woman would do it.

Michael O'Brien basically did all the investigative work for the DA. His office was near the center of downtown Athens in the new Justice Building, a departure from the basically turn-of-the-century Athens architecture. The Justice Building stood just a block from the three-story redbrick courthouse. Distances in town were measured from "Courthouse Square," because everyone knew where that was. And typical of small towns, most trusting Athenians didn't lock their cars around the courthouse.

In less than fifteen minutes, Rose took Becker to meet with O'Brien for the lie detector test. In a small, sterile room, both men watched the polygraph technician place a blood pressure and pulse cuff on Becker's arm, then the respiration tube around his chest. First he asked Becker test questions, telling him to answer yes or no to all of them. He showed him an ace of hearts, and asked if it were a queen of diamonds. When Becker answered, "Yes," the chart indicated a false reply. After answering the test questions, the technician began asking the important ones.

"Did Gerald Albright give you information about Betty Beets?

"Yes."

Rose and O'Brien watched the moving chart that indicated Becker had told the truth.

"Did Betty Beets murder her husband, Jimmy Don Beets?"

"Yes."

The questions continued, covering every aspect of Becker's information. The chart registered all his answers as truthful.

"Ron, I know you want to stay anonymous," O'Brien said. "Let's play 'what if.' Say Albright lies through his teeth and says Betty didn't say any of this. Are you still good for the info?"

Becker thought a moment.

The investigators knew he'd rather be charged with possession than go in front of a courtroom and squeal on someone he knew.

But Becker said, "Sure. Call me. I'll testify."

He left, and Rose opened the sheriff's file on the Beets case he had brought with him. He showed the thin file to O'Brien. It held only a copy of Betty's miss-

ing person's report and the supposed sighting of Jimmy
Don by his niece in Dallas. No evidence suggested that
Betty Beets had been questioned. There were no follow-
ups.

"Looks like we've just reopened the case," O'Brien
said.

A month after Betty Beets secured the "Determination of Death" for Jimmy Don, the news trickled down
to his son, Jamie—an heir Betty had forgotten to mention. Jamie had not been served notice of Betty's action,
and therefore could not protest. He called the declaration premature and improper, and asked for a new declaration trial to set aside the judgment that favored only
Betty.

Bobby Branson leaned against a tree in his yard,
laughing with a friend. They were enjoying the balmy
spring evening until Ray Bone pulled up and parked in
the driveway. He nodded to Bobby and went inside the
house.

"Who's that?" his friend asked.

"Some jerk," Bobby said. "My mom's boyfriend."

"He acts like he owns the place. What's he doing
here?"

"Good question. I'll go ask him," Bobby said with a
glint of mischief in his eyes. He ran up the steps of the
trailer and found Ray in his mother's bedroom.

"How come you're hanging around? Mom's not
here."

"I'm going to take a nap. Do you mind?"

Bobby minded, but said nothing and went back to
his friend, who by then had hopped on his motorcycle
and busily roared through the yard. Dust clouds rose as

he cut donuts in the dirt in the rear of the property. He stopped near Bobby.

While the young men talked, Ray stormed out of the house. "Bobby, come here! Tell your friend not to ride his bike in the yard. He's tearing up the place. Your mom would be furious if she knew."

"Mom doesn't care. She lets me ride in the back."

"Tell your friend to stop or I will. And believe me I'll tell him the hard way."

Bobby threw Ray a disgusted look and went back to his friend. "Better stop riding through the yard. You'd never know what that creep will do."

"And your mom lets him stay here?"

"I don't know why we put up with him. He's been an asshole since the day he arrived. I'll be back in a sec," Bobby said.

Bobby shook with nervousness when he entered his mother's bedroom to wake up Ray. "Get the hell out of here," he said with uncharacteristic boldness. "Mom and I don't want you around anymore." Bobby knew that wasn't true—only *he* didn't want Ray around. Ray had told him he'd beat the hell out of him if he didn't do what he said.

"Who says?" Ray asked, looking irritated.

"Me and my mom."

"Like hell." Ray got up and started getting dressed. "We'll just go down to the Cedar Club and talk to Betty. Bet she didn't say anything like that."

Bobby went outside with Ray on his heels.

"Get in that truck, boy. You and me are goin' to see your mom."

"No, I'm not. I don't wanna go."

"You go, or I'll make you go."

Just as they began to argue, Bobby's friend pulled out a gun and shot into the air. Ray's reputation for meanness evaporated like hot air. He took off running like any bully would when actually confronted. Bobby dashed into the house.

A moment later, seventeen-year-old Bobby tore outside with two six-shooters, one in each hand. Bullets blazed from each gun. He kept looking for Ray, but didn't see him, so he went to his truck. When he heard a noise from the direction of the truck, he began shooting, and he continued to shoot until he had emptied both guns. The smell of gunsmoke, along with its haze, permeated the night air.

Then everything was quiet. Bobby laughed at having shot out all of Ray's tires. *That was for good measure. Ray deserved it.* Bobby knew it was mean, but he thought of how Ray treated them, and it felt good. When he looked around, he notice his friend had left.

It seemed like only seconds before the Cherokee Shores security pulled up to his house, and a guard stepped in front of Bobby. No doubt, more than one neighbor had called to report the disturbance.

The guard grabbed the guns from Bobby and said, "Okay. What happened?"

"Ray was trying to force me into his truck, and then he—" Bobby stopped. He saw Ray sitting in the backseat of the guard's car. Words failed to come out of his mouth.

SIXTEEN

The middle-aged woman who lived on the side street backing up to Betty Beets's corner lot had endured four years of being awakened through the night by gunshot. More than once, she and her retired husband peered into the Beets' yard to see Betty's boys outside shooting at tin cans. Sometimes Betty joined them.

One day the neighbor witnessed a knife-throwing contest between Betty and her boys. They were aiming at a sapling oak, and squealed with delight when they hit the skinny little tree.

Tonight the woman's house had been hit by gunfire. Her husband had died the previous spring, and disregarding her fear of confronting gun-toting neighbors, she called the police. Now that the security guard had arrived, she hurried from her house to the Beets's property.

"I reported the shooting," she said. "He had a shotgun."

The guard turned to Bobby. "Were you shooting a shotgun tonight?"

"I used one of those," he said, indicating the firearms the guard had already confiscated.

"No, Bobby," the guard said. "A shotgun. Do you have more guns in your house?"

Bobby nodded, and motioned for the guard and neighbor to follow him. He led them into the trailer through the living room, down the hall, and into the kitchen. He squatted down and pulled out the bottom kitchen drawer. Underneath were five pistols. He handed them to the guard.

"I saw him out with a shotgun earlier," the neighbor said emphatically.

"It's in here," Bobby told them and went to the hall closet and brought back a shotgun.

"I'm taking these," the guard said. "Got to check them to make sure they're not stolen."

When the three went back outside, police had arrived and were examining Ray's truck. It glimmered in the glare of their bright flashlights, and the many bullet holes puncturing it made it look like a casualty of war.

An officer shook his head. "Who got mad at the truck?" he asked.

The guard started to tell him, but the officer's attention was diverted when he noticed a shotgun in Ray's truck. The officer had earlier run a check on both Bobby and Ray, so he knew of Ray's record as a convicted felon.

"Tell me about this, Mr. Bone."

Ray stared at the gun. "That's not mine. I have no idea how it got there."

Rose and O'Brien frequently talked over the Beets's case and discussed what approaches they'd take to gather information.

O'Brien had ten years' experience with criminal investigations, dating back to when he got out of the navy. The navy had sent him from Vietnam to Texas, then recruited him to work security for the naval air station. He continued working with law enforcement to pay his way through college. The native Oklahoman first attended Baylor University, then graduated from the University of Texas at Tyler.

Both men knew they had to question Betty's kids. If their mother was involved in a murder, possibly the family knew about it.

"I'll run down her kids and get some statements," Rose said. "Hopefully I can convince them to spill the beans on Mama."

"Good luck," O'Brien said. "Sometimes there's loyalty to a parent that makes no sense whatsoever. If a parent is all a kid knows, all he has, there's probably a certain amount of fear, some love, and the fact that he doesn't want to see Mama get in trouble. Good luck."

Phyllis Coleman hadn't lived all that long, but she had lived hard. The prettiest of the four Branson girls, Phyllis resembled Betty more than any of the others. Her silky, light blond hair draped past her shoulders, but didn't conceal the tattoos on each arm. A unicorn pranced around her upper left arm, and the sun rose on her right.

The twenty-three-year-old lived in Balch Springs, a small rural town bordering Dallas, with much lower rent than its big neighbor.

Phyllis sat in what charitably could be called a dive in a shabby area of East Dallas. The entire bar was an all-smoking section. Overflowing ashtrays sat on tables, along with empty beer bottles from previous customers. Phyllis, hazy from too much to drink, fingered an embedded ring on the table.

The young woman sitting with her suggested, "Phyllis, don't you think you've had enough?"

"For what I've gone through, I couldn't have too much."

"You're not getting into your 'poor me' thing again, are you?"

"Poor me is right. If you only knew." Phyllis's long earrings swung as she spoke.

"You're like a broken record. You keep hinting at problems in your family, but you just skip around the outside. I have no idea what you're talking about."

"Do you know anyone who's murdered somebody?" Phyllis asked.

"Hell no, and I don't want to."

"What if your own mother murdered her husband?"

"That's it. I'm leaving," her friend said.

"No, wait. Honest. That's what I'm dealing with. My mom, Betty Beets, killed two husbands."

Her friend slid Phyllis's drink beyond her reach.

"I'm telling you right. Not only did she kill them, she buried them in her yard."

Obviously shaken, her friend slowly stood up and moved to the door. She had to get away. She needed a phone. She had to call Crime Stoppers.

Betty Beets screamed, "Why?" when the police contacted her at the Cedar Club with news that they had booked her youngest son, the fair-haired, blue-eyed Bobby, into the juvenile detention center. Her mystification grew when she learned that Ray Bone had been detained in jail.

At almost midnight, she drove to downtown Athens and met with juvenile authorities. It gave her the willys to drive past the lake at night with no moon to light the ripples on the waves. The lake appeared deeper in the dark.

But on the outskirts of Athens, no bright lights shone either. With bars outlawed and churches sitting on almost every corner, at this hour everything was dimly lit.

Once at the juvenile center, the officers told her about the shoot-out in minute detail. They discussed Bobby's aggressiveness and his dislike of Bone.

The authorities would detain Bobby for a couple more days, then release him to a relative.

Now she had to figure out what to do for Ray.

Rick Rose knew Gerald Albright's habits. At eight every morning he could be counted on being in Seven Points having coffee at McClain's, a homey restaurant in Seven Points, known for its rib-sticking breakfasts. The place wouldn't take credit cards, but they'd accept a personal check. McClain's sat at the main intersection. Seven roads came together at that point, hence the name of the town.

Rose went inside and waited for Albright to finish his coffee, then followed him out. He caught up with him in the middle of the block where there was less pedestrian traffic to hear their conversation.

"Gerald, got a minute?"

Albright quickly turned around and smiled. "How's it goin', Deputy?"

"Just want to ask you a few questions."

"You flatter me. You think I'd know something you're interested in?"

"I've been talking with a friend of yours, Ron Becker."

Albright's friendly expression changed. "What's old Ron up to?"

"Actually, we were talking about what you've been up to."

Albright stopped in his tracks. "Ron doesn't know shit about me."

"He seems to think so."

"Like what?"

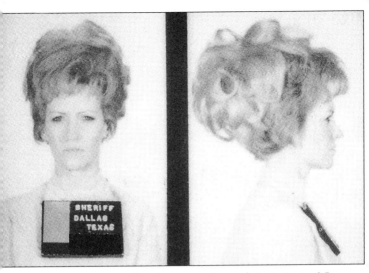

In 1972, two years after they were divorced, Betty Beets, 35, was arrested on attempted murder for shooting Billy York Lane, her second husband.
(*Photo courtesy Dallas, Texas Sheriff's Office*)

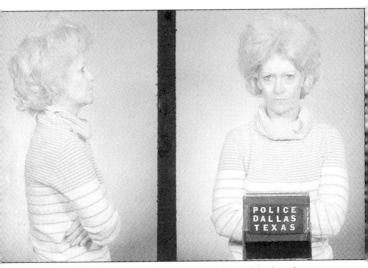

Beets was arrested in August 1979 for public lewdness while auditioning as a topless dancer.
(*Photo courtesy Dallas, Texas Police Department*)

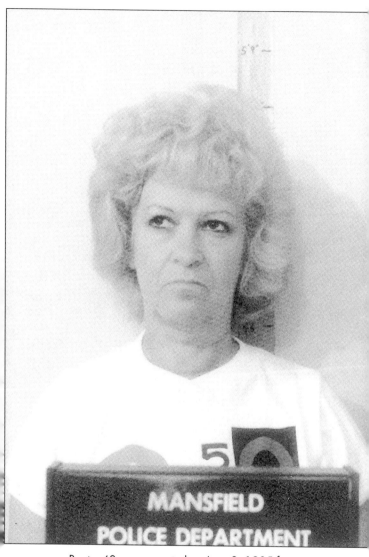

Beets, 48, was arrested on June 8, 1985 for
the capital murder of Jimmy Don Beets.
(*Photo courtesy Mansfield, Texas Police Department*)

Victim Doyle Wayne Barker, Betty Beets's fourth husband. (*Photo courtesy Rodney Barker*)

Victim Jimmy Don Beets, Betty Beets's fifth husband. (*Photo courtesy Susan Beets Huffman*)

Beets (*center*) was a rookie fireman in Dallas, Texas in 1957. (*Photo courtesy Dallas Firefighters Museum*)

Fire Captain Jimmy Don Beets was well-liked by his many friends. (*Photo courtesy Dallas Firefighters Museum*)

Beets celebrated his 44th birthday in 1981, one year before marrying Betty. (*Photo courtesy Susan Beets Huffman*)

In their search for the missing Jimmy Don Beets, police focussed on the Beets's wishing well. (*Photo courtesy Henderson County, Texas Sheriff's Office*)

Police used a backhoe to topple over the well, then dug into the dirt mound inside. (*Photo courtesy Henderson County, Texas Sheriff's Office*)

Jimmy Don Beets's body was found in a near-fetal
position inside a blue sleeping bag.
(*Photo courtesy Henderson County, Texas Sheriff's Office*)

The shed on the Beets's property where they found the decomposed body of Doyle Wayne Barker buried.
(*Photo courtesy Henderson County, Texas Sheriff's Office*)

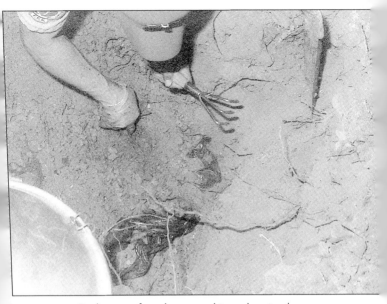

Barker was found wrapped in a sleeping bag.
(*Photo courtesy Henderson County, Texas Sheriff's Office*)

Betty Beets used her .38 Colt Revolver to kill her victims.
(*Photo courtesy Henderson County, Texas Sheriff's Office*)

Deputy Howard Copeland, defense attorney E. Ray
Andrews, and Betty Beets on their way to court.
(*Photo courtesy David Branch, Tyler Morning Telegraph*)

Shirley Stegner, one of Betty Beets's daughters by her first husband, was arrested in connection with the murders after the bodies were found. (*Photo courtesy* The Dallas Morning News/*Lon Cooper*)

Faye Lane, Betty Beets's oldest daughter, leaving court after testifying. (*Photo courtesy David Branch,* Tyler Morning Telegraph)

Beets being escorted to trial by Deputy Rick Rose.
(*Photo courtesy* The Dallas Morning News/*Lon Cooper*)

Rows of sound trucks were part of the national media frenzy over Beets's execution.

Protestors gathered outside the Walls Unit of the Huntsville, Texas prison before the execution.

"What my husbands started

Texas will finish."

Anti-Death Penalty supporters who described Beets
as an abused woman held posters showing her
with facial bruises and a black eye.

Betty Beets shortly before her execution on February 24, 2000.
(*Photo courtesy Charles Stiff, Photographer, Cedar Creek Pilot, Gun Barrel City, Texas*)

Rodney Barker and James Beets attended the execution of their fathers's murderer. (*Photo courtesy Charles Stiff, Photographer, Cedar Creek Pilot, Gun Barrel City, Texas*)

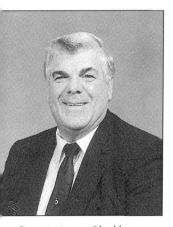

Captain James Blackburn commanded the two-week search for the body of Jimmy Don Beets. (*Photo courtesy James Blackburn*)

Henderson County Sheriff Deputy Ron Shields.

Michael O'Brien, the District Attorney's Office's Chief Investigator for the 173rd.

District Judge Jack Holland.

Jimmy Don Beets was buried in Roseland Cemetery, in Seagoville, Texas.

JIMMY DON BEETS
US ARMY
KOREA
MAR 10 1937 ✝ AUG 6 1983

"Mentioned you were out frolicking with Betty Beets."

"Oh that," he said, striking a match on the sole of his boot to light his cigarette. "I've seen Betty a time or two."

"Actually," Rose said, "it's what she told you that we were discussing."

"Betty gets pretty drunk." He lit his cigarette, then shook out the match. "I always say you can't believe a drunk. It's the whiskey talkin'."

"Well, the whiskey told him what's planted in Betty's wishing well," Rose said.

Gerald inhaled his cigarette smoke, but said nothing.

"Is that what Betty said?" Rose asked again.

Albright exhaled and studied the glowing tip of his cigarette. "Something like that. I'm telling you, Rick"—he stopped to extract a piece of tobacco from the tip of his tongue—"that woman scares me to death."

Officer Diaz Ortega of the Dallas Police Department took the message from Crime Stoppers. The organization automatically forwarded calls to police, but rarely as bizarre a tale as they relayed today.

After hearing the facts that Shirley's friend in the bar had related to Crime Stoppers, Ortega easily recalled the Beets drowning. He remembered that the sheriff's office in Athens had initially handled the case. They'd be the first people he'd want to call.

"Who's working the Beets case now?" Ortega asked the Henderson County deputy who answered the phone.

"That's Rick Rose," the deputy said. "He's not in at the moment, but I can page him on his beeper. It'll be the quickest way to get hold of him."

SEVENTEEN

Betty had spent two hours at the juvenile detention center last night with Bobby, so now at nine in the morning, she had to force herself to get up. First, she'd check with Ray about his bail.

She showered, dressed, and strolled out to her truck, wondering why it looked so much lower than ever before. Several feet closer, she found four flat tires, apparently all slashed with a knife. Could this be some kind of threat, or maybe just teenagers prowling late at night? She didn't know.

She spent the day replacing tires. After she paid the bill, she gritted her teeth at the expense. Then she remembered the Dallas Police and Fireman Pension Committee would meet next week. Once she started receiving that monthly check, life would be wonderful.

However, that could still be a couple weeks away and right now the tires had eaten her bank account. She had no money to bail out Ray. She had talked with him earlier and vowed she'd raise money somehow.

That night, she worked particularly late, and her tips were good. Her story of slashed tires had entertained her customers, and one person had suggested they take up a collection.

Around two A.M., she drove home from work, and when she neared her house, she shook with apprehension. Would someone be waiting outside her trailer with the same knife he used to slash her tires? Distressed, she stopped at the security station for Cherokee Shores, and told the guard about her problem.

"Now you can see why the hell I'm so concerned," she added. "I figured if they'd do that, what else would they try?"

The man nodded sympathetically.

"Would you mind following me to my house and wait till I'm inside?"

"It'd be my pleasure, ma'am. Let me get my car keys and I'll be right behind you."

Betty found it comforting to see the guard's headlights in her rearview mirror.

They curved around the subdivision, each road walled by thick forest and looking ominous at night. Then they turned down her street. As if orchestrated, when both vehicles pulled up to Betty's property, a flash of light exploded, followed by a loud bang; then flames shot out of her trailer.

They both scrambled out of their cars as fast as their feet would carry them and ran to the trailer. Betty grabbed the green hose she always kept handy to water flowers, but found it pathetically inadequate for the fire.

"Oh my God, do something," Betty screamed. "My dog's locked up in the pantry."

The guard had hurried to his car and phoned the Payne Springs Fire Department. They were only five minutes away.

Betty stretched the hose to her kitchen and sprayed water inside.

In another twenty minutes, the fire department had extinguished the fire, but the trailer still smoldered in a hazy gray smoke. Everything looked dark, wet, and soggy.

Betty dashed inside, and came out carrying her dead,

smoke-darkened dog. Her hair and clothes reeked of fumes.

By now, neighbors had gathered. Betty sat on the steps of her front porch, cradling the lifeless animal. "Those goddamn bastards suffocated my dog." Tears rolled down her cheeks. "This is murder, pure and simple. Those bastards murdered my dog," she kept repeating as tears removed her mascara.

A gritty-faced fireman went to her. "Ma'am, just wanted you to know this fire was started by gasoline. It's gotta be arson. The state fire marshal needs possession of the trailer while we get an investigation going."

Sadly, Betty nodded, then affectionately laid her dog on the porch and went back inside the charred shell of her trailer. Moonlight filtered through the smoke-covered windows while the firemen accompanied her, carrying flashlights that cast strange patterns on the damaged rooms.

"Look at this mess," she said. "This bedroom's practically gone. Let's see what's back here." They followed her down the hall to her bedroom. The bed had burned, and the sodden mattress still smoked.

"At lease my closet doors were closed, hopefully I still have clothes." Betty looked at the ruins that had once been her home. She sighed. "Where on earth am I gonna live?"

Rose stopped at the first pay phone he found to return Officer Ortega's call. He spotted two phones mounted outside a small, redbrick grocery store in Cherokee Shores. He listened to the officer and smiled in disbelief when he heard Ortega's report.

"What you're saying fits the scenario of everything we know so far," Rose told him.

Rose had been trying to find Phyllis Coleman ever

since he had talked with his informant, almost a month ago. It turned out that Phyllis had temporarily separated from her husband and was staying in a friend's apartment, so she had no phone listing. Nor could she be traced by a driver's license or credit cards. She had none.

"I've got her temporary address and phone number," Ortega said.

Rose busily jotted down the information.

"What are you guys doing right now?" Rose asked. "Do you have time to run out there?"

"I can if I go right now, but you know homicide. If something breaks I'll be out of here."

"Right now is perfect," Rose said. "How about heading to her apartment and I'll get her on the phone. Hopefully, I can keep her talking until you get there."

Ortega agreed to the plan and Rose called Phyllis's number.

After six rings, a sleepy, slurred voice answered the phone.

"Phyllis Coleman?" Rose asked.

"Speaking."

"This is Deputy Rose with the Sheriff's Office."

"God, what do you want?"

"Just to talk to you. I need you to answer a few questions."

Phyllis sounded apprehensive. "What about?"

"Just a sec," Rose said. He let the receiver dangle down the brick wall while he used the phone next to it and called Ortega. He learned that Ortega had already left for Phyllis's apartment.

"Okay, I'm back. I want to talk about your family. Especially your mother. I've been hearing some things about her and just needed to ask you."

Apparently everything clicked at once, and Phyllis began crying. Her voice sounded garbled and Rose had difficulty understanding her through her sobs.

"What do you want to know?"

"What did she do, Phyllis?"

"What the hell are you talkin' about?"

"Pretty much what you told someone in a bar last night. A person at the next table overheard you," Rose said to cover for the woman who called Crime Stoppers.

"Oh shit. All's I know is what my sister, Shirley, told me. I just couldn't believe it. We were down at Mama's, across the street in the woods, and Shirley kept telling me how scared she was, she didn't know what to do when Mama asked her to help bury Wayne."

"Wayne? Who's Wayne?" Rose was mystified. Could Phyllis be so messed up she didn't know Jimmy Don's name?

"Wayne Barker," Phyllis said. "Isn't that what you're calling about?"

Now a light went off in Rose's head and he was astounded. He'd heard another one of Betty's husbands had disappeared, but didn't dream he'd only gone as far as Betty's yard.

At the time, everyone believed Betty when she said that Wayne had left on his own accord. Just like they believed her now. There had been no investigation, no one coming forth asking authorities to look into Barker's disappearance. Not even his family. Rose's mind went back to his criminal justice courses. The Black Widow killer was the hardest of all to detect for she quietly laid meticulous plans, then struck, and usually at home. Without emotion, she targeted people close to her such as a trusting spouse, and usually for profit. That fit Betty to a tee.

After those thoughts flashed through Rose's mind, he asked Phyllis, "What about Jimmy Don Beets?"

"Just a minute, I'll get to him."

Rose scribbled notes as fast as he could, but the avalanche of new information made it difficult to steady his hand.

"Anyways," Phyllis continued, "we were drinking and when I heard what Shirley had to say, I wanted to keep on drinking. I got so damn sick on Tom Collins that they had to hold me over the toilet.

"Back when it happened, I couldn't believe that Wayne just walked off, but that's what Mama told me."

"When was this?" Rose asked.

"Oh, gosh, three or four years ago. Then one day I went down there and was walking around Mama's backyard, wondering, could this be true? That's when I saw a place that had been sunken in and I thought, oh no, it's just from the rain. It can't be true. Then when Jimmy Don came up missing, I thought, God, it's true. I didn't want to believe it. I told Shirley she had to be lying to me because my mother wouldn't do something like this—I mean someone who raised me up watching *Romper Room?* I just couldn't believe it."

Phyllis continued the sordid details of Barker's death, saying she thought her mother had to be crazy to do such a thing.

"Then around Christmas time in '83, Shirley told me about Jimmy Don. That was when . . . Shit. Someone's at the door."

"Why don't you go see who it is and come back and talk to me?" Rose said. "I'll wait."

After a pause, Phyllis returned to the phone. "My God, it's the Dallas Police Department!"

"They want to talk about this case," Rose told her.

"I sure as hell don't want to talk to them," she said, crying hysterically.

Rose said, "Here's what we've got to decide. You're either in this deal up to your neck, or you're going to help us. It's a fork in the road, take it."

He was met with muffled sobs. "Phyllis? Which fork are you taking?"

"I can't choose." Her voice sounded small and scared.

"Just tell the truth, Phyllis. If you don't, if you lie to us about something, then you can be charged with conspiracy to murder."

Phyllis cried until she was screaming.

"I know it's your mother and it's hard to say anything against her, but Phyllis, the truth needs to come out."

After what seemed to Rose to be several minutes, in a resigned voice, Phyllis said, "I'll help."

Rick Rose couldn't have been happier to hear that Betty's boyfriend had been jailed for gun possession. He had wanted to talk with the man who at this point appeared to be Betty's closest friend.

Ray Bone sat in jail for two days. When the deputies first arrested him, the judge set Bone's bail at $5,000. The afternoon Bone went to court, Rose wrote his Probable Cause Determination and attended the hearing. The Henderson County Court determined that Bone had violated his parole, and now the court had the option of sending him back to prison. Afterward, Rose suggested that Bone accompany him back to his office to talk.

Bone sat across from Rose's desk, looking grumpy and hateful. He had proven his disrespect for law enforcement, but Rose didn't want revenge, he wanted Bone's help in convicting Betty Beets.

He let Bone stew a little longer before he began speaking. It would be easy to send him back to prison for violating his parole, but that wouldn't be fruitful. Nor was it Rose's way to threaten him, but since Rose was six-feet-two, 250 pounds, with broad shoulders, he found that physical threats weren't necessary.

Rose began, "You know, Ray, you're a felon and you've got this weapon." Rose paused for emphasis. "What are we going to do about that?" he said, knowing he'd get more cooperation if the criminal thought he was part of the decision-making process.

Bone shifted uneasily in his chair. "This all is shit. I didn't know that damn gun was there. I borrowed the truck from a friend. Gun was his."

"Whatever," Rose said. "It still remains that you had a gun in your possession."

Ray nodded briefly, but sat frowning.

"What do you think is going to happen now?" Rose asked.

"I reckon it looks like I'm going back to the pen."

"Yeah. Probably does," Rose said without emotion.

Rose waited through the silence, but Bone didn't offer any suggestion. His meanness was legend and whatever he did would be for his own survival. Bone gave the appearance of cooperation, but at the same time Rose knew that the man hated his guts.

"Tell you what, maybe we could do this," Rose said. "How about if you call me every once in a while and let me know what Betty's up to?"

Ray nodded.

"Just fill me in on where she is. What she's doing. That sort of thing."

"Yeah," Ray said. "I can do that."

"Then it's a plan," Rose said, standing up. At that point, he shocked Ray by saying, "You're free to go."

Ray's eyes widened in disbelief.

"I've worked it out with the DA. You're free on your own recognizance."

Rose watched Ray heave a heavy sigh, then get up and plod out of his office. He knew that Ray would probably tell Betty what he was doing, and Betty would probably reply, "No problem. I understand where you're coming from."

Rose put in a call to Mike O'Brien, to update him on the case's progress.

Rose brought him up to speed, then said, "This is too easy. Someone tells my informant what Betty did, Crime Stoppers gets a call a few weeks later about Phyllis, who spills her guts and confirms everything we've heard. Now Ray Bone is calling and letting us know what Betty's up to. When are we going to run into a roadblock? Where's that brick wall that will stop us when we're literally skimming over the waves? I've never had a case go so smoothly."

"But up 'til now, it's sat for two years with absolutely nothing happening," O'Brien reminded him.

"Yeah, but I know luck when I see it," Rose replied. "This is like Hansel and Gretel; all we have to do now is follow the bread crumbs."

Prompted by self-preservation and his desire not to return to the penitentiary, Ray Bone diligently kept in touch with Rick Rose. Bone told him that Betty had been notified by the juvenile authorities that they released her son Bobby to his sister Faye Lane.

Ray reported that since Betty had been burned out of her trailer, he would soon take her to a small house his brother owned on the outskirts of Mansfield, Texas, a community thirty miles southwest of Dallas.

Rose knew the area. The house was probably out in the country, amid gently sloping fields of green cotton. Betty needed the peace and quiet after all she's been through, Rose thought sarcastically.

Bone had called Rose when they first arrived at the Mansfield house and said they'd be there until they decided where they'd live.

The Police and Fire Department Pension Board held their meeting on the first Thursday in June. Their agenda included considering whether or not to award a pension to Jimmy Don Beets's widow. Betty's lawyer saw to it that the board received a copy of the March document pronouncing Jimmy Don "legally deceased."

The board had no access to the case Rose and O'Brien were putting together, and for tactical reasons the investigators didn't want that information made public yet. So after a brief discussion, the board voted unanimously to award Betty Lou Beets a lump sum of $15,852 for back payments and $792 a month, every month, for the rest of her life. They'd mail the first payment next week, on Monday.

EIGHTEEN

The acrid smell of the scorched trailer burned their nostrils as Rick Rose and Michael O'Brien approached it. They knew they'd come out covered with soot and smelling like smoke after their investigation, but like two kids told they could open a box of candy, they weren't about to miss the opportunity to examine Betty's belongings. Any additional information on her became essential now that they were whisker close to making a case against her. With the fire marshal policing the place, they could be reasonably assured that the evidence had not been tampered with.

Many times after Rose had heard of Betty's involvement, he had driven by the trailer, watching the comings and goings of Betty, her family, and her friends. He had never stopped, but he made sure the wishing well and shed were there to substantiate the information his informant and Phyllis gave him.

O'Brien held a notepad to sketch details he'd use in obtaining the evidentiary search warrant. "I'm making sure I include everything the judge will want."

"Good idea," Rose said, "since Judge Holland only goes by the letter of the law."

"I think we're okay unless the judge wants to meet any of the upstanding citizens who gave us the information," O'Brien joked.

As they entered the still smoky trailer, they nodded

to the fireman guarding the front door. They had heard the stories about guns being hidden underneath drawers and inside closets. If that much had been hidden, what more would there be to find?

Rose began sorting through a stack of old letters and newspapers he found in the kitchen. The letter on top was black with ashes.

"Is there nothing you won't touch?" O'Brien asked.

"Nothing," Rose assured him.

One by one he lifted each piece of paper, unfolding it, emptying out envelopes, and reading everything.

"Now this is really nice of Betty. Sweet gal."

O'Brien looked over his shoulder. "A list of her guns? Do you have a rabbit's foot in your pocket or something?"

Rose counted. "Nineteen guns. A woman's got to protect herself, for Heaven's sake." Before he read the description of each gun, he noticed one of them had a red line drawn through it. "This is interesting. Our friend's marked one of them for us. A .38 pistol."

"Sounds familiar," O'Brien said. "Could be one of those confiscated from her youngest son after the shootout, but I bet there's a more definite reason why she ruled through it."

"I've seen this happen over and over in my investigations," Rose said. "There's a certain element in any case that's consistent with the mind. The subconscious is stronger than the conscious mind. It works like a computer. When you submit information to the hard drive, it's there. An expert can find it. Betty consciously listed her weapons, then from the hard drive memory of her own brain, her subconscious, she scratched it out. She knew it was a weapon that could later cause her problems."

"That's eerie."

"Not really," Rose said. "It's about people."

O'Brien went to scrutinize the rest of the trailer, then came back and said, "This will break your heart, but there aren't any more stacks of junk in the back rooms. Looks like the fire took everything there."

"I'm almost finished," Rose assured him. "Oh wait, here's something. Betty's power of attorney."

"Who'd be foolish enough to sign over power to Betty?"

"Well, posthumously Mr. Beets did."

"Figures. Did she use it?" O'Brien asked.

"I don't know. Maybe Betty will tell us." Rose continued to finger the stack of papers with gritty fingers the color of the ashes.

"Here's a bill of sale for a boat, $3,250. That's a tidy little sum. Says it's for a nineteen-foot Glastron."

"That's the empty boat we saw after he 'disappeared,'" O'Brien said. "So that's how she sold it. Convinced someone she was the owner and transferred the title. Completely illegal, but actually pretty clever."

They both stood quietly. Then O'Brien said, "Are you thinking the same thing I'm thinking?"

"Yeah, where's Betty?" Rose said.

"She could be five states away from here. She's probably been feeling cocky getting away with two murders."

"And two almost murders. I found out that Billy York Lane died three years ago of a heart attack."

"Probably brought on by Betty shooting him a couple times."

"It took me a week to find Threlkeld," O'Brien said. "Everybody swore Betty had killed him. He's living in Little Rock. I gave him a call, and he told me when he was leaving her back in '79, she tried to run him down with her car. Said he wasn't worried because he felt he could jump out of the way in time. I dropped in that little piece about her shooting her second husband, which happened right before she met Threlkeld. He had no idea that she had shot Lane, so the guy feels lucky to be alive."

"Let's draw up the warrant and get that gal locked up."

Legal issues were Mike O'Brien's specialty. When he prepared the Evidentiary Search Warrant for Judge Jack Holland's signature, he relied heavily on the informant's statement outlining Betty's revelation to Gerald Albright when they were in the motel.

Rose requested that the informant's name remain confidential. He did this for Becker's protection as well to keep his identity a secret for any possible future information.

In addition to Betty's arrest warrant, O'Brien drew up one on Shirley Thompson. He added facts from the signed affidavit the Dallas police had secured from Phyllis Coleman. Now if everything went as expected, Shirley would be arrested right after Betty.

Deputy Ron Shields, a rookie at the Henderson County Sheriff's Office, had expected to be assigned the less glamorous assignments, but hadn't considered he'd also be handed the dull and boring ones.

He had read about Jimmy Don Beets's disappearance two years before, but considered it no big deal until June fifth when Rick Rose asked him to stake out Betty's trailer.

"There's a possibility that someone might try to break in there tonight," Rose told him. "We can't let that happen. There's too much evidence at stake."

Rose didn't confide that Shields would be guarding two graves. He only said, "Just watch the house. If Betty

Beets shows up, call me. I'll let you know if anything goes down at this end."

At three P.M., Shields drove his green Chevrolet sedan out to Cherokee Shores. He used his own car, equipped with a police radio, because it wouldn't stick out like a police car. He parked up the street at a vacant lot and waited.

At five, another deputy brought him a cold drink. An hour later, Rose called and said they were putting together a search warrant. Around six, another deputy showed up with Shields's dinner. Occasionally, other deputies checked on him until midnight. After that, he sat for eight hours straight fighting off sleep.

Finally, he went home and managed to crawl into bed. A few hours later, his wife woke him, telling him Rose was on the phone.

"Get back out to Betty's house by five," Rose said. "We'll need you."

At seven-thirty on Friday morning, Rick Rose and Michael O'Brien had been up for seventy-two hours straight while they orchestrated Betty's arrest. They hadn't been to bed since the night before Rose spoke with Phyllis Coleman.

They sat in O'Brien's paneled office, putting the finishing touches on the search and arrest warrants. His office appeared tailored. On the walls hung numerous framed plaques and awards. It had a neat, orderly, no-nonsense look compared to Rose's wild animal kingdom.

A secretary came in to compile the material for typing the warrants.

"You guys look tired," she said. "I can't believe the time you've put into this case."

"Don't worry about us," Rose said. "A dog in the hunt don't know he's got fleas."

She laughed, then said, "Do your wives keep pictures of you so they can remember what you look like?"

After she left, Rose said, "Let's not let on we enjoy what we do. We'd stop getting sympathy."

A moment later, the same secretary buzzed O'Brien. The sheriff's office had forwarded a phone number with a message for Rick Rose to call Ray Bone.

Bone had been waiting at a pay phone. He immediately picked up when Rose called.

"What's happening?" Rose said into the receiver.

"We're still over here near my brother's," Bone told him, "but we're getting ready to leave."

"What route are you taking?" Rose asked.

"We're picking up Highway 287 north of Mansfield, heading south."

"If you'd come down 635, I could meet you," Rose said.

"Nah. I'm coming down 287. It's about thirty minutes faster."

"Okay, can you be a little more precise about when you'll be leaving?"

"Probably around eight or so. In just a few minutes."

"Is Betty overhearing our conversation?"

Bone sighed. "You got that right."

At eight-fifteen on a clear morning outside of Mansfield, Texas, the police dispatcher broadcast a 10-29, an urgent message to all officers in the area: "Be on the lookout for a red-and-white Chevrolet pickup bearing Texas license plate KJ 3409. The truck was last seen traveling southbound on Highway 287 from J. Rendon Road. Occupant is Betty Beets. There's a warrant on her from the Athens Sheriff's Office for murder. She's possibly armed."

Two Mansfield police officers, Wallace and Hostettler, moved their squad cars to the bridge on East Broad that spanned the highway. They could sit there with an expansive view of the road beneath them and wait for Betty's truck, then notify officers on the highway. Other officers in the area headed to the same location. In less than ten minutes, Hostettler radioed that the red-and-white truck had just passed below them.

A quarter of a mile north of Willow Bend, three Mansfield police cars, with lights flashing, caught up with the truck, and surrounded it. The officers motioned the driver to the side of the road.

Bone opened the driver's door, and an officer said, "Both of you, get out with your hands up."

Once Ray Bone and Betty stood in the bright sunlight with their hands raised, they were told to step back toward the patrol units, one at a time. Two officers reached out and clamped handcuffs on both of them; then an officer took out his printed card to read the Miranda warning.

Before the officer began the first line, Betty blurted out, "This couldn't have anything to do with my husband's drowning, could it?"

The officer fought to ignore her and finished Mirandaizing them, while another officer quickly wrote the words she had spoken.

The police began searching their vehicle and discovered a high-standard, .22-caliber, two-shot derringer under the front seat, a .22-caliber, one-shot derringer under the floorboard, and three boxes of ammunition. Various bags of clothing, along with some jewelry and beer cans were also found.

The Henderson County Sheriff's Office had told the

Mansfield police, "We aren't requesting a hold on the vehicle. Just confiscate all the weapons."

An officer checked with the dispatcher and learned that Athens didn't want to arrest Raymond Bone, so they unlocked his handcuffs.

Ray rubbed the circulation back into his wrists, and turned to Betty. The officers were filling out her arrest forms. During that serious moment, she showed no emotion, but occasionally glanced at Ray.

Then in the middle of the highway, Betty turned her truck over to Ray—the truck that had belonged to Jimmy Don. Ray hugged her before an officer pulled her away and led her to a squad car. They whisked her off to the Mansfield Police Department jail, where she was booked, photographed, and fingerprinted. Before being placed in a holding cell, a judge set her bond at $100,000. Then they waited for Deputy Rick Rose.

Deputy Herman Kite had been sent to Cherokee Shores when Bobby Branson decided to run off Ray Bone, in what everyone now called the "shoot-out." Kite was in the office when the call came from Ray Bone that he and Betty would soon climb into her truck and take Highway 287.

The deputies would normally assume that Betty would come back to the lake area because of her family, but now with what they knew of Betty, her children might not be enough incentive for her to return. She could go anywhere.

Once the Mansfield police notified the sheriff's office that Betty had been locked up, Rick Rose asked Deputy Kite to accompany him to retrieve Betty and bring her back to Henderson County.

Since the case had dragged on for two years, many of the other deputies looked skeptically at Rose as he left to collect Betty. Rose had invited a couple of the deputies to accompany him, but they gave him a "We'll believe it when we see it" glance.

The trip to Mansfield took an hour and thirty minutes, past the southern tip of Cedar Creek Lake. They crossed miles of rolling pastureland before reaching Mansfield.

Rick Rose didn't doubt that it would be the mean Betty who greeted them when the police unlocked her cell. He couldn't have been more correct. At first, Betty shot him a hateful look. Her chin jutted out and her mouth clamped shut.

All the way back to Athens, her mouth stayed locked. They only saw a reaction when Betty occasionally flashed them a hostile glare.

Sheriff Charlie Fields ran the jail for Henderson County—one of his many jobs. He had long known of Betty Beets, ever since he went to inspect her husband's boat that stormy night at the lake. Now the slick woman was locked in a cell in the county jail, a separate building from the sheriff's office.

Fields had spent three years in the navy and he'd been told by his deputies that Betty knew swear words that he probably hadn't heard. Fields wanted to talk with her and make sure she understood the jailhouse rules.

He had Betty brought into the interrogation quarters where he could sit at a desk with her. She came in wearing handcuffs and white jail garb, which consisted of a rough cotton shirt and drawstring pants.

Shields took the chair opposite her. She smiled as he sat down.

"Just want to lay down the ground rules, Mrs. Beets," he said.

"Yes, sir," she said demurely.

"We don't allow any profanity in this jail."

"Oh no, sir."

"And we won't put up with any sloppiness."

"I always like things as neat as a pin," she replied, quite honestly.

"Okay. Now we expect you to be cooperative here and not cause a ruckus."

"No, sir. That's not my way."

He told her the time she would be expected to get up, when meals would be served, and other intricacies of jail routine.

"All right then," he said. "I'm glad you understand how things are going to be." He left the room after a guard took Betty back to her cell.

"How'd it go?" a deputy asked Fields as he left the jail.

Fields smiled and said, "Just fine. She's a cute lady."

Judge Jack Holland had great respect for Michael O'Brien. He knew him to be meticulous about legal procedures, as well as a completely honest person, so he wasn't overly concerned with the request for an evidentiary search warrant. O'Brien had personally carried it into the judge's spacious, carpeted office for his signature.

The judge sat back in his leather chair and read the document.

"This is good, Mike."

"We got lucky with an informant," O'Brien said.

"And I see you have collaborating testimony from a family member."

"Yes. We've substantiated the informant's testimony by interviewing two people. Here's Gerald Albright's signed affidavit," he said, reaching across the judge's dark mahogany desk. "He's the man Betty told about killing and burying her husband."

Holland perused the documents. "I think you've covered all your bases," he said as he signed the warrant.

A guard unlocked Betty's cell to again take her to one of the rooms lawyers used to converse with their clients. This time she would talk with Michael O'Brien.

O'Brien waited for Betty to be brought in. Once she entered, he said, "I've got this search warrant Judge Holland signed so we can look for the body of Jimmy Don Beets."

Betty looked blankly at him, not appearing interested.

"We're going out to your property on Cherokee Shores and you're sure welcome to come along."

She shook her head.

"You could help by telling us where the body is buried so we don't have to dig up your whole yard. We're taking a backhoe with us."

She shook her head again, almost in an unconcerned manner.

"While we're out there, we're going to look for Doyle Wayne Barker's body too. Would you like to come along?"

Betty's blue eyes flew open, turned black, and shot daggers at O'Brien. "I want my lawyer!"

O'Brien looked into those eyes and found it easy to read Betty's mind. She must have figured that investigators had put two and two together, he reasoned, and it now became a whole different ball game.

"You're sure welcome to come with us if you like."

"No!" Betty shut her lips and raised her chin. "I want my lawyer," she hissed. "That's all I'm sayin'."

NINETEEN

The crowd stood anxiously on the street, restrained by the crime-scene tape the deputies had strung. By now the investigators' reason for digging up the yard had spread throughout the multitude, and murmurings of "I knew it all along," flowed from lips of people who hadn't known anything.

A warm wind blew across the lake, but it offered only slight relief. When the crowd realized the investigators would soon be recovering bodies, the scene chilled them more than anything else could.

After the sun had set and the sky grew dark, the fire department brought in portable generators and lit the grounds to daylight brightness. With such visibility, the deputies worked to shroud the investigators' activities from the onlookers. Once the deputies extracted the sleeping bag supposedly containing Jimmy Don Beets, Michael O'Brien stepped forward. With forensic expert Charles Linch at his side, O'Brien inspected the bag and saw what he believed to be human bones. When he found the skull, he knew. Another deputy encased the remains in a body bag to guard against contaminating the evidence.

Deputy Ron Shields found the proceedings anything but boring, even though his job was to sift dirt from the graves to make sure that bullets or bone fragments were not overlooked. He discovered a bullet in the dirt under Beets's grave that had worked its way out of the rotted hole. When he revealed his find, he received high fives and pats on the back. Thanks to his diligence, another important piece of the puzzle filled a gap in the case.

After deputies had picked Jimmy Don's grave clean, O'Brien ordered the backhoe driver to move the machine to the rear of the property. There, the machine crunched toward the eight-by-twelve-foot shed and knocked it over. It landed in one piece. A sunken spot under the shed became readily apparent in the spotlights' glare.

O'Brien directed the deputies' shovels toward that area. They had to dig deeper than for the first grave, since Wayne Barker did not lie atop the ground as Jimmy Don had. But having tasted success, the deputies' enthusiasm drove them to keep shoveling.

Ben Ashley, always carrying his camera, continued flashing pictures, and O'Brien's wife took copious notes of the proceedings. She was a probation officer, but liked to assist her husband on special cases. They had dropped off their children at their grandparents' for the evening so she could be free. She listed every graphic detail to convince the trial jury of the premeditation of the two murders.

Four feet under the ground, deputies uncovered a flatter-looking sleeping bag, although the bag itself was identical to the first one. Four years of decomposing had obviously reduced Wayne Barker to virtually a skeleton. Some bones were still tangled by tendons, plus a wrapping of flesh in a few places. Barker's black hair had slipped from his skull, but his own natural teeth remained in place. When the deputies lifted the bag onto a gurney, the disconnected bones gathered essentially to one end of the sleeping bag.

O'Brien again inspected the bag and turned it over

to the medical examiner. After both victims were in body bags, deputies transported them to a waiting ambulance. The curious crowd parted to allow the vehicle access to the road, and onto the highway back to Dallas.

Reporters in the street roamed the area, asking questions of neighbors, and trying to find people who would admit to knowing Betty Beets.

The residents of the Cedar Creek community were relieved when reporters told them of Betty's arrest. One woman related how she had forced her young son to take karate lessons to protect himself from Betty's family.

"And those friends of hers that were always hanging around!" another neighbor complained. "They were the boot-stomping, cowboy-hat, pickup-truck kind of people."

Mrs. Rosenberg, who lived down the street, said, "I walk my dog, Bubblegum, along here every night, and he about tore my arms out of their sockets trying to get over to that well. He used to sniff like crazy before I could pull him away and get on with our walk. Guess he knew something I didn't."

"Her arrest doesn't surprise me one bit," said a man who requested that his name not be used. "Betty moved into this area four years ago and look at this," he said gesturing toward the yard. "Turned it into a killing field. The whole family's had a history of gunfights and disturbances."

A tidy little woman waited her turn to speak. "Saw it with my own eyes," she told the reporter. "The family used to stand in their yard and shoot turtles with a rifle."

Newspapers throughout the state had erased their planned headline stories and ran the gravedigging photographs as front-page news. Television channels broke into scheduled shows to reveal the action going on at

Cherokee Shores, and ran up-to-the-minute videos of Betty's front yard. Quickly, the story spread nationwide.

Shirley Thompson, now Shirley Stegner, had just returned from her honeymoon the day after her mother's arrest. She had no knowledge of the arrest, nor of the drama that had taken place in her mother's yard the night before. A sheriff's deputy knocked on her front door that Sunday morning.

The deputy entered her small apartment in Balch Springs. He asked to speak to Shirley alone.

"This is my husband," she said proudly, "whatever you have to say, he can hear."

"All right, ma'am. Don't know if you heard we arrested Mrs. Betty Lou Beets yesterday."

Shirley sank down in a chair and her husband went to her, taking her hand.

"Because?" Shirley asked hesitantly.

"We found a couple bodies in her yard."

"What?" her husband screamed.

Shirley looked at the floor.

"Ma'am, I'm here to arrest you on two counts of murder."

"Two?" Shirley's hand covered her mouth. "Did my mother tell you that?"

"No, ma'am, but we have reason to believe you were involved in the murders of Jimmy Don Beets and Doyle Wayne Barker," he said as he took handcuffs from his pocket. "You have the right to remain silent. . . ."

Employees and customers alike at the Cedar Club sat around bemoaning Betty Beets's arrest. The brightly lit neon that outlined beer signs on the walls seemed festive and out of place for the somber mood permeating the room.

The club manager was the most shocked, since she had enthusiastically hired Betty. "She was great," she said, looking at her customers. "Brought in a good crowd and everybody loved her. She knew everybody in town and everybody knew her."

"I really liked her," said a middle-aged woman. "Listen, there are two types of waitresses. There's the kind that pays attention only to men. The other is fair to both men and women. That's Betty. She was always nice to me."

A man in jeans and cowboy boots sat slumped over the bar, numb with disbelief. "Y'all, I've got to say that Betty's a great person. Did you ever hear her get into an argument with anyone?"

The patrons shook their heads.

"I just can't believe she did what she's been charged with."

A man in the back of the club listened to the conversation that floated around him as he shot pool. The click of his cue stick swishing balls across green felt was all the others heard from him, until he cleared his throat to speak.

"Seems to me it was just this week that Betty bragged about getting a whole bunch of money." He stopped to pocket the seven ball. "This is the truth, I swear. She told me she was going to collect on Jimmy Don's life insurance and his pension."

"I talked to Betty a lot," another man said. "We always had fun and I asked her out. Then I said something one night that she didn't like. Hell, can't remember what it was now, but her entire face changed. Her eyes turned to slits and her bottom lip jutted out. Still gives me shivers to think about it."

* * *

Rick Rose sat in his office sorting out the growing stack of documents in front of him. He had already taken numerous interviews from people who knew Betty Beets, and a pattern emerged.

The people she wanted something from, including her bar customers, or people who could do her favors, reported that they just loved the little woman. An officer with the security company who patrolled her area said, "Mrs. Beets was as polite and pleasant as you could ask for. She was always very neat."

Betty's neighbors, not necessarily in a position to be of service, all gave negative images of Betty. Added to their chagrin that Betty had brought devastation and disruption to their lives on the scenic shores of Cedar Creek, she had snubbed them. If they said hello, she ignored them. When they waved from their automobiles, they received no response. The neighbors unanimously labeled Betty Beets a very unfriendly person.

Chad Higgins had been a real-estate developer for years in the Cedar Creek area. He told his next-door neighbor about a conservative, very polite, quiet-spoken woman who had approached him a couple of years earlier.

"She was interested in buying the Frontier Club in Seven Points," he remembered.

"One of your famous blue-collar, biker bars?" his neighbor replied.

"Yes, and now that I've seen Betty Beets's picture in the paper, I know for sure that's who I talked to."

His neighbor shook his head, and said, "The parking lot's always full. What's that bar like on the inside?"

"How would I know?" Higgins replied. "I don't even go into my own clubs. They're rougher than hell."

* * *

Rick Rose looked up when Ray Bone strolled into his office. Everyone thought of Ray as a handsome man. Rose only saw the hate in his yellow eyes. "Eyes as yellow as a chow dawg," Rose would say.

"Sit down, Ray. I just wanted to touch base with you. Since Betty's been arrested, I know where she is and you haven't had to call me. I've just been wondering what's going on?"

"I talked with Faye Lane the other day," Bone said. "You know, Betty's oldest. She sure made it plain that Phyllis and Shirley did the killings."

"Do you believe her?"

"I don't know what to believe. Phyllis told me about the killings a while back and she said I'd be next. I took it all to be bullshit."

Bone glanced out of the window. "But as it turns out, the bodies were in the places I'd been told. Before all this broke, Phyllis kept saying if I knew what was under the wishing well, I wouldn't spend another night in that house."

Sunday afternoon at two-thirty, Shirley Thompson Stegner stood before Justice of the Peace O. D. Baggett, who charged her with murder.

Night arrived by the time Shirley had been booked, photographed, and fingerprinted. She refused to speak, and asked for the only attorney she knew, E. Ray Andrews. By phone, Andrews insisted that she not say a word to anyone.

Shirley had a history of drug abuse, and now shaking and scared, she probably would have liked something to calm her nerves, but in jail, she assumed they'd give her nothing. However, no drug could prepare her for what happened next.

After a female deputy gave Shirley the white prison

garments to change into, she marched her into the women inmates' section. Further segregated cells separated inmates with minor infractions from those who had been charged with felonies.

Shirley caught a glimpse of her mother in her cell. The deputy continued to take her closer. Shirley wanted to run away. She had enough of hearing her mother talk about killing and burying Wayne Barker, and she had tried to stop her every time she wanted to rehash the story of Jimmy Don's murder. For the last several months, she had tried to avoid her mother because she felt so uncomfortable around her.

The deputy turned down the aisle housing Betty's cell. Then to Shirley's horror, the woman unlocked the very next cell to Betty's and ushered Shirley inside.

TWENTY

Jamie Beets became very much a part of the action once his father's body had been found. Mike O'Brien kept him apprised of everything his office did.

When Jamie heard of Betty's bail being set at one million dollars, he could see his father's assets evaporating to buy Betty's release and pay for her defense. Two days after her arrest, he filed a motion for a protective order of his father's property, declaring that he was the rightful heir to his father's estate.

Betty had asked for a tablet and pen, then spent the next hour composing a letter to Ray Bone:

"Well, Ray," she wrote, "here we are at the crossroads again. Only the cross is a lot larger this time." She talked about her utilities being turned off and the bank repossessing the trailer. She elaborated on how hard she had worked to get the trailer, but didn't mention she had killed Doyle Wayne Barker to keep it.

"You said one time how much you needed me. Did you ever stop to think how much I needed you too?" She talked of wanting him to rescue her, but knew that wasn't possible. She admitted turning to the bottle to forget her troubles, but professed that it hadn't helped. She lamented that her family was gone, and gave her children as the reason she had tried so hard all these years.

"Please, Ray," she continued writing, "don't hurt me anymore. Don't put me in that corner." She admitted feeling lost and alone with no one to turn to. She had wished Ray would have been that person, and now questioned why she ever thought he could be.

She ended her letter by telling Ray to take care of himself and stay out of trouble.

Then she signed her name. Betty's signature was proud. Written with a heavy hand, the "Bs" were large and wide. Her name appeared stylized, artistic, and self-assured.

Rick Rose and Michael O'Brien were still putting pieces of the puzzle together, and help kept pouring in.

Phyllis Coleman's husband, William, called Rose to tell him about a time in May of 1983 when he had gone to the Beets's trailer and saw Jimmy Don building a shed. William spoke of Jimmy Don's irritation over Betty's insistence that he build the shed in the exact spot that she chose, the spot that turned out to be Wayne Barker's grave.

The next day, a neighbor who lived on Red Oak Drive, a few houses down from Jimmy Don's blue-painted house, contacted Rose. "I just couldn't keep this to myself," the neighbor began. "There was a time shortly after Mr. Beets disappeared that Betty Beets's oldest son was digging in the backyard over here. It was between one to three in the morning."

"What first made you aware of this?" Rose asked.

"Because they made so damn much noise. They played loud music, they were always talking loud and fussing. Someone inside the house was yelling at somebody else."

"Betty's oldest son's name is Robby," Rose offered. "Did you see him do anything else besides dig?"

"Yeah. He'd also get into his truck, which was bronze and tan. Then he'd rev his engine, making even more noise when he left the addition. A few minutes later, he'd be back and start digging again. Guess this went on for three nights or so.

"Then the next thing I knew, they moved a couple Doberman pinschers onto the property. Had them chained up in back like they were guarding something. After a while, Betty and her sons moved out, but one of them would come back a few times a week to feed and water the dogs."

Rick Rose thanked him for his information, but he had already visited with many of Betty's neighbors. They had all mentioned the dogs, and at the time the neighbors thought they were there guarding Jimmy Don's body.

Rose put more stock into testimony from family members, or ex-family members. So when Shirley Stegner's ex-husband, twenty-eight-year-old Jody Ray Thompson, visited Rose at the sheriff's office, Rose let him know how much he appreciated his coming forward, since Shirley wouldn't say a word to law enforcement.

"Just felt I should get here and tell you all I knew about it," Thompson said. "Shirley and I were married when Jimmy Don Beets was reported missing. I sure did like that man. He seemed to get along so well with Betty. Really thought they had a good marriage."

Thompson went on to relate Shirley's call from her mother around six-thirty P.M. on August 5, 1983, and how upset Shirley was, wanting her husband to drive her immediately to Cherokee Shores.

"Are you sure of that time?" Rose asked.

"Yeah. Remembered it was light outside."

Rose pondered this. Shirley had told her sisters that

Betty had called her around midnight and that it was after one A.M. before they got to their mother's house.

"I stayed outside while Shirley went in to talk with her mother. While I was out there, Jimmy Don never came out. I thought that was odd because his pickup was still there.

"After about fifteen minutes, Shirley and Betty both came out, looking like they were in a really good mood. We stayed outside and talked for another forty-five minutes, then came on back to Dallas. Shirley was in a good mood all the way back, but never mentioned anything her mother had told her."

"When did she tell you Jimmy Don was missing?"

"She didn't. I had to hear it the following Monday morning when I went to work. Shirley and I broke up a month later. I never saw Betty again after that Friday night in August."

Rose had to sort out all the information. People's memories would dim or play tricks with them. He looked for facts that were verified by others' testimony or physical evidence they had. There were still many hours of searching ahead of him.

Newspaper reporters had found Wayne Barker's brother, Jackie Barker, and asked him about his brother's disappearance.

"I called Betty after I hadn't heard from Wayne for a while," Barker said. "She told me that he left one night to get a package of cigarettes, and just didn't come back. That's all she said. I couldn't imagine he'd do something like that and leave a new pickup just sitting there."

"Did you know Betty Barker?" the reporter asked.

"Yes. I was my brother's best man when he married Betty for the second time in July of 1981. When Wayne never showed up, I suspected foul play, but I was never suspicious of Betty. She was just too super-nice when I was around her."

It was late at night in the DA's office. Rick Rose had gone to see Mike O'Brien to review the case. They were both disappointed that Shirley Stegner refused to talk. Without her testimony, there could be no first-hand witness of Betty Beets's actions. All they had so far was second- and third-hand information. If Shirley had been involved in burying anyone, she would have been an eyewitness to at least seeing the body.

"Do we know for sure that she helped bury both men?" O'Brien asked.

"Wayne Barker, for sure," Rose said. "You know, if someone else did help Betty with Jimmy Don, then we'd have an additional witness out there. Let's go back to Phyllis, because she's the first to break the news."

The next day, Rick Rose contacted Phyllis Coleman and convinced her to meet him at the Seagoville Police Station, not far from her home in Balch Springs. He took Deputy Ron Shields with him as a witness, thinking it was about time Shields saw another part of law enforcement other than waiting in cars and digging through dirt.

Phyllis Coleman's appearance surprised both deputies. She was pretty. Her long, shiny blond hair and blue eyes made her look like a young Betty Beets. Her thin body bordered on anorexia, and her nervousness made Rose think she was speeding on something. The large tattoos on each arm indicated she had seen the seedier side of life.

Phyllis came into the police station, frowning with a "now what?" attitude.

"We just needed to clarify some things," Rose told her.

They sat in a small room that held a Coke machine, a few chairs, and a couple of tables covered with detective magazines.

"You told us that Shirley helped your mom bury Wayne Barker."

Phyllis nodded.

"So did she also bury Jimmy Don?"

"Nah, Shirley wouldn't have done that. She was furious with Mama. We all loved Jimmy Don. Shirley didn't want Mama to kill him for anything. So no way would she help bury him."

"So your mother buried him herself?"

"No, she got my brother Robby. He helped put Jimmy Don in the well."

Rose tried to hide his amazement. Inside he reeled, hearing about the bizarre participation of Betty's family. "Did your mother happen to mention Jimmy Don building that well right before he died?"

"No," Phyllis said, looking surprised. "She told me she built it herself."

Like waiting for the other shoe to drop, Robby Branson continued working as a crane operator for his father's construction company, all the while knowing Shirley had been arrested for helping their mother bury Wayne Barker.

As time slipped by, he became more puzzled. Wouldn't Shirley tell the investigators that he'd helped bury one of his mother's victims? Was his sister protecting him by keeping quiet about his involvement?

Then one day at work, Robby glanced over his shoulder and saw a man approaching him with a white Stetson, cowboy boots, and a gold star. He wasn't surprised.

Karen Warner, another investigator for the district attorney, had been out of the state on a two-week vacation when the case broke. Her area of expertise primarily involved child-abuse and sexual-abuse cases, but she helped in other areas when they needed her. Rick Rose had asked her to assist with the statement by Robby Branson, who was now sitting before them, tapping a pencil and avoiding everyone's eyes.

When Robby first walked into the district attorney's office, his large, muscular body made him appear older than his twenty-one years. The dark skin he inherited from his father was even darker from his hours of working outside in the hot summer sun.

Rose read him his rights, which he promptly waived and readily agreed to give them a written statement.

TWENTY-ONE

A tape recorder captured Robby Branson's words as he related a tale of the worst child abuse Karen could imagine. Robby kept his head down as he spoke. He appeared frightened, and he probably was, but Karen could only feel sympathy for him. O'Brien had told her earlier that when he first met Robby, he thought of him as a good kid, but presumed his home life with Betty Beets would invite anyone to go astray.

Robby reported his mother's nonchalance when she told him that she planned to kill Jimmy Don that night and would need his help. Everything seemed so matter-of-fact and acidly cold of Betty. Robby related each detail about leaving the house so his mother could shoot Jimmy Don, then coming home and dragging the body out to the well. He, too, mentioned how good Jimmy Don had been to his mother.

"Have you told anyone other than your sisters about this?" Rose asked.

"Yeah," Robby said with some hesitation. "My common-law wife. She lives in California. About eighteen months after I helped bury Jimmy Don, I just had to get it off my chest. So I told her about it, and how my mom planned it. I also said that Mom killed Wayne Barker too. So this morning I called her and told her not to tell the police what I had said about the murders, but that was before my arrest."

Karen found it difficult to listen. *How could a mother involve her own child in a murder? Even in the wild, female animals fight to the death to protect their young, and here his mother had used him as an accomplice to murder.*

Betty Beets wanted out of jail. E. Ray Andrews convinced her that he could make that happen if only he could get her bail bond reduced. He'd have that opportunity at her habeas corpus hearing tomorrow. But today on June 13, the law required that she be brought before a magistrate to determine her bond and clarify charges.

Michael O'Brien had begun thinking about Betty's indictment before her arrest. After reading volumes of case law, he decided to base it on the "Candy Man" killing in Houston. A Houston dentist, Ronald O'Bryan, had taken out massive life insurance policies on his two young children, then fed them cyanide-laced pixie stick candy. His daughter became violently ill, but his son died. Once law enforcement found the newly purchased insurance policies, they established premeditation, and found O'Bryan guilty of capital murder.

From the affidavits of Betty's children and fire department chaplain, Denny Burris, O'Brien felt certain he knew Betty's motive. Especially when he learned the amount of insurance Jimmy Don had. Today, O'Brien wrote the charge against Betty that would form the basis for her indictment—an indictment the prosecution would have to prove at her trial.

Deputies escorted Betty from her jail cell to the Henderson County Courthouse. The three-story, redbrick courthouse graced an entire city block in the center of Athens. Built in 1919, the Georgian-style building boasted four imposing columns on every side before each entrance. Eighty-year-old live oaks and magnolia trees gave the grounds a parklike setting.

Betty stood before Justice of the Peace O. D. Baggett. After a clerk swore her in, Judge Baggett read her charge:

"Betty Lou Beets, on or about the 6th of August, 1983, and before making and filing of this complaint, in the County of Henderson and State of Texas, did then and there unlawfully, intentionally, and knowingly cause the death of an individual, Jimmy Don Beets, by shooting him with a firearm, for remuneration and the promise of remuneration, to wit: an insurance policy from employment with the City of Dallas by the said Jimmy Don Beets in which the said defendant is the beneficiary."

Then Judge Baggett charged her with capital murder and ordered her to be held without bond. Now Betty's only hope was her habeas corpus hearing the next day.

Rick Rose made a quick call to investigators in Pasadena, California, and asked them to visit a Jennifer Cook. In a taped and written statement, she admitted everything that Robby had told her, thoroughly corroborating his story.

The officers asked if she had told anyone.

"Just my grandmother," Jennifer said. "She didn't believe me and said she thought I could really come up with the whoppers. Told me not to tell anyone else because they'd think I was daft."

"What did you tell the investigators?" Betty asked her daughter while she clung to the bars separating their cells.

"I haven't said a word," her daughter replied. "E. Ray

told me not to talk. But I'm scared shitless. I could end up in the electric chair. Damn it, Mama, you got me into all this."

"So you wanted me to take the abuse?"

Shirley closed her eyes. "Do we have to go over that shit again? You know you didn't have to kill Wayne, and goddamn it, Jimmy Don never laid a hand on you."

"Okay, we don't have to go over that shit again." Betty stayed quiet for a moment, then said, "It was only a matter of time before Jimmy Don started beating me. He'd given me some pretty angry looks lately."

"Mama, can't we talk about something else? I just got home from my honeymoon. Jay calls every day wondering when in the hell I'm getting out. This is no way to start a marriage."

These discussions made Shirley long for a cell far removed from her mother's, but once when she complained about being thrown into this particular cell, a deputy told her that the jail had very few spaces for female felony inmates.

Rick Rose opened the ballistics report that had just arrived. The document outlined the testing on the bullets found inside the sleeping bags of Wayne Barker and Jimmy Don Beets. It had been difficult to test the semi-jacketed, .38-caliber bullets because of their corroded and oxidized condition, but they were similar enough to indicate that both men could have been shot with the same gun. All of the bullets had six land-and-groove impressions with a left-hand twist. What a coincidence was that? In the same house where two people are killed is a weapon that generally fits the same description. Rose knew that the weapons having this style of rifling were primarily Colt revolvers.

He reached for his file, which had grown thick in the

last six weeks. Pulling out the list of Betty's guns he had taken from her trailer, his first glance rested on the one with the red line drawn through it. Betty's highlighting drew his attention to the .38 Colt police special revolver.

He immediately left for the evidence locker. Deputy Kite had locked up the two guns Bobby Branson had used in his shoot-out. The deputy in charge of the locker retrieved the guns and handed them to Rose.

Rose compared serial numbers. One matched perfectly—an antique Colt revolver, probably sixty years old, with an ornately carved ivory handle. He instantly put in an order to have the gun test fired. Then he'd compare those bullets to the ones taken from the bodies.

Judge Jack H. Holland presided over Betty Beets's habeas corpus hearing in the 173rd Judicial District Court. The tailored courtroom held no carved molding or unnecessary decor. Its straightforward design resembled a plain but distinguished church with dark paneled walls and matching pews of the same dark wood. Twelve brown leather chairs awaited the jurors, and a V-shaped table in the center of the room accommodated both the prosecution and defense.

The District Attorney, Bill Bandy, would do anything to keep Betty incarcerated. The short, witty, down-to-earth attorney had earned his law degree while working days, and attending South Texas College of Law in the evenings. He still considered that easy compared to the combat he'd seen in Korea as a foot soldier. Now he was in a different kind of combat with E. Ray Andrews, a man he had known for many years.

E. Ray came to court in a huff. He insisted he had only heard about Betty's habeas corpus hearing yesterday. Having had no time to prepare, he asked for a delay.

District Judge Holland, a thin, distinguished-looking man, was the first and only judge, since the 173rd District had been formed in 1970. The respected judge spoke softly, for he never found it necessary to raise his voice. He sat patiently in his brown leather chair on its raised platform, listening to E. Ray carry on.

"Since this is a capital murder case and you say you just learned about it," the judge told him, "we can afford you more time if you need it."

E. Ray said, "Your Honor, I really do. I mean, I was just crossing the street when I heard a rumor out yesterday afternoon, and I couldn't understand them bringing her over here without my being here."

Then Andrews tested the water by asking if the prosecution would allow a $100,000 bail. Bandy quickly rejected an amount that Betty might somehow be able to pay and obtain her freedom.

Having that attempt fail, Andrews decided to go ahead with the hearing after all.

Bandy called Rick Rose to the stand and took him through all the legal proceedings that led up to Betty's arrest. Then it was E. Ray's turn to question Rose.

The first thing he wanted to know was about Rose's connection with Ray Bone.

"You had him in jail last week, didn't you?" Andrews asked.

"Yes, for unlawfully carrying a weapon."

"You knew at the time he was on parole for murder."

"Yes, sir."

"How come you let him out?"

"All the case I had said that he was unlawfully carrying a weapon."

"Well, someone talked to Ray Bone a few minutes before they arrested Betty."

"That's correct. I told him to call me."

"And did Ray Bone tell you what highway they were coming in on?"

"He sure did."

"How come he done that?" E. Ray said, slipping into the vernacular that made him a favorite with many rural Texas juries. Some court reporters quoted him verbatim, while others tried to clean up his grammar for the official transcript.

E. Ray tried to establish that Betty knew of Bone's calls, and that she understood police would be waiting for her on the highway, and regardless of having that information, she still didn't run.

Rose retorted, "I don't know what her destination would have been if she hadn't been caught and arrested in Mansfield."

Unable to dispute that, E. Ray asked his trademark question that he used on everyone who wasn't an eyewitness. "You're not telling me that you saw this woman kill anyone?"

"Absolutely not."

Andrews let that response hang in the room as he excused Deputy Rose.

After hearing more witnesses, Andrews called Betty Beets and established that she was being held on a one-million-dollar bond. He said, "Before you was incarcerated in the Mansfield County Jail, where was you working at?"

Betty said, "The Cedar Club in Seven Points." She testified that she worked as a barmaid, making only $150 to $200 a week, depending on tips, so she had no way to pay the bond. She also stated she had no relatives who could help.

"Is it your intention to enter a plea of not guilty?" E. Ray asked.

"I am not guilty. I haven't killed anyone."

"Did you know they were planning to pick you up for murder?"

"Yes, sir. As soon as Ray got to me, he told me."

"You didn't run, did you?"

"No, sir," she said calmly.

"How come?"

"I had nothing to run from. I heard Ray tell Deputy Rose what highway we'd be on, and that we'd be in the red-and-white Silverado pickup."

Bill Bandy now had his opportunity to delve into her past.

"You say you haven't killed anyone, but have you shot anyone?"

Betty remained silent as Bandy held up a document for her to see. He said, "I have a copy of a 1972 indictment against you for intent to commit murder against Billy York Lane."

"That charge was dropped to a misdemeanor."

"Now we learn that Jimmy Don Beets had a considerable amount of insurance and you are the beneficiary," Bandy said.

"I didn't know a thing about any insurance until his family told me I was the beneficiary."

"You got yourself appointed as administratrix of his estate." Bandy showed her the "Proof of Death" document that she had also requested. "Is this your signature?"

Unable to deny her signature, Betty said, "Many papers were put in front of me that I signed without reading. I had no idea what they were."

Bandy continued questioning her about the insurance, attempting to assert before Judge Holland that Jimmy Don's insurance provided Betty's motive for killing her husband. Then he shifted to the evidence.

"Assuming that the bodies of your two former husbands were found at your address, do you have any idea how they could have been buried out there having died two years apart?"

"No, I do not. I did not kill anyone. I was living there, but I'm not home all the time."

"Isn't it true that you were out planting flowers and vines in the wishing well right afterwards?"

"No."

"But the neighbors saw you."

"Then they're mistaken. I planted them prior to August 6, 1983. I set them out every year."

Betty testified that she didn't know where either body had been found, and was surprised to know that Jimmy Don had been in the wishing well, and just as surprised that Wayne Barker was under the shed.

At the conclusion of the testimony, Bandy maintained that Mrs. Beets was not only guilty of murder, but in the case of Jimmy Don Beets, she had committed capital murder by maliciously killing him when she was the beneficiary of his insurance. He asked the court to deny her bond.

E. Ray Andrews insisted, "This just don't all fit because this woman never ran off, even when she knew she was being sought for serious charges. She could have hooked 'em. So it's a miscarriage of justice to keep her in jail." He asked that she be granted a reasonable bond.

Judge Jack Holland listened patiently to both sides, then said, "The court, after hearing the evidence, finds that the proof is evident, and bond will be denied."

Rick Rose and Michael O'Brien talked numerous times every day, sorting out information and strategizing how to learn more facts. Not being able to talk with Shirley Thompson Stegner became a major frustration.

"The poor kid doesn't know what's best for her,"

O'Brien said. "As long as E. Ray's her lawyer, he can shut her up so she can't testify against her mother. It's a clear conflict of interest to even pretend he's representing Shirley."

"But Shirley's got to ask for another lawyer," Rose said. "We can't do that for her. Maybe we can convince one of her sisters to paint a clearer picture for her. She's got to know that her mother will take her right down with her as long as E. Ray remains her attorney."

Jamie Beets had seen how manipulative Betty could be, so the young man had realistic concerns that she could somehow get his father's insurance to use for her lawyer's fees. He went to his attorney, telling him that he worried about his father's life insurance because it still held Betty's name as the beneficiary. In order to protect Jamie's interests, his attorney drew up a constructive trust on the insurance, placing it out of Betty's hands until after the trial. Unless the court found Betty innocent, Jamie would be the sole heir.

E. Ray Andrews sat in his favorite bar in Seven Points, sipping his second drink, a double shot of Wild Turkey.

"Hey, E. Ray, you gonna get our girl off?" Another customer at a nearby table called to him.

"You can put money on it," he said. Then laughing, he raised his glass and toasted the man. "I've got a real big surprise for y'all. Just be there at the trial and you'll see."

A large E. Ray following in Athens believed if he said his client was innocent, then his client was innocent. E. Ray's admirers always packed his trials. He was ceaselessly cordial to the ladies, and even people who questioned his ethics, liked him.

One time, police arrested him for public intoxication, and the state bar temporarily revoked his license. He was sent to an "al-kee-hall" center, as he called it, to dry out. Soon after his return, he'd started tippling again.

As a kid, E. Ray was easily the smartest person in his class, but became known as a rebel even then. The nickname "Thin man" fit him perfectly because he only weighed 130 pounds at six-foot-two, although he had added another 30 since. Many friends back then were surprised he had survived adolescence, let alone that he had reached middle age.

Rick Rose thumbed through reports he received on the polygraph results. He noted Betty Beets had refused to take the test. Gerald Albright, who confided to the informant and broke the case wide open, had done well. He had answered all questions truthfully, according to the machine, even the one asking, "Do you believe Betty Beets killed Jimmy Don?" Gerald had answered with an emphatic, "Yes."

Raymond Bone had trouble with honesty, which came as no surprise. According to the polygraph, when he drove his friend's car containing the shotgun, he knew the gun was there. But he truthfully said that Betty never told him she had anything to do with Jimmy Don's death, nor did he have any information that would solve the case.

Robby Branson eagerly took the lie detector test that revealed he had not shot Jimmy Don, nor was he present during the shooting. He again honestly told the investigators that he had helped his mother place Jimmy Don in the wishing well.

* * *

Two weeks after Betty Beets's arrest, E. Ray Andrews wanted to know exactly how much evidence the State held against his client. He filed an examining trial in the court of Judge Venita Lucas, a magistrate from another precinct. The hearing would in no way benefit the State, for it was a hunting expedition for the defense.

At the opening of the proceedings, the first person Andrews wanted to interrogate was Michael O'Brien.

"At that time you talked to Betty in the jail, did you say you knew everything and you were going down to her yard and dig up bodies, bones, whatever?"

"No, I didn't tell her that."

"Did she tell you she wouldn't stop you because you wouldn't find anything?"

"No, she didn't say that."

"Are you positive?"

"Well, she didn't say it in that way. I told her we had a search warrant to look for a body, and while we were there, we'd look for a second body. But I didn't threaten her with a search warrant."

"Well, you was the one who told her you had a warrant the judge had signed."

"That's correct."

"Betty Beets didn't tell you she killed anyone, did she?"

"No, she didn't. She didn't admit to any wrongdoing."

"What killed Jimmy Don Beets?" Andrews asked.

"Gunshot wounds."

"That's what you've been told. You don't know that for a fact."

"I have a death report from the Southwest Institute in Dallas."

Skirting around any presentation of factual evidence in the case, Andrews said, "Those forensic reports don't tell you when these people were killed, when they were buried, or who buried them. Other than what you speculate and what someone's told you, you don't know anything about these alleged murders?"

O'Brien shrugged. "I have no personal knowledge, no, sir."

He was excused and Bill Bandy brought in another witness for the prosecution, Phyllis Coleman. Bandy had Phyllis reiterate what Shirley had told her about the killings.

After walking her through all the information, Bandy asked, "Did that shock you?"

"Yes, sir. I didn't believe it."

Bandy passed the witness to Andrews.

Andrews asked, "Do you believe today that your mother killed Mr. Barker?"

"No." Phyllis crossed her legs and shifted uneasily in her chair.

"Didn't I ask you to come here voluntarily?"

"Yes. I asked for an attorney, but the investigators said I didn't need one." Her hands were clutched tightly in her lap until her knuckles turned white. "They said I would be charged with murder if I didn't sign a statement that Rose wrote out. I told them that my sister Shirley was drunk when she told me all this."

"I don't mean to embarrass you, sweetheart," E. Ray said in a fatherly tone, "but you've had some problems with drugs."

"When I talked with Rose I was high on drugs. I couldn't have written a statement. I was too confused and too upset about it. It's hard for me to sit here right now, but I'm not under the influence." Tears welled, then rolled down her cheeks. "I don't know if I'll ever stop using drugs."

"So when you gave the statement, you were under the influence of drugs?"

"Yes, methamphetamine. Shooting it in my arm."

"You didn't see your sister or your mother kill anyone, did you?"

"No, sir. My mother never told me she ever killed anyone."

"So the statement you gave wasn't true?"

"Yes, I was very high. Very upset and crying. I couldn't walk into my apartment. I didn't know half of what I was saying. Rick Rose and everyone told me I'd get a conspiracy of murder if I didn't sign the papers. I told them I didn't know that Mama done any of this. It was all hearsay." She buried her face in a Kleenex.

"Did Rose go easy with you, sweetheart?"

Phyllis raised her face to his. "No. When Rick Rose phoned me, he said, 'I know you were there. I know you saw everything.' But I didn't. I love my mother and I don't believe she did this."

Once he had finished with Phyllis, leaving her sobbing and physically drained, he called Faye Lane to the stand.

Faye appeared to have come from a different planet than some of the others testifying. She wore a conservative, printed cotton dress, and had no tattoos or dangling earrings. She testified that no one had told her of the murders, nor did she know of her siblings' involvement. She knew none of the facts until the police dug up bodies in her mother's yard.

However, at the grand jury hearing, Faye would flip-flop and say, "I knew that Shirley helped bury Wayne's body. Shirley told Phyllis exactly where the bodies were. That's why I'm having a hard time thinking. I love my mother and I love my sister Shirley. I just can't believe they'd do that. And I don't believe anything Phyllis tells me. She runs off her head so much, I just told her to go and leave me alone."

A grand juror asked, "Can you mention any of your mother's husbands that you liked?"

"I liked my dad and Jimmy Don Beets. Bill Lane was okay to be around, but I've seen him beat my mother until she couldn't open her eyes. One time I had to go to jail to bond her out after she shot Lane."

But at today's interrogation, Faye just shook her head, saying it was impossible to believe this actually happened in her family.

E. Ray wanted more positive things said about Betty Beets, and it appeared the only person who would do that was Betty herself, so he called her to the stand.

"Do you know anything about the death of Jimmy Don Beets?"

"No, I don't."

"Do you know anything about the death of Wayne Barker?"

"No, sir."

"Do you know why Phyllis or any of your kids would say anything to hurt you?"

"No, sir. We've always been a close family."

Andrews explained that capital murder involved killing someone for money or something similar, such as insurance.

"I didn't do that," Betty said. Showing no emotion or remorse, her reserve contrasted sharply with her daughters' emotional displays.

"Have you collected a quarter in insurance money from any husband?"

"I haven't collected anything from anybody."

Andrews knew he had to mention Betty's going to court two months before to have Jimmy Don declared legally dead before the prosecution brought it up. He asked, "Did you intend to wait seven years for the insurance?"

"I never wanted any money from him. I don't know how much insurance I have coming."

"Now you testified that you were standing next to Ray Bone when he was on the phone telling Deputy Rose what highway you'd be fixin' to come in on. Why'd he have him do that?"

Bandy objected to Andrews questioning what the investigator was after, calling it a "fishing expedition."

"If this is a fishing expedition," E. Ray retorted, "I haven't caught anything."

That comment abruptly brought the hearing to a close, and Judge Venita Lucas decided to bind Betty Beets to the grand jury.

Jimmy Don Beets received a second burial on June 21. His family held his funeral service at Roselawn Memorial Garden in Seagoville, Texas. He was laid to rest amid the East Texas rolling hills decorated with red and pink begonias. A host of Dallas Fire Department officials participated, and several gave glowing eulogies for their friend. In the weeks ahead, he would have a granite headstone with a bronze military plaque because he had served in the U.S. Army.

Few of the people standing before his flag-draped casket knew that Jimmy Don was being buried without his skull.

TWENTY-TWO

By July 11, over a month after the skeletal remains were discovered, there was more action going on in the courthouse corridors than in the courtroom, and only hours from the grand jury hearing.

Rick Rose and Michael O'Brien clustered in a hallway with Robert Branson, Sr., and Jay Stegner, Shirley's father and new husband. Both Branson and Stegner looked drained and stressed from the ordeal.

"I really want to help her," Mr. Branson said. "But that can only happen if she's willing to help herself."

"Let's get Phyllis to talk some sense into Shirley," O'Brien suggested. "Phyllis tells us all the time how unfair she thinks it is that Shirley's locked up for something her mom did. She also affirmed that E. Ray's telling Shirley to keep her mouth shut."

O'Brien marched the group closer to a corner in the hallway, farther away from the growing crowd.

"Here's what we should do. Let's bring Shirley over here to the courthouse and find a room where they can be alone. Then Phyllis can explain the situation to her."

The jail sat several blocks away from the courthouse, and O'Brien called over there to request a deputy pick up Shirley Thompson Stegner and bring her over.

Now the two sisters huddled together in a small room.

Bookcases lined the walls with volumes that were fat with criminal cases.

"I am so damn scared," Shirley complained. "I'm worried about my life."

"I bet," Phyllis said sympathetically. "I know in my heart that you were only trying to help Mama. So listen to this. You need to tell the truth about her; then they'll know you didn't kill anyone. Also, you have to ditch E. Ray, 'cause he's just on Mama's side."

"They want me to testify against Mama?" Shirley said, appearing concerned.

Phyllis nodded.

"But I'll still need a lawyer, won't I?"

"Daddy will get you one. He told me that a little while ago in the hall. He'll pay for the lawyer and everything."

"Then what happens to me?"

Phyllis thought for a moment. "They didn't really spell that out, but I'd think without that extra murder charge, you'd get your bail reduced. Then Daddy would get a bail bond and you'd be outta there."

A broad smile brightened Shirley's face. "Hell yes, I'll do it!"

With all the publicity about the trial, Betty received numerous letters people sent to the jail, but only after a deputy first read and thoroughly inspected them.

In late September as her trial approached, an anonymous writer sent Betty one of her more unusual letters:

Dear Mrs. Beets,

Don't let anyone read, hear, or see this letter. I am writing in regards to your case. I am the only one who can help you. Do everything that I tell you.

Tell the jailer that someone is in the cell with you

and you are hearing voices. Begin running back and forth like you have lost your mind.

When they take you to the doctor, don't say anything to him. Just start touching things on his desk. Fall on the floor and move your body up and down. When they touch you, stop and act like you don't know what is going on. This will make everyone think you are having a mental breakdown.

When you see your attorney, don't say anything to him or anyone for that matter. Then they will take you before a judge and have you committed to an institution. When you decide to be yourself, you must tell them you don't remember anything. This will save your life. They cannot prosecute you, for you will be classified as a mentally ill person, and no one can touch you for as long as you don't remember.

If you don't do what I say, you will die. Destroy this letter. I do this because I like helping people.

"I don't know a lawyer," Robert Branson said after Phyllis ran out to tell him of Shirley's decision.

"There are lawyers all around this courthouse square," Mike O'Brien told him, pointing to the street outside the building. "Just head in any direction and you'll find one."

Twenty minutes later, Robert Branson came back with a lawyer in tow. Jay Stegner threw his fist in the air, screaming, "Yes! Shirley's getting out!"

Investigator Karen Warner waited in the DA's office for Shirley Stegner to give her long-anticipated statement. Shirley's newly hired attorney ushered her into a long, carpeted room that could have been used for a board meeting. Michael O'Brien and Rick Rose walked in behind them, and they all gathered in chairs at one end of the table. A fresh tape had been placed into the recorder.

Warner, a pretty woman, was always professional. Now she needed that professionalism to help camouflage her inner softness, for when she first saw Shirley, Warner thought her heart would bleed for the painfully thin young woman who had lost many a bout to drugs.

Karen Warner looked into Shirley's eyes and saw old eyes—nothing sparkled. Shirley appeared to have seen too much in her short life.

As a state's witness, Shirley was surrounded by people who wanted to help her, but she remained wired tight and very nervous.

It had been over a month since Shirley had been read her rights, but now with her own attorney present, she waived her right to be silent.

Rose said, "Why don't you start at the very beginning, and tell us when you first knew about your mother's plans?"

"I believe it was October of 1981 when my mother, Betty Lou Beets, told me she was going to kill Wayne Barker. We were in her backyard on Red Bluff Loop at Cherokee Shores sitting around a bonfire . . ."

Everyone saw the stress on Shirley's face and heard it in her voice, but she continued, relating everything that had happened from when she first heard her mother's plan until she helped bury Barker in the backyard. When she spoke of her mother getting someone with a backhoe to dig the grave for Barker, O'Brien jotted down a note.

Warner artfully pulled details from Shirley by continually asking questions. "What happened right before that occurred?" or "Once your mother did that, what immediately followed?" She forced Shirley to search back in her mind four years and come up with details that would provide the missing pieces to their puzzle.

Shirley's information established that her mother had minutely planned Barker's murder. "Betty told me that she was going to wait until Wayne went to sleep and that she would shoot him while he was in bed."

After Shirley finished describing the first murder, she said, "Approximately one year later, Betty married Jimmy Don Beets. Their marriage was the best I recall Betty ever having. Jimmy Don was loved by all of Betty's children, and he treated Betty and all of us better than we had ever been treated by a stepfather. I lived with them for three months. Jimmy Don let me stay there to help me through a marital crisis.

"In July of 1983, Betty told me she believed she was going to end up killing Jimmy Don. I told her, 'Mama, you promised me that you'd never do anything like this again. I just can't help you because all of us love Jimmy Don. We all loved Wayne too.'

"A week before his death, she told me she was going to ask Robby, my brother, to take Jimmy Don's boat out on the lake, set it adrift, and make it appear that he had disappeared in a boating accident."

She reached for the Coke Rick Rose had placed in front of her and took a big gulp, then wiped her mouth on the back of her hand.

"Around the first part of August 1983, Betty called me. At that time I had remarried and was living with my new husband, Jody Thompson, in Dallas. When Betty called, I asked, 'Have you done it?' She said, 'Yes.' By that I knew she had killed Jimmy Don.

"Betty wanted me to come down to Cedar Creek to see her because she was upset. She told me to tell my husband that she and Jimmy Don had been fighting and that Jimmy Don had left and gone to Dallas. So my husband and I drove down around one in the morning. I no sooner walked in her door when Betty said, 'Everything's been taken care of. You can go back home.' By that I understood she had got Robby to help bury Jimmy Don.

"After that, I've had very little contact with Betty until our arrest for the murders of Wayne and Jimmy Don. Since we've been in custody at the Henderson County Jail, Betty again confirmed that she had shot Jimmy Don and buried him in the wishing well."

During the time Shirley was making her statement to the DA, Betty Beets had been lying on her cot trying to take an afternoon nap. She had awakened intermittently, concerned that her daughter had been absent for almost three hours.

Her greatest fear was that the investigators were forcing Shirley to talk.

By late afternoon, Shirley came down the jail corridor. Once her daughter went inside the next cell, Betty sat up and squinted in disbelief.

Shirley had changed into street clothes, and now hurried around her cell, collecting her few personal belongings.

"Why the hell are you dressed like that?"

Shirley said nothing.

"Where're you going?"

Shirley turned around, a brush in one hand, a shoe in the other. "I'm going to where I should be," she said. "I'm going home."

With the combination of Robby's and Shirley's statements, Rose and O'Brien finally had their hands on two sworn affidavits that completed the picture of what had happened during both murders.

Their case against Betty Beets grew stronger by the day.

* * *

Mike O'Brien began searching for the man who dug Wayne Barker's grave.

Fire Captain Hugh DeWoody knew everyone in the area, so O'Brien called him. He explained the situation to DeWoody, and told him that finding the backhoe operator would corroborate Shirley's testimony.

"I know some of those people," DeWoody told him. "Many of the subdivisions have maintenance crews because they have to fix their own ditches and roads. I'd guess most of them would have backhoes."

"The man would probably be running off his mouth by now, unless he thinks I'm after him for accessory to a murder," O'Brien said.

"That would keep him quiet," DeWoody said. "I'll give you a call as soon as I know something."

After all the testimony had been given in the preliminary hearings, the grand jury's decision appeared a foregone conclusion. It surprised no one when on July 11, 1985, the grand jury returned two murder indictments against Betty Lou Beets, and one against Shirley Stegner for Wayne Barker's death.

A letter from Betty to another inmate had been intercepted by jail authorities. In the letter, Betty questioned Phyllis's statement to Rick Rose and told the other inmate that Phyllis "was on drugs real bad." She wanted to know if the statement would stand up in court because of Phyllis's drug-fuzzed mind. Betty knew better than to divulge anything incriminating in her letter; in fact, she did just the opposite and questioned if the police knew how the two men found in her yard had been killed. If the investigators hoped to find a jailhouse confession from Betty, they were disappointed.

A few hours later, Hugh DeWoody was back on the phone with O'Brien. "Fortunately, Betty is just one of those women that men remember," DeWoody said, chuckling. "We found an Oscar Reemers who worked for the Cherokee Shore's maintenance at the time. Said Betty needed the hole for a barbecue pit. Sound familiar?"

Friction began growing in the Branson family. As Betty sat alone in her jail cell, fingers were pointed at siblings who had testified against their mother.

They suspected Shirley of buying her way out of jail at her mother's expense when she gave her statement to the investigators. Robby had stopped talking to his brother and sisters altogether after he had called Betty in jail. He admitted to his mother that he had told authorities the truth.

Ray Bone had heard that Shirley and Robby had committed the murders and he told them to do the right thing—"Get down to the jail and tell the truth so Betty can get out."

Phyllis told Bone that wasn't true, and added, "If I had known that Mama killed Wayne before Jimmy Don died, I would have warned Jimmy Don, because I damn sure didn't want it to happen to anyone else. I just don't understand how Mama could have done something like that to someone like him. And it's not fair for us kids to go through the hell of this."

But the family also suspected Ray of lacking loyalty for having turned Betty over to authorities in Mansfield.

Investigators frequently questioned Ray Bone because

of his closeness to Betty, but with his past history, they didn't place much credence in his responses.

After one long discussion where Bone continued extolling Betty's innocence, an investigator asked, "Ray, do you happen to have a life insurance policy with Betty's name as the beneficiary?"

Ray's yellow eyes loomed large when he said, "Oh, God, I hope not!"

The pretrial hearing of *Texas* vs. *Betty Lou Beets,* kicked off on September 11, 1985, with E. Ray Andrews pleading for a change of venue.

Judge Holland watched E. Ray parade all of the local newspaper reporters into court, along with their head-lined articles displaying pictures of digging up bodies on Betty's property. He had reporters give their circulation numbers, and held up articles leading with such headlines as: BEETS SHOT HUSBAND IN THE BACK.

After naming all the newspapers, television channels, and radio stations, Andrews said, "Your Honor. There's just no way we can get a fair trial here with this kind of publicity. The whole area would be prejudiced against my client."

Then he led a procession of dozens of witnesses who lived in Henderson County. One man testified how the local bars and restaurants buzzed with stories of Betty, and most everyone had decided she was guilty. He questioned a woman who said she didn't have time to read the newspapers, but from talking with her friends, she was sure of Betty's guilt.

E. Ray called on a man who described reading everything he could get his hands on about Betty.

"Do you think she's guilty?" E. Ray asked.

The witness said, "You shouldn't have asked me that. Sure, I think she's guilty."

Then Andrews called a man to the stand named Frank Steinsmith. E. Ray questioned him about his access to newspapers, radio, and TV, and asked if he'd had any discussions with his friends about Mrs. Beets and the murders. The man nodded, and asserted that he had talked with his barber, the grocery store clerk, the guy down at the filling station, and many of his friends.

"Would you say this case is widely discussed?"

"Absolutely. By everyone in town."

Before allowing Steinsmith to leave, Bandy questioned him and learned he'd been a long-time friend of E. Ray's.

Taking another tack, E. Ray held up a copy of the *National Enquirer.* The supermarket tabloid's front page headline, printed in inch-high letters, read: SELF-MADE WIDOW. Under the headline, a large photograph depicted Betty Lou Beets handcuffed to Deputy Rick Rose.

"Just look at this!" E. Ray shouted. "It accuses Mrs. Beets of murdering two husbands."

Bandy rose to thank E. Ray for making that point. "That paper is proof that this case has received nationwide as well as statewide coverage. There's no place in this country that hasn't heard of her. Mrs. Beets should be tried by a jury of her peers and they would be found right here in Henderson County."

Judge Holland announced, "The motion for change of venue is overruled," and pounded his gavel.

"But, Your Honor," E. Ray pleaded, "people are just waitin' to be picked for the jury so they can find this lady guilty."

TWENTY-THREE

Haggling over the change of venue consumed the entire morning, and now lawyers spent the afternoon questioning 150 prospective jurors. Because it was a capital murder case, they questioned each prospect individually.

E. Ray Andrews's chatty demeanor included such questions to prospective jurors as, "I think I know you. Didn't you pick cotton for my old daddy?" He intended to be their friend from the beginning, and he easily made friends. Many times he had counted on an amicable jury to find his client innocent because they liked him.

The entire voire dire procedure consumed five days, from September 23 through September 27.

Finally, on October 7, 1985, the long-awaited trial began.

Athens, Texas, a town of 10,000, was known as the "Black-Eyed Pea Capital of the World." The lowly cowpea had been used for livestock feed until someone came up with the ingenious idea that it brought good luck. The town leaders began a festival in 1917 to celebrate the black-eyed pea, and forty years later Neiman Marcus began packaging the vegetable in fancy containers, calling it "Texas Caviar."

But regardless of that notoriety, nothing compared to

the trial of Betty Lou Beets. Every major newspaper across the country and all the main national television networks sent reporters to cover the case, all drawn by her "Black Widow" image and the bizarre facts surrounding her case. The streets were clogged with media vans.

Long lines stretched from the courthouse out to the street as people waited for the maintenance crew to arrive and unlock the doors. Many held sack lunches and planned to make a day of it.

In spite of handcuffs circling her wrists, Betty Beets managed a smile as Deputy Copeland escorted her to the courthouse. Copeland always found the good in people, and he tried to see some in Betty. He treated her gently and with respect, and she rewarded him with frequent smiles and thank-yous.

Betty wore a gold ring on her left hand, presumably her wedding ring from Jimmy Don. Her lacy blouse, tucked into a gored, print skirt, showed her still trim waistline, and she wore high heels. Everyone expected to see the forty-eight-year-old's signature blond hair and carefully applied makeup, and they weren't disappointed.

People roamed the corridors, unable to get into the packed courtroom. If anyone inside the room had to leave for the restroom, they reserved their place with a newspaper or their sack lunch. Frequently, someone in the hall would hurry to sit in their place, not respecting squatter's rights.

Many firemen had driven the seventy miles from Dallas to Athens with their wives to show support for Jimmy

Don, and some of them were stranded in the hall as well.

Before the trial began, all of the witnesses were assembled inside the courtroom, where the district clerk swore them in en masse to save time and remind them from that moment on they couldn't discuss their testimony or the case with anyone.

Case #A-2144, *The State of Texas* vs. *Betty Lou Beets,* came to order in the 173rd District Court with Judge Jack Holland presiding.

A very capable Henderson County attorney, Allen Boswell, assisted DA Bill Bandy. Boswell himself normally handled misdemeanor cases, but in important cases like today's, he also helped the DA.

E. Ray Andrews had pulled in an attorney "fresh out of law school," as he told everyone—a young man by the name of Gilbert Hargrave.

Judge Holland motioned to the attorneys to approach his bench, and leaned over to tell them, "I need to warn the prosecution not to bring up the killing of Doyle Wayne Barker nor the shooting of Billy York Lane unless the defense does it first." The judge also told Bandy to instruct witnesses not to mention Barker.

The court had finally selected a jury of eight women and four men. All jurors were white except for the one black alternate. A deputy went to a door to the left of the judge's bench and opened it for the jurors to file into the courtroom, then directed them to their leather chairs.

The boomerang-shaped table in the center of the courtroom held E. Ray Andrews, Betty Beets, and Gil Hargrave on the right, with DA Bill Bandy and Allen Boswell on the left. The point of the "V" remained empty to give some semblance of separation.

For all of the turmoil surrounding the case, everything started smoothly, with Billy Bandy's reiteration of the facts that the people of Henderson County knew by heart from their newspaper, the *Athens Daily Review.*

Bandy, always a natty dresser and possessing a flair for the dramatic, stood before the jury summing up his presentation. "The evidence is going to *shock* you," he said, punching his· fist in the air for emphasis. "It will *appall* you, and it is a necessity that this evidence be brought before you. I make no apology for it because I didn't create that necessity. At the conclusion of this evidence, the only reasonable verdict will be guilty of capital murder."

E. Ray Andrews, wearing a suit, ostrich-skin boots, and a serious expression, waived his right to make an opening statement.

Bandy called his first witness. Deputy Johnny Marr entered through double doors in the middle of the long wall in the large courtroom. Witnesses were cloistered in an anteroom off the foyer to the courtroom entrance.

Marr testified about his visit with Betty Beets and taking her statement regarding her missing husband. Everything flowed uneventfully as he answered all of the questions with well-documented proof.

Then came E. Ray's turn to cross-examine. "Just why are you so sure it was August sixth when you questioned Betty?" he asked, frowning.

"I logged it in my book," Marr said, showing Andrews his report.

"Did you do that at Betty's house or did you wait until you got back to the office?"

"I wrote out everything when I talked with Mrs. Beets."

"Would it surprise you to know that on August sixth Betty Beets was in Dallas shopping?"

"It was Saturday morning."

Marr stayed firm in his testimony and accurate with

his written details. E. Ray couldn't fight that, so he took off on another tangent.

"Are you testifying that somebody shot someone? Or buried someone? You're not trying to tell these people over there," Andrews said, pointing to the jury, "that you saw any of that, did you?"

"No, sir."

Andrews's questions flicked away Marr's written report like yesterday's newspaper. Instead, he questioned Marr about witnessing a murder, a murder Marr never claimed to have seen.

Next, Bandy called for Mike Warren from the Texas Parks and Wildlife Department. Lil Smith had phoned him the night they found the boat, and he had come to inspect it.

"At the time I thought the boat could have drifted away from somebody's dock," he said. " 'Course, after examining it closer, I saw the possibility that someone might have been working on the motor and fell overboard."

On cross-examination, Andrews asked, "How deep is the water over there where they found the boat?"

"I really don't know," Warren said.

"Think about the area from the Redwood Marina back to the shore. Could a lady put her feet on the ground in that lake and walk to the nearest highway and get out of there?"

"No, sir."

"So if a lady couldn't swim, she couldn't get out of there?"

"I would think not," said the parks' representative.

Andrews excused the witness, and Bill Bandy called Captain James L. Blackburn to the stand. Bandy led him through the three-week search that Betty allowed to continue despite knowing Jimmy Don was not in the lake.

Blackburn told of organizing the search, of the hundreds of people involved, and the hours everyone spent searching.

"How did Mrs. Beets appear?" Bandy asked.

"She was very, very calm. She didn't appear to be grieving in any way."

Andrews objected. "Your Honor, that calls for a conclusion by the witness."

The judge overruled his objection and Bandy proceeded.

The DA asked, "You've been around a lot of grieving people and you've seen them act in different ways?"

"No, I just didn't see her grieve. She appeared the same on all other visits. She never appeared distressed."

During the cross-examination, E. Ray would have a high hurdle to jump because Blackburn came across as a hard-working, sincere witness, who had gone to a lot of trouble because of Betty's grand scheme. E. Ray needed to pull the jury out of that sympathetic mood.

"Mr. Blackburn, where do you live at?" E. Ray asked.

Appearing surprised by the unusual question, Blackburn answered, "[   ] Wisteria in Dallas."

"Really?" Andrews said with a neighborly smile. "I used to live on that street.

Blackburn nodded at the information, probably wondering what difference it made.

"Okay, y'all volunteered to come down here and search for your friend?"

"Yes."

"You understand what this lady's being charged with here today?"

"Yes, sir."

"You didn't suspect her of any foul play at that time, did you?"

"No, sir. Not at *that* time," Blackburn said.

The next witness, Chaplain Denny Burris, stated that his job included general counseling, hospital visitation, crisis intervention, and death counseling.

"How did Betty appear when you first saw her that Sunday morning?" Bandy asked.

"She was wringing her hands," Burris replied, "but there were four or five people in her trailer so I couldn't sit down and talk with her. I went back the next day."

"How did she appear then?"

"About the same. Didn't appear in a grief-stricken manner, just a little nervous, uncomfortable. Tell you the truth, that made me feel a little nervous and uncomfortable."

Bandy nodded as he paced toward the jury so Burris would have to aim his next answer in that direction. "Did she ask about insurance?"

"Yes: I told her I'd check and find out what kind of insurance there was with the city of Dallas."

"So you had to return a third day?" Bandy clarified. "What did you find out about insurance?"

"I learned he had twice his annual salary, with a $15,000 life insurance policy on top of that. Plus, he had life insurance with Republic National Life which amounts to about $24,000."

"Who was the beneficiary on these policies?"

"Betty Beets."

On that note, Bandy passed the witness, and E. Ray stood to cross-examine.

"Okay, you go out and discuss insurance. Are you aware that she never drew any insurance?"

"Yes, sir," Burris answered.

"Are you aware that it is alleged in this indictment that she *did* draw insurance?" E. Ray said, eyes wide with his own astonishment that the prosecution had lied.

"No, sir, I wasn't aware."

Bandy almost knocked his chair over as he rushed to stand and object. "That's a misstatement of law, Your Honor!"

Judge Holland replied, "The jury will remember what the indictment said."

"Did she cooperate with you?" E. Ray asked.

"Yes, sir."

Having heard that Betty had too many people around her to talk with the chaplain on his first visit, E. Ray felt safe to ask, "The first time you was there, did Betty ask about insurance?"

"No," Burris said, giving his answer to E. Ray's final question.

Betty's son, Robby Branson, the alleged accomplice to Jimmy Don's murder, was the closest to being an eye-witness the court would ever find. Robby's good looks compensated for his outdated, tan leisure suit.

Robby took the stand, never once looking at his mother, and Bandy led him through the scenario that he had previously told Bandy was the worst night of his life.

"When did you learn that your mother first planned to kill Jimmy Don?"

"It was just that night. We didn't talk about it first. She just told me. Expected me to help her." Robby was breathing hard and his words came out in short gasps.

"Start right before your mother told you about her plans."

"I had been out riding my bike and went home to

get a drink of water. That's when she said she was going to shoot Jimmy Don.

"I was almost sick to my stomach. I couldn't understand why she was doing this."

Robby went on to describe the entire evening, and his answers didn't waver from the first time he told the investigators about the night of the killing. He also explained the elaborate scheme with the boat that his mother had concocted the next day that served as her alibi.

Now E. Ray stood to cross-examine the witness. He strolled to the youth, looking sternly at Robby as if he hadn't turned in his homework assignment on time.

"Did you ever tell anyone about the alleged shooting?"

"Yes, sir, my ex-wife. It was just bugging me and I thought I should tell her."

"It was bugging you because you really killed Jimmy Don Beets with a handgun."

Bandy and his assistant, Allen Boswell, were in shock. At the grand jury hearing, a rumor had circulated that E. Ray would attempt to pin both murders on Robby. After the hearing, Robby told the prosecution, "Just let them try. I never met Wayne Barker in my life. I was living with my dad then."

Now Andrews had revised that scenario, labeling Robby only the killer of Jimmy Don Beets. The prosecution searched its collective minds for clues about Robby killing Jimmy Don, but there were none. No sister had hinted about Robby being the triggerman. They had uncovered no evidence suggesting Robby had a motive. And if Betty had been wrongly accused, E. Ray would have been screaming "false arrest" long before now. Still, E. Ray had a lot of fans in Henderson County, and some could have found their way to the jury, so the prosecution would have to start shooting holes in E. Ray's new theory.

Now at the trial, Robby sat gasping at E. Ray's accusation that he was the murderer. Finally, he shouted, "No, sir!"

"Your mama and stepfather just got off a vacation. You didn't always get along with Jimmy Don Beets."

"Yes, I did," he said defensively.

"Didn't you hot-wire his boat while he was gone?" Andrews asked with an "I know you did this" tone to his voice.

"Yes, sir," he said, his voice now quiet.

"Didn't he really get hot about that?"

"We didn't get into an argument," Robby replied.

"He didn't like it one bit, did he? You wrecked one of the motorcycles."

"Yes, sir."

Having set the stage, E. Ray said, "Okay. Take us back to August fifth now. Where was your mother in the house when she said, 'I'm gonna kill him'?"

"In the kitchen."

"Okay, your mother says she's gonna kill Jimmy Don, and since she's in the kitchen, you say, 'Pass me something to eat.' "

"No, sir."

"But it took you until right now, some two years later, to get religion, didn't it?"

"I guess so."

"Buying your story, the State was right in on it. What did they offer you for your testimony?" E. Ray stepped closer to Robby as he questioned him.

"Nothing."

"You went before the grand jury to testify against your own mama, didn't you?"

"Yeah."

"So you could have a little soul cleaning. Put it on

someone else. That would be just fine, wouldn't it?" Now E. Ray stood only a few feet from Robby.

"No, sir."

"You don't care what happens to her. You don't care if they put her to sleep, do you?"

"Yes, sir," Robby said, frowning.

"You sure do. You know your mother never killed anyone. You know you did. You know your mother took up for you. You can come up here and say, she's forty-eight. Let her die because my soul's clean."

Now E. Ray stood almost nose to nose with Robby. Bandy objected, saying Andrews was standing too close, badgering the witness.

Andrews waved his hand at the objection. "I'm tired," he told the judge. "I'm gonna sit down anyway." He went back to his chair, dropped into the seat, but continued the questioning.

"Robby, she took the rap for you. You called down here on the jail telephone and she asked if you told them everything. Remember that?"

"Yes, sir."

"But you didn't tell them everything. You didn't tell them that you killed Jimmy Don, did you?"

"I didn't have no reason to tell them that I killed him 'cause I didn't," he said, his voice sounding like a pleading child's who'd been unfairly blamed.

"You didn't kill him, just like you didn't have any arguments with him. You came down here to the DA with your story that your mother killed him and they let you go anywhere and live your life scot free. That's what you got promised, didn't you?"

"No, sir. They didn't promise me anything."

"You never come down to the jail. You completely abandoned the lady. How come you just kept this a big secret for a couple years?"

"Because I was protecting my mother."

"Your mother was protecting you," E. Ray fired back. "When have you been in trouble that she hasn't helped you?"

"I was in trouble a couple times for burglary."

Bandy jumped to his feet. "I object, Your Honor. This is not relevant to the case."

"Branson's credibility is certainly at stake," E. Ray said.

When the judge overruled Bandy's objection, he sat down, disgusted. It wasn't fair. Andrews's own credibility was at stake because he knew all of Robby's legal problems, having defended him. Now he was using that confidential attorney-client information against his previous client.

Andrews pulled his lanky body out of his chair. His boots scuffed on the carpet as he closed in on Robby again. "It would be a lot easier if someone else took the trip, right, partner? Is that your mother?" E. Ray asked, as he pointed to Betty Beets, forcing Robby to look at her. "Has she always been good to you?"

"Up until now."

"What's she done to you now?"

"She's lying now, saying that I killed him when she did."

"She's gonna take the stand. Does that surprise you?" E. Ray asked, a faint smile on his lips.

Robby glanced at his mother, but said nothing.

"In truth and in fact, you got into a fight with Jimmy Don Beets and shot him in the back of his head and buried him under the wishing well and tried to put the blame on your mother. Have you got anybody to say that you didn't?"

"No, sir. There were no witnesses, unless she wants to come forward and say that she did it."

"She's going to take the witness stand, my friend. I can promise you that.

"You say you told your wife. You weren't married at the time you killed Jimmy Don Beets?"

"No, sir."

"Did you understand what you just said?" Andrews gloated.

Bandy, enraged, stood up immediately and objected that E. Ray would try a basic trick question like that.

The judge sustained the objection and let Bandy explain to Robby that he had just been hoodwinked.

With a smug look because he got away with something, E. Ray Andrews turned Robby Branson over for Bandy's redirect.

Bandy wanted to show Robby's willingness to testify, to prove he had nothing to hide.

"You were subpoenaed to come here?" Bandy asked.

"I would have come anyway because I want to cover my back just like she's trying to cover hers."

Bandy said, "You weren't subpoenaed to go to the grand jury, but you testified voluntarily."

"Yes, sir."

With that reply, Judge Holland closed the first day of the trial.

Robby Branson left the courtroom, and a television camera caught him with his arm around a pretty brunette. Robby continued down the courthouse's marble staircase, appearing relieved as he chatted with his girlfriend and smiled broadly.

Bandy and Boswell went to the prosecutor's office to consider Andrews's surprise "Robby did it" angle. O'Brien followed them inside.

"There can't be anything to it," O'Brien said. "If it were true, E. Ray would have been screaming 'false arrest' when we picked up Betty. Besides, whoever killed Jimmy Don had to also have killed Barker, or Betty had loaned him the gun. And you just don't have a couple different people wanting to start using Betty's yard as a cemetery."

"That has to be right," Bandy said. "The bullets were identical. Let's just see how this plays out. It wouldn't be the first time E. Ray painted himself into a corner."

TWENTY-FOUR

Shirley Thompson Stegner, the first person called when court reconvened the next day, ranked only second in importance to her brother Robby. DA Bandy led her through her mother's planning to kill Jimmy Don.

"Your mother wanted you to help her? To be an accomplice to a murder she committed?" Bandy asked, as he stood near Betty so all eyes in the courtroom would be centered on her.

"I told her I wouldn't help. She knew I didn't want her to kill him."

As the jury heard Shirley relate her role in the murders, she verified everything that Robby had told the court.

Afterward, Andrews jumbled the facts again.

He looked Shirley in the eye and said, "You didn't like Jimmy Don Beets, did you?"

Shock painted her face. "That's a lie," she said. "I cared very much for him."

E. Ray placed his hands on his hips. In a stern voice he said, "I didn't ask you to call me a liar."

"I'm sorry. It's just that I did care for him. He was the best stepfather I ever had."

"Just a few minutes ago you said you conspired to murder him."

"No, I didn't," Shirley said, visibly shaken. A chain-smoker, she had had to leave her beloved cigarettes outside, and her hands shook for the security of the nicotine between her fingers. "My mother had talked to me about killing him and I told her I didn't want anything to do with it. I didn't want to discuss it."

On Bandy's redirect, he asked Shirley, "If you thought Jimmy Don Beets's life was in danger and you were so fond of him, how come you didn't tell somebody?"

"Because I was afraid of my mother."

"Has your mother ever done anything to you?"

"No, but that doesn't mean she wouldn't."

Betty, sitting close to E. Ray, frequently whispered in his ear. She seemed especially agitated by Shirley's last remark.

Then Bandy stood in front of Shirley and said very slowly, "Has your mother ever put you in that kind of situation before?"

"Yes, sir."

Knowing what was coming, Andrews rose to object, but Bandy asked the judge for permission to approach his bench.

After the judge excused the jury, Bandy presented the prosecution's artillery to fight E. Ray's accusation of Robby being the murderer. Bandy said, "Introducing the death of Doyle Wayne Barker becomes very relevant at this point. Here are two bodies that are inextricably entwined. Both men were shot by the same gun using the same type of bullets. This shows Betty's design. Your Honor, this is very important because Shirley's testimony can rebut the defense's theory that Robby Branson murdered Mr. Beets."

The judge agreed with the DA. E. Ray tore off his wire-rim glasses and objected, but Judge Holland reiterated that the testimony would continue. The bailiff strolled over and opened the door to the jury's quarters.

Bandy began patiently and deliberately. "Shirley, I call your attention to October of 1981. You're sitting around the campfire. Do you recall having a conversation with your mother at that time in reference to the killing of Doyle Wayne Barker?"

"Yes, sir."

"What did she tell you?"

"She said she was going to kill him because he had beat her so many times and she just couldn't stand it anymore. She said if they were to get a divorce he would end up with the trailer because it's in his name."

"Did she say how she was going to do it?"

After Shirley recounted how her mother murdered Barker, Bandy knew that the jury had heard the most damaging evidence against Betty Beets. He passed the witness.

When E. Ray began his redirect, he didn't want to venture over the dangerous ground of Shirley's testimony. Instead, he decided to malign Shirley.

"Have you been heavy into shooting drugs?" he asked. Then not waiting for an answer, he continued, "Do you pass out frequently? Have loss of memory?"

"I used to do drugs, but I don't anymore."

"Now you're a pot head?"

"No, I just drink Budweiser."

Andrews hurried past the snickering in the courtroom. "You're charged with murder and you had a bond set at a million?"

"Yes."

"Okay. You're out of jail now. What's your bond?"

"The charge of Jimmy Don Beets's murder was dropped so my bond was set at $5,000."

"Only $5,000?" His eyes rolled in disbelief. "And you've been told you're not going to the penitentiary or anything of that nature?"

"No, sir."

"They just came by and told you to come over and tell us this and we'll reduce your bond?"

"No, sir. It was my decision to make my statement."

Trying one more time to discredit her, E. Ray said, "I understand people can hallucinate under LSD or methamphetamines."

"I don't do drugs anymore, sir," Shirley said firmly.

George Chaney had been a document examiner for thirteen years while he worked as a special agent with the Secret Service. Now he held the same profession in the private sector. He had spent hours scrutinizing the handwriting of both Jimmy Don and Betty Beets.

Bandy asked, "When you reviewed the J.C. Penney insurance policy, did you inspect the signature on the bottom of the application?"

"Yes. It was not Mr. Beets's authentic signature. It was not genuine."

He had examined numerous checks of Betty's, the bill of sale for the boat, the transfer of title, and called Betty's writing, "very unique." In his opinion, the signature "J. D. Beets" on all the documents had been in Betty Beets's handwriting.

Bandy passed the witness to E. Ray, who couldn't refute what the writing expert had said. However, E. Ray shined brightest when he had to come up with smoke and mirrors.

"Sir," E. Ray began pleasantly. "You said you were with the CIA?"

"No, sir, the Secret Service."

"How much are you getting paid to come down here and testify?"

"Five hundred dollars, which is not our normal fee; we usually charge more."

"Five hundred dollars?" E. Ray said appreciably. "You expect to get paid, don't you?"

The man frowned at the question. "Yes, sir, hope so."

"I hope you do too," E. Ray said, turning away from him and pacing by the jury. "You've never been mistaken about any of your documents that you compared?"

"Not to my knowledge."

"You've *never* been mistaken?" E. Ray said, mustering an expression of disbelief.

"If I have, no one's told me."

"How many times have you testified in court?"

"Roughly sixty times," Chaney said.

"Okay, you're the man from the CIA from Dallas, Texas, who's never been mistaken," E. Ray said, followed by lighthearted snickers from the courtroom.

"Would it surprise you to know that we're not denying that Betty signed 'J. D. Beets' to this title up here?"

"I didn't know that," Chaney said.

"If they'd asked you that, we wouldn't have had to pay you that money, would we?"

"Probably not, sir."

"Then we could have done without you," E. Ray said in an attempt to discredit the prosecution for bringing an unnecessary witness.

That was enough for Bandy, who was on his feet to protest. "Your Honor, can't we keep this to questions and answers?"

"I'm sorry, Your Honor," E. Ray offered.

Bandy wanted more apology out of Betty's defense lawyer than that. "I'd like the court to admonish counsel about his sidebar remarks."

"If I say I'm sorry, isn't that a sidebar remark?"

Now Judge Holland had had enough. "Mr. Andrews, if you would, *please.*"

As the days of the trial rolled on, E. Ray Andrews tried to discredit any witness the State threw at him.

When he questioned Rick Rose, Andrews referred to Rose's breakthrough information as from his "Confidential informant, second-hand information."

The jury sat attentively listening to each side without letting their expressions divulge any opinions they might have already formed.

Dr. Charles Petty, the chief medical examiner from Dallas, carried a brown cardboard box into the courtroom. The slightly built, bespectacled man was highly accredited, but when the rumor went through the room that the box contained the actual skulls of both Wayne Barker and Jimmy Don Beets, the courtroom crowd saw Dr. Petty as weird.

"The skulls will be there," he had previously told the investigators, "just in case the photographs fail to show every detail."

Bandy led him through his impressive credentials, then asked, "Did you perform an autopsy on Jimmy Don Beets?"

"If you want to call it that," Petty replied. "All I received were the bony parts of the body."

Bandy picked up an enlarged photograph that had been facedown on his desk. It depicted the bones of Jimmy Don Beets on a stretcher that just happened to include another stretcher showing the bones of Wayne Barker.

E. Ray vigorously objected to the State getting in a shot of Barker's skeleton. But since Barker's death had already been introduced, the judge overruled his objection, and allowed the photo to be passed to the jury.

Dr. Petty testified that he had X rays taken of Jimmy Don Beets's skull for positive identification of the body, since Beets had dental X rays made shortly before his death. Beets's dentist supplied the doctor with X rays that matched perfectly. Then Petty picked up a large, detailed photograph of Beets's head and pointed to the bullet hole that entered at the base of his skull. Another photograph showed part of his rib cage and a bullet hole in his trunk that was close to his heart. Petty noted the four areas of fractures: at the base of the skull, on the cheekbone, and one above each eye.

In Wayne Barker, Dr. Petty had discovered three bullet holes that resulted with fractures to his ribs and jawbone. Barker's third bullet attested to the practice shot Betty had discussed with Shirley.

As the doctor spoke, jurors looked down at the photograph of the two murdered men, then glanced at Betty before passing it on to the next juror.

By the time E. Ray had his turn, he'd had his fill of technical jargon. He asked, "Do you know who killed these people?"

Petty frowned at the audacity of the question, "No, of course not," he huffed.

Then Andrews said, "What did you say about the presence of a fracture on Jimmy Don Beets?"

The doctor again discussed the four areas of fractures.

"Could that skull fracture be caused by a fight with another man?"

"Yes, it could."

E. Ray grinned while jury members glanced at each other, appearing that they had heard a whole new scenario. "So you're just basing the cause of death on your medical opinion because of the presence of bullets?"

"Yes," the doctor admitted.

Andrews surprisingly scored a few points with Dr. Petty's testimony, especially that Jimmy Don's skull could have been fractured during a fight with another man, taking the killing off Betty's shoulders.

When Bandy redirected, he asked, "Doctor, could

that fracture have been caused by a shovel hitting the body after it had decomposed?"

"No, in my opinion, it's not the type of injury one would expect with a shovel."

"Could that fracture have been caused by a bullet entering the back of the skull?"

"Not in my opinion."

Bandy frowned and began pacing. The answer didn't seem logical to him. Then he looked back at the photo. The bullet had obviously made a round hole. The damage was to the soft tissue, like the brain.

"Doctor, would it be compatible with the body being dragged down some steps?"

"Yes, it could be."

Bandy went back to his chair, thinking of how Jimmy Don had been yanked down the steps of the trailer. But did any of this really matter? The man had obviously died from the bullet wounds.

Allen Jones, a firearms examiner with the Dallas County Forensic Lab, entered the courtroom through the double doors from the outside foyer. He had fourteen years experience with firearms and was an SMU graduate who had trained at the Smith & Wesson Handgun factory. He had attended the FBI Academy at Quantico, and now taught about firearms in police academies.

Having heard enough of his credentials, E. Ray threw up his hands, and said, "Judge, he's got to be an expert, just gotta be!"

Bandy gave E. Ray a "There he goes again" glare and asked Jones, "Did you have occasion to examine the projectiles received from Dr. Petty on or about June 10 of this year?"

"From both bodies," Jones said, "we detected that the bullets were a special type of .38-caliber, semijacketed hollow point bullets manufactured by Remington. They came from a weapon having six grooves in the barrel that turned with a left-hand twist."

Bandy handed him State's Exhibit 11, a Special Colt revolver.

"We test fired this gun," Jones explained, "and found that test bullets showed this gun gave the bullets the same spiraling detected on those bullets found with the bodies. It's my opinion that all of the bullets could have come from that gun."

"So you're saying that those projectiles were fired from that revolver?" Bandy asked.

"Could have," Jones reiterated, "but because of the oxidation of the metal, I cannot state that they were."

Listening to the expert answer Bandy's questions, E. Ray picked up on the difficulty of describing minute details of the bullets because of the condition of the metal. On cross, he concentrated on that difficulty.

"You can't state to this jury that these bullets that were introduced up here were fired from that pistol, can you?"

"That's correct."

"In fact, you can't tell us anything for certain outside of your education."

"You're right," the gun expert had to admit.

Court recessed for lunch, and Deputy Maureen Pagent took Betty Beets to the ladies' room. The many women in there immediately stopped talking, and only gawked until Betty had washed her hands and left. In court, they thought of her as evil, but up close, the petite woman looked normal and vulnerable as she smiled at them.

The conversation resumed, every woman giving her opinion of Betty's hairstyle and clothes. Then they left for the Jubilee House for lunch, or tried to grab a quick burger at a drive-through. Others took their sack lunches and ate under the trees on the courthouse grounds.

The afternoon session began with a petite redhead, Hilary Benton, from Garland, Texas, who had purchased Jimmy Don's boat on July 24, 1984. Betty Beets had sold it to her after the two met in a Cedar Creek boat repair shop. Mrs. Benton identified Betty in the courtroom as the person from whom she bought the boat. Bandy admitted the bill of sale into evidence.

"At the time you made the purchase," Bandy asked, "did you know that Mr. Beets was missing?"

"No, I did not."

"You carried that title to work and had it notarized, didn't you?"

"Yes, she had a power of attorney."

"Did you know that a power of attorney ceases when the grantor dies?"

"No, sir."

"So you assumed it was legal?"

"I didn't read the instrument. It was a half piece of eight and a half by eleven paper with 'Power of Attorney' at the top, and some legal writing under that. It looked legal."

Andrews passed his opportunity to cross-examine.

In a surprising move, especially to E. Ray Andrews, the prosecution rested.

E. Ray nodded to Bandy and the other lawyers to accompany him to the judge's bench to have a conversation out of earshot of the jury.

Andrews said, "Judge, I've not released any of these

witnesses that have been subpoenaed. I intend to use them, but I asked to be given ample notice. Now all of a sudden Bandy rests. It's gonna rush me up."

Bill Bandy said, "I didn't make the decision to rest until the minute I did. I had several more witnesses that I anticipated calling, and probably would have run until noon tomorrow, but the way it went, I decided just to shut it down."

E. Ray Andrews crossed his arms over his chest. "You think it's going that good, huh?"

TWENTY-FIVE

The Henderson County courtroom was large, but not large enough for the growing crowd wanting in. Now people began lining up as early as 6:30 A.M. in front of a building that didn't open until 8:00. Once the doors were unlocked, onlookers ran up the white marble stairs to form another line in front of the second-floor courtroom. People crowded and pushed, jockeying for better positions than they had had outside.

E. Ray Andrews began his fight for Betty's life, and he summoned her oldest daughter, Faye Lane, as the first defense witness.

Slipping back into his "good ole boy" role, Andrews asked, "You wasn't subpoenaed by me, was you?"

"No."

"Did your sister tell you anything about helping your mother bury anybody?"

"No."

Bandy objected as it being hearsay, but Holland overruled.

"Did you ever talk to your brother, Robby Branson, about—"

"No."

"Hold on here, let me finish, about helping your mother bury Jimmy Don Beets?"

Faye, an obviously friendly witness for the defense, couldn't wait to say things that would help her mother.

But this time she again flipped from previous testimony, now saying she knew nothing about the murders.

"Did you ever know anything about your mother trying to collect insurance?" E. Ray asked.

"No. Well, I knew there was some insurance on Jimmy Don where Betty's the beneficiary, but not that she's trying to get it."

Faye went on to testify that she'd only been around Jimmy Don five or six times, but that she liked him. She said he and her mother got along well, and she'd never heard them quarrel or saw them fight.

"Have you ever talked to Mr. Bandy before?" E. Ray asked.

"No. I only talked with Rick Rose and Mike O'Brien."

"Did you tell them the same thing you're telling me?"

"Yes."

"They subpoenaed you here today and you know nothing whatsoever?"

"That's right."

After ascertaining Fay knew Ray Bone, E. Ray walked closer to the witness, and asked in a confidential manner, "Did he ever tell you that he made a deal with Rick Rose?"

"No," Faye said.

E. Ray looked disappointed, for he probably hoped Faye would substantiate that a deal had been made by the prosecution.

"Is your brother, Robby Branson, capable of murder?"

Bandy, on his feet with both open palms extended toward the judge, said, "Your Honor, he's usurping the province of the jury."

When the judge overruled his complaint, the DA looked stunned that Holland would allow E. Ray that much range.

"Now listen carefully," E. Ray cautioned Faye as if she were a small child, "in your opinion, Robby Branson, who's testified here, is he capable of belief—"

"I've always believed in my family," Faye said.

E. Ray's faced reddened with annoyance. "No, ma'am, I'm not talking about have you always believed him, but in your opinion is he capable of belief?"

"I've always believed him, but he's never told me about any of this."

Tired of trying to get Faye to admit that Robby was capable of murder, E. Ray ventured onto another subject. "Your sister Shirley, have you known her to have blackouts?"

"When she gets drunk."

"Oh, she drinks!" said the known alcoholic, with a condescending frown. "Does she take dope?"

"Not anymore. She used to."

"You've visited your mother twice a week at the jail," Andrews said, establishing Faye's loyalty.

"Yes," she replied.

Knowing that Faye Lane would only say what supported her mother, Bandy passed on questioning her.

E. Ray Andrews had made a contractual agreement with Betty Beets for her media rights, since she couldn't pay for her defense. Then he promptly signed the rights over to his son, affording E. Ray clean hands if anyone questioned his ethics, for he knew Betty's book rights would be more valuable if she were found guilty. Her other attorney, Gil Hargrave, was promised twenty percent of the royalties.

The only witnesses E. Ray allowed Hargrave to question were Betty's mother and brother. The two drove twenty-four hours from Virginia to attend the trial. They told the jury how loving Betty was, and how she never exhibited any childhood outbursts or violent tendencies.

When Bandy questioned Betty's relatives, he concentrated on Betty's behavior at her brother's funeral two years prior. Her mother remembered Betty openly crying at the funeral home when she first saw her brother in his casket and also the next day at his funeral.

After Mrs. Dunevant told how much she liked Jimmy Don, Bandy asked, "Did you know any of her other husbands?"

"None other than Branson. I'm sorry, I did know Bill Lane." Under further questioning she revealed never hearing the names Ronnie Threlkeld or Wayne Barker.

Hargrave wasn't going to let the listing of Betty's husbands go unchallenged. He fired back, "Did you know that Jimmy Don Beets had four wives?"

A commotion in the foyer outside the courtroom caught a deputy constable's attention as he mingled with the hallway crowd. He had a shiny fake-gold badge pinned to his shirt, and a pink bald head narrowly fringed with hair. He considered himself a ladies' man, but no one understood why. Now he busily eyed Shirley Stegner, the only person he recognized in a group that stood illegally discussing the trial. He stared at a short, stocky young man in a leisure suit, knowing he'd seen his face before.

The constable leaned in to catch their conversation, but he only heard the young man say, "While I was on the stand, I was asked . . ."

Although he had wanted to hear more, he felt he had heard enough. At the next trial break, he rushed to E. Ray's office and told him what had happened. Andrews had hoped for something like this. The constable's information could lead to a mistrial, since discussing testimony with other witnesses had been expressly forbidden by the judge.

The next morning, E. Ray eagerly recalled Robby Branson to the stand. The young man plodded into the courtroom, looking perplexed at having to testify again.

E. Ray pulled answers from Robby, getting him to admit to speaking with his sisters about the trial, and perhaps, Robby hedged, he might have mentioned his testimony and the questions he was asked.

When Shirley Stegner had her turn, she appeared more savvy and street smart than her younger brother. Andrews zeroed in on what she knew about the possibility of Robby being the murderer.

"I heard something about you accusing him of killing Jimmy Don, but Robby didn't tell me directly. I knew we weren't to discuss the case, but I didn't know we weren't supposed to discuss the newspaper."

"What was in the newspaper?" Andrews asked.

"Quite a bit. Some of my testimony was wrong and so was other people's."

"How'd you know about other people's testimony? That's just hearsay," Andrews told her.

"Everyone talks about hearsay," Shirley replied.

Now the constable would have his turn. He padded into the courtroom and swore to tell the truth.

Bill Bandy asked him, "What do you make a year?"

"A dollar fifty-eight a year," the man said without apology.

"A dollar-a-year man," Bandy said, in a tone that indicated the man's cheap badge had cost more than that. "What do you *really* do for a living?"

"I work for Ronald Waldie."

"Is that the same lawyer who represents E. Ray Andrews in his disbarment action?" Bandy fought the smile forming on his lips.

E. Ray quickly objected, but Bandy had turned to go back to his chair and left the constable with Andrews.

Andrews took the constable through everything he'd heard and seen in the hall and how his civic duty as a concerned citizen required his bringing it to the court's attention. Then he asked what else had happened yesterday.

"Mr. Bandy called me up to his office. He wanted to know if my loyalty was to Mr. Waldie. He tried to humiliate me. He also called me to the sheriff's office and I went there and talked with Mr. Bandy, Michael O'Brien, and Rick Rose. Rick accused me of using my constable position to help my investigations for Mr. Waldie."

On redirect, Bandy forced the constable to admit he'd seen the composite drawing of Robby Branson at Mr. Waldie's house and not on television as he earlier testified.

Andrews brought back Rick Rose.

"Did you have an occasion to talk with the constable yesterday?" E. Ray asked.

"I did."

"How did you know what the constable reported?"

"He told me what he reported."

"How did you know he'd be called into Mr. Bandy's office?"

Rose managed a straight face and said, "It was a good guess."

Bandy cross-examined Rose and asked, "Did you see the constable hanging out in the hallway yesterday?"

"I certainly did."

"What was he doing?"

"Creeping."

Bandy sat down and E. Ray redirected, "What's creeping?"

"Lurking."

"What's lurking?"

"Snooping."

Andrews had enough and decided to act quickly. He turned to the judge. "Based upon the testimony heard here today and yesterday, I ask the court to declare a mistrial. We ask that Robby Branson be held in contempt of court, as well as Billy Bandy and Allen Boswell."

Judge Holland apparently considered the testimony had been clouded with ulterior purposes and wasted no time in overruling Andrews's motion.

Many contrasts in appearance and personality existed among the Branson children. One of the most notable was slim, sensitive Bobby, when compared to his older brother Robby who outweighed him by seventy-five pounds. Bobby's lighter coloring resembled his mother's, and except for the shoot-out, he rarely showed any of Robby's bravado.

Because of Bobby's age, only seventeen, no one had been allowed to quiz him without his father's being present. Andrews began by asking Bobby about the family trip to Virginia, where he had accompanied his parents. He asked if Bobby had an occasion to hear Jimmy Don and Robby having a discussion.

"When we got back," Bobby said, "they argued because Robby wrecked my motorcycle and did a whole bunch of other stuff. He took out the boat and messed it up and messed with my mom's truck."

"Mr. Beets was pretty upset about it?"

"Yes."

"Did your brother get upset about it?"

"A little bit. Not much."

Andrews had Bobby agree that Robby had argued with Jimmy Don, who was also upset over Robby quitting his job. Then, without pressing him further, E. Ray passed his witness to the DA.

Bandy asked, "Bobby, you said that Robert and Mr. Beets had a heated discussion about the motorcycle being wrecked and the other things that were done. How did Robert and Jimmy Don get along?"

"Fair. They did argue some."

"Well, did you argue with Jimmy Don?"

"No."

But Bobby said that he too had argued with Robby, and that Robby was strong and could get violent at times.

Bandy asked, "Did Robby and Jimmy Don have any vicious arguments?"

"Not that I know of."

"You never saw the two men fight?"

"No," Bobby answered.

"Who told you about Barker's disappearance?" Bandy asked.

"I asked Mom about it a few days later. She really wouldn't tell me. Just said he was gone."

TWENTY-SIX

The next morning started off with something unique. Up to now, the witnesses had been either technically proficient experts or family members with important insider information. Now E. Ray Andrews announced a witness who appeared not to give a damn.

Ray Bone strutted in looking as though he had just slid off a horse. His jeans were tight, his shirt wrinkled, and his cowboy boots had never seen saddle wax or shoe polish.

Andrews asked, "You know Mrs. Beets?"

"Yeah."

"Have you lived with her?"

"For a year."

"What are you on parole for?"

"Manslaughter."

"You remember coming to my office?"

"I've been to your office several times," Bone said, in a tone that indicated E. Ray should have known.

"We talked about the Beets' case, remember?"

"I told you what her kids told me, and I said I didn't think the woman was guilty."

"What did you base your opinion on?" E. Ray asked, then rested his foot on his chair, getting comfortable for an extensive tribute to Betty's innocence.

"Well, the only basis I have is that I lived with her for over a year and the way she treated me. I don't know nothing about the rest of it, but the only thing I can tell you is that the woman always treated me decent."

"You had a run-in with one of her sons. What started the argument?"

"He and a friend were riding their motorcycles in the backyard, and I told them to get their motorcycles out of there. I said if his mama came home, she was gonna be hot."

"Did they listen to you?"

"Paid me no attention. When I told them the next time they saw my truck parked there, they better keep on going, 'cause that meant I was there. Guess his friend didn't like that. He pulled out a gun and started shooting. Next thing I knew Bobby come runnin' out of the house with a pistol in each hand."

"So that's when you ran into the woods?"

"I mean, it'd take a *fool* to stand there with him havin' two guns."

"How many times did he shoot at you?"

"I don't have no idea," Bone said, shaking his head. "He shot out three tires. There were seven or eight bullet holes in the truck. I don't know how many times altogether."

"Then what happened?"

"A security guard came and took me to a friend's house over in Arlington."

"You were arrested for having a gun in your truck. Tell us what happened."

"I was arrested in Arlington. Mr. Rose came and brought me back here."

"You aware Robby Branson talked to the DA's office?" E. Ray asked, appearing paranoid of witnesses getting a word to his competition.

"No."

"Did you talk to anybody when the grand jury was in session?"

"Talked to Robby."

"Did you know about him getting into any trouble?"

"I heard of some trouble, but I don't know what it was."

"Assault to murder?" E. Ray asked, and was probably surprised that Bandy didn't object to his putting such inflammatory words in front of the jury.

"No, I never heard that, but I heard him say he was on probation."

"Okay, you spent two days in jail because of a gun in your truck. How'd you get out on bail?"

"Gerald Albright got the bond for me."

"After that, did you have a conversation with Rick Rose?"

"Yeah. I called him. I was over in Mansfield and I called him from a little grocery store."

"Was Mrs. Beets with you at the time?"

"She was in the truck with me."

"What did Rose want?"

"He wanted to know when we were coming back down here, and I told him we were on our way. Taking 287."

"Did you tell him what you were driving?"

"No, I didn't have to, he already knew."

"How many times have you talked with Rick Rose?"

"Not since Betty was arrested."

"I didn't *ask* you since Betty got arrested," E. Ray said sarcastically.

"Then make yourself plain, fella."

A few jurors smiled in disbelief at Ray Bone.

E. Ray frowned. "I'll make myself plain. How many times did you talk with Rose?"

"I didn't write it down in my book," Bone snapped.

"Three or four times?"

"I don't have the slightest idea. Your office called Gerald Albright's house and left the phone number for me to call the jail."

"Does it surprise you to know that I don't know where Gerald Albright lives?"

"No, Ray, I don't have any idea what you know," Bone said, turning his shoulder to E. Ray as if he was bored by the conversation.

"Do you know anything about Jimmy Don Beets?" Andrews asked.

"I don't have the slightest idea. I didn't know he'd been killed 'til I read it in the paper."

"Okay, back to when you called Rick Rose. Did you leave the number of the pay phone for him?"

"Yeah. He called back in five or ten minutes," Bone said.

"He just wanted to know, Ray, when you comin'?" Andrews asked.

"No, he wanted to know when Betty was comin'."

"How long after you hung up from Rick Rose was Betty Beets arrested?"

Bone scanned the ceiling of the courtroom, trying to come up with a time. "Oh, probably thirty minutes."

"When they arrested her, did they arrest you too?"

"They arrested me, then they turned me loose."

"When you're talking about being arrested, did they put you alongside the car?"

"No, they put me down face first in the middle of the highway."

"Then you weren't arrested."

"I had handcuffs on me and I was pretty well arrested as far as I'm concerned." Bone smirked.

"After Betty got to the jail here, did you call down and talk to her?" Andrews asked.

"Yes."

"What did you talk about?"

"I was asking what she wanted."

"Such as?"

"Well hey, what I talk to Betty about ain't none of your business."

Murmurs rumbled through the courtroom at Bone's disrespect.

"I bet it's the court's and the jury's business," E. Ray shot back.

"We weren't talking about this case," Bone said, looking down, suddenly interested in his fingernails.

"What was you discussing?" E. Ray asked.

"Betty had nothing to tell me," Bone said, probably remembering his recent prison term where nothing was lower than a snitch.

"Was she talking about you and Gerald Albright?" Ray Bone and Gerald Albright fascinated E. Ray because they were friends, and because a drunken Betty Beets had lain in bed with Albright and confessed to burying someone in her yard.

"Betty has nothing to tell on me or Gerald Albright. I've known him for forty-two years."

"When was the last time you talked with him?"

"I haven't the slightest idea."

"You don't have the slightest idea when you talked to someone you've known for forty-two years?"

"That's right."

"Where does he live?"

"I don't have the slightest idea."

"Ever been to his house?" E. Ray moved closer and his brows drew together in an angry frown.

"I've never been to his house."

"Does he live in Kauffman County?"

"I don't have the slightest idea," Bone said, continuing in his sullen manner.

"Well, where in the last forty-two years has he lived?"

"I don't have the slightest idea. I take care of my business, and Gerald takes care of his."

"What kind of business does he do?"

"He keeps an ad in the paper. You just have to look in there."

"What does it say, hot cars?" Now the testimony had degenerated to nasty insinuations, with attorney and witness trying to out-nasty each other. "Have you run an ad in the paper?"

"No, I haven't lately. Did you read in the paper that I had an ad there?"

"I don't have the slightest idea," E. Ray said, happy to zing one of Bone's lines back at him.

Judge Holland grabbed his gavel to silence the laughter, but the courtroom crowd took the hint and quieted down.

"You seem to be talking about all this stuff that you should have been asking a long time ago," Bone said. "You should have gone to the DA's office to get some charges filed against me, because it seems like you know a lot that I don't."

In exasperation, E. Ray turned to Judge Holland. "I'm trying to ask him some questions, Judge."

"Mr. Bone," Holland said, "please answer the questions that are asked by the lawyers."

"How long had you been in the penitentiary?" E. Ray said.

"Seven or eight years."

E. Ray took off his glasses and rubbed his eyes. He looked drained as he passed the witness to Bandy and gratefully fell into his chair.

Bill Bandy picked up some photographs from the evidence table and handed them to Bone. "Could you please identify these for me."

Ray thumbed through the pictures. "This is the wishing well, that's the shed, and that's Betty's trailer."

"Mr. Bone, who looks after those flowers out there in the wishing well?"

"Betty."

"Does she mow the yard?"

"She never did want anyone else to mow her yard."

Bandy went to the bar in front of the jury. Leaning on it, he said, "She spent a lot of time looking after those flowers?"

"I know she had flowers all over the porch and everywhere else. She spent a lot of time in her yard, period."

"Did you know at the time you were living there that Doyle Wayne Barker was buried out there under the shed?"

"No, sir."

Bandy passed Ray Bone to Andrews for redirect.

"Did you know at the time or did Mrs. Beets tell you that Robby Branson killed Jimmy Don Beets?"

"No, sir, she never told me anything like that."

"She didn't tell you that *she* killed anybody?"

"No."

E. Ray sighed in relief and released Bone, who swaggered out the door.

The witness who had been promised stepped daintily to the stand. Betty Beets smiled shyly at E. Ray and nodded briefly to the jurors.

To add to her demure pretense, Andrews cautioned Betty, "Now you're gonna have to talk loud enough for everyone to hear you."

"All right," she said softly.

"Have you ever been in trouble before?"

"Not that ever amounts to anything," Betty answered.

"You might want to tell me about a misdemeanor offense in Dallas. Something that concerned a husband, correct?"

"Yes, my second husband, Bill Lane. He told the judge that my shooting him was his fault, so the court reduced my charge to a misdemeanor and fined me one hundred dollars. Another fifty dollars in court costs."

Having that antiseptically out of the way, E. Ray led her through the facts that by now were well known to the court, and everyone else in Henderson County. He talked about her trip to Virginia where her mother had testified that she and Jimmy Don got along well.

"If I asked if Jimmy Don Beets was missing in the lake," Andrews said, "would that be true or false?"

"False," Betty answered.

"What happened to Jimmy Don Beets?"

Betty started at the beginning of Jimmy Don's last day, itemizing whom he had talked with, the errands he ran, and continued describing a very ordinary day for two people who lived at the Cedar Creek Lake.

"We took the boat to get gas for the races the next day, and Jimmy Don began griping about all the work he put into the boat and what a mess it was after we returned from vacation.

"We went home and watched TV, then got ready for bed."

"Do you sleep in the same bedroom?"

"Yes, but we never went to bed."

"How come?"

"When Jimmy Don had gone to the bedroom, I went to put my dog in the kitchen like I do every night. By the time I got to the living room, Robby came in."

"Now Robby is the older boy?"

"Yes. Jimmy Don heard him come in. Jimmy Don had been drinking all day and he was pretty well drunk, and he was mad."

"What did he do when Robby came in?"

"Jimmy Don came into the living room and said, 'Robert, did you quit your job?' Robby said he did.

Then Jimmy Don started griping about the messed-up boat and the motorcycle. Also about my truck. I had four flat tires and it was all muddy. The house had been a mess. Coins we owned were thrown all over a dresser.

"I asked Jimmy Don to calm down, that we'd talk about it in the morning. He turned and went back to the bedroom, and Robby went into the bathroom. When Robby came out, I heard them fighting. I was startled at first. I didn't know what was going on."

"They were fighting in the bedroom and there were loud voices?" Andrews said, making sure the jury had heard.

"They were yelling at each other. I had started for the bedroom when I heard a shot."

At this point in her trial, Betty made a production of manufacturing tears. She sniffled loudly while tightly clutching a Kleenex. Snickers filtered through the courtroom.

"Did you hear one shot or more?" E. Ray asked.

"I only remember hearing one shot."

"What did you do then?"

Betty reached for a fresh Kleenex and dabbed her eyes. "I got to the bedroom and found Jimmy Don on the floor. Robby was standing just inside the door. I sat down beside Jimmy Don."

"Did Robby have a gun in his hand?"

"No, but I found one a few minutes later."

"Did it look like that gun there?" Andrews asked, pointing to the gun that the prosecution had placed into evidence.

"It looked similar to it."

"Do y'all have two guns that look like that?"

"We have three guns that look like that."

Realizing he should have cleared that point with Betty so the jury wouldn't think she owned an arsenal, E. Ray hurried on. "Was Jimmy Don facedown, or how was he laying?"

"He was kinda on his back and side. His head was bleeding and there was blood coming from his mouth."

"What did you do then?"

"I reached up and got a bedspread. I don't remember anything about a sleeping bag, but I do remember a bedspread. I was sitting beside Jimmy Don, and Robby said, 'Mom, I'm sorry. I didn't mean to.' Then he asked me to help him."

"Did you try to talk with Jimmy Don?"

"I held Jimmy Don for a few minutes and tried to tell him what I was doing and why. I told him how much I loved him. And I know if he could be here, if he could see me, he'd say he understood that I had to help Robby," Betty said, as if she had rehearsed a script.

"How come you felt like you had to help him?"

"I remember when he was a little boy of eight, I took him to live with his daddy. He looked up at me and asked when he could come home again. I said soon, but I knew that wouldn't be. He didn't come to live with me 'til he was eighteen."

Betty ran through the facts of the case, telling about Robby going on a bike ride, Shirley coming down with her husband, and everything else that had been attested to by her family, but she cleverly rearranged the facts so they suited her story. At E. Ray's prompting, she frequently added new details.

"Back in the bedroom," Andrews said, "did you put a sheet over Mr. Beets?"

"I put the bedspread on him. When I rolled him over onto the spread, the gun was under him, so I picked it up and put it in the nightstand."

"When Robby came back in, had Mr. Beets already been placed?" Andrews asked.

"He was still laying in the bedroom," Betty told him.

Then disregarding the fact that Robby had to have seen Jimmy Don if he had killed him, Andrews asked, "Did Robby ever see him?"

Incredulously, Betty answered, "No," telling her attorney that the son she accused of killing Jimmy Don hadn't seen the man.

She also turned around the fact that Robby had helped her bury Jimmy Don to that she had helped Robby. She denied having peat moss hidden under her trailer, ready to cover the grave, and insisted she bought it the next day.

"Would your check for that peat moss be dated that next day?" E. Ray asked.

Betty assured him it would, but she produced no check as evidence.

Again, E. Ray revisited the reasons for Betty helping her son.

"Robby was on probation," Betty told him. "He had just gotten six years. I said to Jimmy Don, 'I couldn't do anything else.' " Then she turned to the jury and said, "I guess I could have too. I could have told the truth, but I had to help him."

Then there was the matter of the insurance that Betty had tried to take out with J. C. Penney, in addition to hiring lawyers to have Jimmy Don declared dead so she could collect on his policies and pension. E. Ray continued trying to put out fires, and establish that it was Jimmy Don, not Betty, who suggested trying to collect on the life insurance policies.

He asked, "Do you know how much insurance Jimmy Don Beets has?"

"No."

"Do you know how much his retirement fund was?"

"I didn't even know anything about a retirement fund."

"You heard the lady testify about the J. C. Penney

insurance application, and we didn't object to that, and that's in evidence. Did you sign his name?"

"Yes, I did," Betty admitted, adding that Jimmy Don had never objected to her signing his name when he was living.

Betty also acknowledged signing her husband's name to sell the boat, cleverly sliding over the fact that she didn't own it, and never mentioning her fictitious power of attorney.

Andrews still had another task. He needed to clarify that Betty wasn't the hard-hearted woman who could dump a dead husband in a planter and get on with her life. He asked, "Did it bother you that Jimmy Don was out there in the front yard, dead?"

Through more sniffling, she said, "Oh yes. Every day. It bothered me and it always will. I had to move out of that trailer for a while. When it'd go dark, I couldn't leave the living room and I couldn't go outside."

After keeping Betty on the witness stand all morning, Andrews prepared to wrap up his questions, and wanted to leave on a positive note.

"Are you owning up to your part in covering up for your son?"

"Yes, I am."

"They have this indictment that you pulled the trigger on the gun that killed Jimmy Don Beets. Is that the truth?"

"No. I could never hurt Jimmy Don."

"Did you love Jimmy Don?"

"I loved him. No one's ever been as good to me as he was."

"Do you love your son Robby?"

"Who?" she asked, adjusting her hearing aid.

"I said, do you love your son Robby?"

"Yes. I love all my children. No matter what they say, what they do, it won't ever stop that."

* * *

At noon, the judge called for a lunch break, telling everyone to be back at one-thirty.

Billy Bandy interrupted. "Your Honor, before we break, may I just ask Mrs. Beets just one question?"

The judge nodded, and Bandy approached the sniffling woman. "Mrs. Beets," he said, "is this testimony upsetting you?"

Indignantly, Betty said, "Wouldn't it you?"

"Then why are there no tears?" he asked. The round of courtroom laughter blanketed her answer.

After lunch, Allen Boswell, Michael O'Brien, and Karen Warner accompanied Billy Bandy back to his office to formulate more ways to shoot holes in Betty's testimony. Since Betty had changed many of the facts, Bandy made notes of his new approach. The bailiff tapped on their door to tell them court was ready to reconvene.

Bandy said, "Let's get going, it's show time."

As Billy Bandy approached Betty on the witness stand, she continued sniffling into her ever-present Kleenex.

Bandy said, "You stated that you could not leave the house at night and that you sat in the living room because your former husband, Jimmy Don Beets, was buried in this planter."

"Yes," she whispered.

"Were you aware that a former husband, Doyle Wayne Barker, was also buried on your premises?"

"No, I was not." A hint of hostility crept into her voice.

"You testified earlier under oath at your habeas corpus hearing that you were unaware that Jimmy Don Beets was buried in that planter. Do you recall that?"

"Yes."

"My question, Mrs. Beets, is"—he paused for emphasis and at the same time paced toward the jury making sure everyone there was listening—"were you lying then or are you lying now?"

"I was lying then," Betty said evenly.

E. Ray had brought up Betty's shooting Billy Lane to deflate the importance of it, but instead, according to Judge Holland's initial admonition, he had opened the gate for the prosecution to question her about it.

"Mrs. Beets, you testified about only one prior arrest, a misdemeanor conviction concerning a former husband, Bill Lane. Is that the offense when you shot him twice in the back?"

"He was shot in the side and stomach," Betty insisted.

Bandy ignored her response and demonstrated how well the prosecution had done its homework. "Isn't it true that you were convicted in Dallas County of public lewdness arising out of an indecent act at Charlie's Angels Bar in Dallas? You were assessed thirty days in jail. On August 23, 1979, a situation arose where you allowed your breast to be fondled in a public place?"

"That wasn't true."

"You were convicted of it, were you not?"

"I went to court over it."

"Did you plead guilty?"

"I don't remember the plea."

"Do you remember Archie Phillips?"

Betty glanced at Bandy and her eyes squinted hatred. She caught herself and said, "Yes, I admit I was tried after being arrested."

"You were jailed for thirty days, then placed on probation and fined?"

"Yes, for a year."

Bandy had captured Betty in an outright lie, but she showed no emotion or remorse.

He quizzed her about trying twice to collect insurance on Jimmy Don's burned house. She admitted to trying once to collect, but she said she never knew why the insurance company wouldn't pay. Bandy filled her in, explaining that she hadn't been paid because the insurance company suspected arson.

After hearing one lie after another, he phrased his next question, "Regardless of what you say or may not have known, you've heard people testify about the $86,000 in life insurance, another $24,000 in life insurance, $15,000 in back pay, and $792.40 in monthly retirement benefits. And further, another policy for $43,400.32 naming you as the beneficiary. Did you hear that testimony?"

"Yes. That's the first I heard the amounts."

"Going back to Saturday, August 6, 1983, do you recall telling Deputy Johnny Marr that Jimmy Don Beets was missing?"

She looked Bandy straight in the eye and said, "I've never talked to Johnny Marr about Jimmy Don at all."

Bandy scowled, then looked down at his notes to make sure he had the right date and name. After he assured himself he was correct, he wondered why she would lie about something so easily documented.

In a voice louder than he customarily used in court he asked, "Are you saying that his testimony was in error when he stated that he came out to your house at eight-thirty Saturday morning?"

"I'm saying that his testimony was not true. That Saturday morning, I went out and bought peat moss; then the boys and I went to Dallas."

Bandy showed her the blue sleeping bag Jimmy Don had been found in, but she said she didn't recognize it. He asked why she didn't come forward at the habeas corpus hearing and tell that Robby killed Jimmy Don during a fight.

"I don't know," Betty answered lamely.

"When your son Robby broke into that house, did he have a lawyer?"

"Yes, E. Ray Andrews."

"The same E. Ray Andrews who accused him of murder in this courtroom?"

"That what?" Betty said, appearing not to have heard the DA, but that was unlikely, for at this point Bandy shouted at her in disbelief.

"Mrs. Beets, do you recall Chaplain Burris from the fire department coming out and talking to you?"

"Yes."

"And you discussed insurance then?"

"I don't remember discussing insurance with him."

"You heard his testimony, did you not?"

"Yes, but I didn't discuss any insurance with him."

Bandy stood for a moment staring at the woman. She had shown not a shred of emotion while telling the court that all the prosecutions' witnesses had lied. Her children, the fire chief, the sheriff's deputies, the entire DA staff, and now the chaplain—they were all liars.

Bandy, drained and exhausted from pulling answers from Betty, turned her over to E. Ray for redirect.

At this point, E. Ray may have questioned the wisdom of having Betty testify, but Judge Holland saved him for the moment by announcing that court would recess for the day.

Fifteen minutes after court adjourned, Bobby Branson rushed to E. Ray Andrew's office to discuss the case. Bobby had watched E. Ray question his mother and it made him wish she had a different attorney. He remembered E. Ray arriving for court that morning with bloodshot eyes and shaking as though he had jangled nerves from a hangover.

Now Bobby sat across the desk from the attorney and smelled whiskey on his breath. As he saw it, the man defending his mother from capital murder could only think about his next drink. Andrews apparently had gulped down several slugs of Wild Turkey as soon as he returned to his office.

TWENTY-SEVEN

After Betty had been pounded with Bandy's questions for most of yesterday afternoon, Andrews strolled up to her the next morning, hands in his pockets, trying to do some damage control.

"Mrs. Beets, did you and Robby talk about what to do if later on someone were to find Jimmy Don's body?"

"I told him that if Jimmy Don was found, for him to say that he knew nothing about it and I would take the blame."

"How come you're now testifying to the truth?"

"Because you told me you wouldn't represent me unless I leveled with you."

"You didn't tell me this to start with, did you?"

"No."

"Didn't I tell you that I was going to have the truth or you could find someone else?"

"Yes," Betty said, sounding like she had rehearsed a script.

On recross, Bandy asked Betty, "You told Robby, who was a teenager at the time, to say nothing about this and you'd take total blame. Why then do you suppose he would admit his complicity in carrying the body out of the house and putting it in the wishing well?"

"I think he was under pressure."

"By whom?"

"Rick Rose."

"What kind of pressure?"

"The same kind of pressure he put all my children under when he questioned them. He told them that if they didn't tell what he wanted to hear or what they knew, they were going to be charged with murder."

"Are you referring to Phyllis's testimony that if she didn't sign the statement that she might be charged with murder?"

"Yes," Betty answered. "And that she didn't need an attorney and not to worry about it."

Bandy moved on to Betty's motive for the murder.

"Mrs. Beets, why did you think you were entitled to Jimmy Don Beets's retirement benefits after you disposed of the body?"

"I never felt like I was entitled to anything."

"Well, you made application back in February of '85, some sixteen or seventeen months after you reported him missing."

"At my attorney's request."

"He talked you into it?"

"Yes," she said, nodding.

"What were you going to do with the money?"

"I didn't expect it to be approved."

"Then why bother?"

"Because I didn't have Jimmy Don."

Betty's circuitous answers did nothing to move the testimony forward, but Bandy suspected that may have been her intent. His questions were met with only partial answers, or essentially non-answers.

Bandy called Fire Chief Hugh DeWoody, who had accompanied Marr to Betty's house, to verify Marr's testimony.

"Did you see Deputy Johnny Marr at the Henderson County Sheriff's Office on the morning of August 6, 1983?"

"Yes, Johnny told me about the possibility of a drowning and he was going to check it out. I accompanied him to Jimmy Don Beets's house to see if there actually was a drowning. We talked with Mrs. Beets."

"Did Mrs. Beets appear upset?"

"No, sir, she did not."

E. Ray Andrews couldn't let Betty's testimony rest on that note, so he recalled her.

"We have admitted your part of the murder, have we not?"

"You mean who contacted me first?"

Now it was Andrews's turn to be frustrated over not getting a straight answer. "No, now listen to me. I said that we admitted that you helped bury Mr. Beets."

"Yes."

"Put him under a planter, is that correct?"

"Uh-huh."

"And you heard Johnny Marr say that he was the first person who contacted you when they found Jimmy Don Beets's boat floating in the lake."

"It was the Coast Guard. I'm positive. But I know Johnny Marr."

E. Ray leaned over until he stood only inches from Betty's face, and spoke slowly through clenched teeth. "You're not understanding my question. Did you see the State put on any witness from the Coast Guard?"

"I don't remember all of their names. That lady from Redwood Marina called later, but this guy from the Coast Guard called first."

Bandy tried to sort some order out of Betty's answers. "You've heard Johnny Marr's and Captain DeWoody's testimony that they talked with you."

"I heard them say that, but they didn't talk to me Saturday morning."

"So you're saying that both men lied?"

"I'm saying that their testimony wasn't true."

Bandy shook his head and turned to another point. He asked, "What kind of work were you doing when Bobby got into the fight with Ray Bone?"

"I'm a barmaid and waitress. Ray came by to see me that night, but that was before he had the run-in with my son."

Andrews returned to redirect. "Okay, so we can be sure what Mr. Bandy is trying to establish here," he said to Betty. "You have a history of working in beer joints, is that correct? Tell this jury over here that you've worked in clubs before for a living."

Betty faced the jury. "Yes, I have," she said.

"And these clubs sell beer and mixed drinks. Are you ashamed of working in these clubs to support your family?"

"No, I'm not."

"Have you conducted yourself in a ladylike fashion?"

"Yes, I have."

Bandy tried to hide a smile before asking his first question on re-cross. "Were you conducting yourself in a ladylike fashion in Charlie's Angels Club at the time you got arrested for public lewdness?"

"I wasn't working. I never worked there. I was only auditioning that night."

"What kind of dance?" Bandy asked.

"It's a topless place," Betty replied.

Bandy decided that the lewdness testimony showed the true character of Betty Lou Beets and reasoned it a good place to end the trial. He said, "I have nothing else, Your Honor."

Judge Holland read the charge to the jury. Then told them they could find Betty Beets guilty of capital murder, murder, or not guilty.

DA Bandy stood to make his closing address. He went directly in front of the jury and paused a moment until every eye rested on him.

The jurors straightened in their chairs, waiting expectantly.

Bandy said, "The evidence that the prosecution presented was strictly on the guilt of Betty Lou Beets in the death of her husband. She did in fact shoot him for remuneration: his insurance policies, his estate, and his retirement benefits." Bandy retraced, step by step, all evidence placed into the court record, and emphasized the inconsistencies in Betty's testimony.

Betty whispered something to E. Ray, who jotted notes on a yellow tablet in front of him.

"Robby testified that his mother instructed him to leave the house on the night of August fifth. Now this is a domineering woman. She has a forceful personality." Bandy held up a picture of the wishing well. "This was taken on June eighth of this year. You can see it's well tended. Mr. Barker didn't fare too well; he had a storage shed placed over his grave.

"Now, Robby gets nominated as a killer. The worst thing Robby ever did was get into a neighbor's house, pled guilty and was placed on probation for taking some swords. And I think it's interesting that the lawyer, E. Ray Andrews, who represented him over there, used that same information to accuse him of this *murder!*" Bandy's voice rose to a crescendo as he thumped his fist on the wooden rail in front of the jury.

E. Ray sat quietly, staring off at something in the courtroom, appearing not to be interested.

Bandy reiterated Shirley Stegner's involvement in the death of Doyle Wayne Barker, emphasizing what a planner Betty had been, and what a conniving, greedy, self-absorbed woman she was. "He's been beating me, and if I get a divorce, I'll lose his trailer," Bandy quoted in a falsetto voice, then shook his head.

That line forced Betty to glare at the district attorney. "Now Betty says her son got into a fight with Jimmy Don Beets and she heard a shot. Just one shot. Now if there are two shots fired inside a house trailer, and there are two bullets found with the body, you're going to hear those shots from a .38.

"Now if two men are fighting," Bandy said, flailing his fists in front of him to demonstrate a fight, "it isn't likely that one of them is going to get shot in the *back* of the head," he said, pointing to his skull.

Bandy asked, "Did she try to do anything for Jimmy Don? Did she call an ambulance? Did she try to get someone to determine if this man, 'Whom I'm deeply in love with,' to see if he was really dead? No, she just put him in a sleeping bag and pushed him in the wishing well."

A juror sitting close to Bandy mouthed, "No," to each question.

"Lil Smith from the marina called her a brave woman. But what Betty Beets was is *cold*. Cold as a well chain throughout it all. She took all of this care of the yard and didn't know that Doyle Wayne Barker was buried in that yard?" Bandy said with sarcasm. Now that he reached the end of his statement, his voice resounded like a Baptist preacher's. "That's tragic! It's horrifying! It's shocking that such a crime as that could be committed by someone residing among the God-fearing citizens of Henderson County, Texas.

"She's been brought to justice and the proof is there, and under the evidence I ask you to find her guilty of the offense of capital murder."

E. Ray Andrews stood slowly. This would be his only chance. He approached the jury, smiling, as if to say, "Remember, we're still friends? I'm the good ole boy from Henderson County." He stood by the rail, touching his fingers together, prayerlike. "Mr. Bandy would like you to believe that Robert and Shirley should be blessed for any of their actions or their testimony. He wants you to think they didn't do a thing in the world.

"The prosecution told you they were going to bring ninety-five people here to testify. They actually used about fifteen or twenty. Now, where are those other seventy people?" he said, gesturing toward the DA.

"Now you saw Robert Branson. Did you see him leaving here waving and smiling? God bless you, Mom. God bless you, Daddy." E. Ray smiled as he imitated Robby. But then he frowned, knitting his dark eyebrows together and said, "Robby's cold blooded. He admitted he was cold blooded [a fact not supported by Robby's testimony] and I subject him to you as a cold blooded killer.

"And the State brought in this other body over my objection. They couldn't prove a case against Jimmy Don Beets, so he's got to go out and bring in other things. He brought that in simply to inflame your minds. He's done that, but Bandy don't go back in the jury room with you. Thank the Lord.

"But remember Dr. Petty. He's a good doctor. We talked about that fracture in Jimmy Don Beets's skull. I asked him, 'Could that have been caused by a blow to the head in a fistfight?' He said, 'Yes.' When I passed the witness and Bandy asked, 'Could it be caused by a bullet?' Petty said, 'No.' You have the benefit to carry that back in the jury room.

"Robby Branson took the stand and admitted killing Jimmy Don Beets one time," he said, gesturing with his raised forefinger. "That's the only time he told the truth.

"Robby tells this old story about helping his mother. These lies that were repeated a few minutes ago. That just didn't happen. That old dog just won't hunt. Huh-uh. Have you ever seen anyone so cold blooded? Anybody that would turn on their mother that way? Then go out of this courthouse waving at people, waving at reporters, laughing and smiling."

E. Ray again insisted that Betty knew nothing of Jimmy Don's insurance and never pestered him or anyone to get her the proceeds, so he maintained that this couldn't have been a capital murder case.

"The State has no evidence whatsoever that put a gun in Betty Beets's hand. She didn't run, but took the witness stand and told you that she did her part in this to protect her macho-man, the liar. Who knows what a mother would do to protect her child? Robby wouldn't have a care in the world for his mother to rot in the penitentiary. It wouldn't bother him for them to put her on a table and put a needle in her arm."

One juror turned toward Betty, giving her a sympathetic glance.

"Now Ray Bone. Me and him's almost got into a little hassle up here," E. Ray said and grinned. "Convicted killer. He was *Bandy's* witness.

"Then we put Mrs. Beets on the stand and you heard Bandy asking that poor woman, how come you didn't cry? And how come you lied in the previous hearings? And she told you she lied to protect that waving, grinning cat, cold-blooded-killer son of hers.

"How come Betty Beets got up here? It's always been

my theory living in a rural area, being a country boy, that the jury wants to hear both sides.

"The DA did not prove every element of the indictment beyond a reasonable doubt. All he did was throw in red herrings. Red herrings about another body. Red herrings about fan-dancing auditioning. Just stick to the evidence of this case alone. That's how it should be tried.

"I have no doubt in my mind that you fair people in Henderson County will return a verdict of not guilty. I thank you very much."

Bill Bandy had been taking notes on E. Ray's closing. Now he laid down his pen, and went back to the front of the jury to make his final plea.

"Members of the jury. It's a strategy in law, if you don't have a defense, try the prosecutor."

The jurors smiled and nodded.

"Betty's plan hit a snag. Texas law has a seven-year waiting period before a missing person is presumed dead.

"What kind of wife would shoot her husband as he lay sleeping on their bed? What kind of mother would seek to pin the murder on her own child? What kind of person would turn this town into a killing ground?" Bandy's voice rose with each question, and the jurors hung on every word.

"There is a need for justice in this case, a strong need that calls out from Jimmy Don's family, his son, his mother and father. Those who loved him, from the men he worked with fighting fires. The men who turned out and looked for him so diligently. This case has been investigated, indicted, and it has been proved. Members of the jury, it is your responsibility, and I ask you to do your duty and find her guilty of capital murder."

The hushed courtroom sat silently after hearing Bandy's appeal. Then Judge Holland announced that since it was one P.M., they would take a lunch break. After lunch, the jury would begin its deliberations.

TWENTY-EIGHT

While the crowd of media and onlookers waited for the jury to reach its verdict, they wandered through the shops and walked past the businesses surrounding the courthouse. All the buildings on courthouse square are turn-of-the-century architecture, and built about that time or shortly thereafter. The structures have a look of heritage and stability about them. The largest buildings throughout Athens are not fancy shops or elaborate stores, but churches, some dating back to the nineteenth century. That influence marks the community, and some of the movers and shakers in Dallas trace their roots to Henderson County. One, Clint Murchison, became the first owner of the Dallas Cowboys football team, and Rita Clements, whose husband, Bill, was a Texas governor. Both men made their fortunes in oil.

Once word spread that the jury had reached a decision, those milling around the courthouse, and out on the spacious grounds surrounding the building, scrambled back inside to find a seat. In moments, they'd learn Betty's fate. The jury must have heard the snickers in the courtroom as Betty pretended to cry, but her attorney was E. Ray Andrews, and how many chosen jurors could have been his cult followers? He had won more than his fair share of serious felony cases.

Everyone waited expectantly as the somber-faced jurors, who had deliberated for six and a half hours, filed into the room. Judge Holland asked the jury if they had reached a verdict. The foreman nodded and handed the written verdict to the bailiff to take to the judge. He glanced at it for a second and asked Betty and E. Ray to stand.

The judge read, "We, the jury, find the defendant, Betty Lou Beets, guilty of the offense of capital murder as charged in the indictment."

Betty blinked, but showed no emotion. E. Ray muttered an expletive under his breath. Four of Betty's children sat in the courtroom, paralyzed by the news, and too numb to cry.

In Texas, the punishment phase is a separate procedure, and it would begin the following Monday. Judge Holland announced he'd sequester the jury as a cautionary act. Because Betty had been found guilty of a capital charge, the judge didn't want to take any chance that jurors would read the newspapers or be swayed by a friend or family member who held their own opinion without the benefit of having heard the testimony.

Judge Holland told the jury they'd be in the Holiday Inn all weekend. He looked at them sympathetically and said, "I hope it won't be too confining for you."

After Betty's verdict had been read, her same four children who had attended the verdict announcement—Faye, Connie, Phyllis, and Bobby—waited outside the courtroom for their mother to emerge. The courthouse had no way for the jury, defendant, or observers to leave other than through the double doors exiting to the main marble lobby. After the judge left, a deputy escorted the jury to the bus that would transport them to the Holiday Inn; then the large body of spectators filed out. Several minutes elapsed before Betty appeared in the doorway. Deputy Copeland held on to her arm; her wrists were still locked together.

Her children ran to her, sobbing, all trying to hug her at the same time. With everything that had transpired, they still loved their mother.

Reporters waited in the rear of the courtroom to grab comments from the families as they departed after the announcement.

Doyle Wayne Barker's sister, Peggy Campbell, appeared happy with the verdict. "I finally know how my brother died," she said.

Jimmy Don Beet's only son, Jamie, told reporters, "I think justice has been done. Now my dad can rest in peace."

A reporter approached a tired-looking Robert Branson, Sr., the father of Betty's children. "I just feel like this has been hell on the kids," he said.

No one had spoken in Betty's defense, so her oldest daughter, Faye Lane, stepped forward. "I know my mother didn't do this," she said. "I know down in my heart she's innocent. It was all an accident."

One of Judge Holland's clerks locked her files and headed toward her office door. It had been a long day because the jury's verdict hadn't been announced until nine P.M., and she wanted to go home. But when she reached the foyer outside her office, she stopped. She had never heard such crying in her life.

After Bobby Branson's sisters had left, he still clung

to Betty. "Mama, Mama," he sobbed. "They can't take you."

The clerk hid in the shadows, not wanting to intrude. Betty appeared stoic, but her son locked a hug around her neck that bent Betty toward him.

On the threshold of manhood, the seventeen-year-old cried like a baby. "Mama, tell me everything's gonna be all right. It's gotta be."

The clerk hid deeper in the shadows as she watched the pathetic scene unfold and listened to Bobby's heart-wrenching cries as they echoed down the hallways.

In the punishment phase the following Monday morning, Judge Holland charged the jury to answer two questions. The first: "Were all questions of the defendant's guilt of capital murder resolved beyond a reasonable doubt?" And the second; "Would the defendant commit future acts of violence and therefore constitute a continuing threat?"

Bandy again spoke first. He looked more formal today in a navy suit, and white-and-navy striped shirt. Adjusting his red tie as he stood to speak, he headed for the jury, maintaining that when they voted for the verdict, all questions of capital murder beyond a reasonable doubt were answered.

"Betty's act was deliberate with the reasonable expectation of death." He paced in front of the jury, then stopped and pointed at them, not in an accusatory way, but indicating, "You have the responsibility."

"You saw the evidence the investigators found on Jimmy Don Beets's body—two deliberate shots. Death was expected. She told her daughter Shirley that she was going to do this. Deliberate, planned, carried out without mercy," he said in even, measured tones, as if counting each of Betty's actions.

When he addressed the possibility of future acts of violence, Bandy said, "She told you of shooting Bill Lane twice. We know of the other two she killed. We must judge a person by their actions. She is a continuing threat of future acts of violence if given the opportunity. Members of the jury, I ask you to vote those questions 'yes.' "

E. Ray pulled himself out of his chair and slowly made his way toward the jury. His shirt collar lay wrinkled under his suit coat. Squinting, he said, "Both of those questions resolved Friday? Was all questions in your mind resolved? Then how come it took over six hours? No, all question was not resolved Friday. You had a job to do, but I certainly disagree. I heard a person say the other day, 'Can we go to church while we're at the Holiday Inn?' I would have liked to answer that question—yes, please go to church. You can correct a wrong here today. The burden of proof is still on the State of Texas. You can correct this wrong by reconsidering in favor of Mrs. Beets. When you get back there, I'm asking you to answer 'no' to both of those issues. Don't listen to anyone else. Can you find her guilty of capital punishment and live with it? Look in your heart and do the right thing. I have faith in you.

"Please don't take it that I'm scoldin' you for your decision on Friday. You can be back out here in forty-five minutes and rectify a mistake. Come back here and answer both of these questions 'no,' and let's stop this thing."

Bandy had one last chance in his rebuttal. He said, "The fact that it took you six and a half hours to arrive at the verdict speaks well for your sincerity. The issue of guilt of capital murder has been finally resolved. That's over with, so don't get that trip put on you. The answer to both of these issues must be 'yes,' unanimously. It's your case."

The jury came back in forty-five minutes, but not with the answers Andrews had requested. The judge read the jury's answer of "yes" to both questions as Betty stood listening; then he told her she could sit.

"The jury having found you guilty of capital murder in the punishment phase," Holland said, "the punishment is hereby assessed as death."

The reality of the decision finally struck Betty. "No," she screamed, "I didn't do it." She buried her face in her hands as E. Ray patted her back, then handed her a Kleenex.

Judge Holland had paused at her brief outburst, then continued. "You are remanded to the sheriff of this county to await the decision of the Texas Court of Criminal Appeals on the appeal of your case."

TWENTY-NINE

The reality of prison aged Betty Beets five years in the three months she'd been incarcerated. The gray hair around her face and her puffy eyes were easily noticed when she came back in January of 1986 to start appealing her murder conviction.

Three guards accompanied her from the women's prison, housed in the Mountain View Building, 150 miles away in Gatesville, Texas. She shared death row with three other inmates. One was Karla Faye Tucker, a sweet, pretty, and now religious woman. Tucker had been found guilty of hacking two people to death with a pickax during a robbery. The women made up a little more than one percent of the death row population.

Gatesville housed the women's death row in a red-brick building surrounded by a twelve-foot-tall chain-link fence topped with swirls of razor wire. Inside were six ivory painted cells, five by eight feet, with a red tile floor. In the dayroom, afghans were draped over benches, and books sat neatly stacked in bookcases, including one entitled *Why Do Women Kill?*

Each woman had her separate cell with a stainless-steel commode and mirror, but the four shared a shower and the dayroom. In the dayroom, Betty and the others painted blue eyes and red lips on faces of dolls, and sewed intricate dresses for them. Betty saw it as a way to make time go faster. A *Dallas Morning News* reporter described the process as "Dolls that are brought to life by women waiting for death."

The dolls sold for twenty-five dollars, but the inmates profited nothing from their efforts, save for the camaraderie of working together, as the revenue went directly to the Texas Department of Corrections.

A fenced recreation yard adjoined Betty's building. The soil of the yard had once held grass, but now was bare from the pacing of women's feet as they sweated out their appeals or waited for their execution dates to be announced.

Betty Beets needed a lawyer. She swore before Judge Holland that she had no money for an attorney. She didn't have money to pay an attorney at her murder trial and that was why the unusual compensation of her story rights went to E. Ray Andrews.

E. Ray now stood beside her. He still hadn't collected a penny on Betty's story, but he, along with Gil Hargrave, had offered to represent Betty at her appeal on a contingency basis. If her case was overturned, she'd still be eligible to receive the insurance and pension. If she lost, the county would pay the two defense attorneys. With the agreement that they wouldn't be paid until the aftermath of the appeal, Judge Holland appointed Andrews and Hargrave to represent her again.

Michael O'Brien felt confident about the outcome of Betty's appeal. He had read numerous criminal cases before writing her indictment based on the 1974 "Candy Man" case in Houston. He had copied that case's verbiage for Beets's indictment. The Candy Man case had traveled smoothly through every appellate court in the land, including the U.S. Supreme Court, and every time, the courts rejected the appeal. O'Brien had nothing to worry about, especially since the Candy-Man murderer, Ronald Mark O'Bryan, had already been executed before Betty's trial began.

On November 12, 1987, Michael O'Brien left the front entrance of the District Attorney's Office. One of the reporters, who routinely hung around the building, approached him as he walked down the steps.

"Mr. O'Brien, what's your opinion of the Criminal Appeals Court's decision to reverse Mrs. Beets's verdict?"

O'Brien thought the man was joking. "What's this all about?" he asked.

That's how Athenians learned of the appeals decision, and the entire community was thunderstruck. The Court of Criminal Appeals of Texas in Austin had rejected the trial court's findings that Betty Beets had killed for remuneration. On a vote of six to three, Judge Teague wrote the majority opinion for the appellate justices who took away Betty's death penalty.

The appellate court's thinking skirted the issue of killing for an expected future gain. They decided that killing for remuneration only applied to hired killers, and an individual couldn't hire himself to kill someone. The judges agreed with Betty that the prosecution offered no evidence to show that she had entered into an agreement to be paid for murdering Jimmy Don Beets. That required a third person.

DA Billy Bandy's overall reaction at first was disbelief. Then after thinking it over, he became madder than hell. A furious Billy Bandy condemned the court's ruling, and demanded a rehearing.

* * *

The grumbling started anew in Henderson County. Many people thought Betty didn't flee when she knew of her impending arrest because she had successfully slid through Wayne Barker's killing without a ripple. Her cockiness tripped her when the court found her guilty of murdering Jimmy Don Beets. Now again she felt untouchable with the appeals court canceling her execution.

The highly controversial and unpopular appeals decision received heated criticism from newspapers throughout the state. In a state where judges have to stand for reelection, they're forced to listen to the electorate. A Houston newspaper dug into the case and learned that none other than Judge Teague, an unpopular judge with the newspaper, had been the defense attorney for Ronald O'Bryan, the "Candy Man."

Giddy reporters pointed out that Teague never supported the death penalty, regardless of the circumstances. His previous client, O'Bryan, had no insurance on himself or his wife, but took out $100,000 policies on each of his small children before poisoning them. Obviously, the judge wanted to reverse the case any way he could so Betty could get off with her life.

Ten months later, in September of 1988, in a rare and precedent-setting move, and after many negative editorials and newspaper articles, the appeals court reversed itself.

Judge W. C. Davis said in the majority opinion, "We have examined this issue and now agree that the remuneration statute includes the killing of a person in order to receive a benefit like an insurance settlement on the life of a deceased victim."

* * *

Following along with her one-appeal-a-year schedule, Betty Beets's lawyers ambitiously took her case to the U.S. Supreme Court. The court refused to hear it, thus letting the reversal decision of the appeals court stand. Betty could now be executed. She'd be the first woman in Texas since the Civil War to die for her crime.

In 1989, as Betty waited for her execution date to be set, she began giving interviews to garner sympathy for her plight. Once described by newspapers as "sullen and haggard" at her arrest, now when she talked with the press, they said she had a softer look. Newspapers portrayed her gray hair as neatly coifed, and mentioned her "pink nail polish that matched her dark pink lip gloss." The papers made her seem more human, almost playful, by referring to the Garfield-the-cat scarf she wore around her neck with her prison whites.

Soon E. Ray Andrews became the target of Betty Beets's bitter attacks. "He gave me poor representation," she'd say to anyone who would listen. "He failed to tell me that the district attorney offered a life sentence in exchange for a plea of guilty."

A quick check with the court showed no such offer had been made.

But Betty continued. "E. Ray persuaded me to sign over the book and movie rights to my life, and wants to profit from my execution."

Asked by the *Dallas Morning News* to respond to Betty's tirade, E. Ray said, "I went overboard to help this lady. But if I were on death row, I might be grabbing at anything I could too." In August of 1989, the court granted E. Ray's motion to withdraw as Beets's attorney.

Betty's life continued to change. She found religion. "I've got Christ in my life," she told reporters. "Every night before I go to bed, I hold hands with my cellmates and pray; then we give each other a hug."

Two years after entering prison, she took classes and received her general equivalency diploma. Then she began correspondence courses in business and accounting.

After moving away from E. Ray's representation, Beets relied on a legal resource center from the University of Texas School of Law.

A dark hammer fell on Betty's life in August of 1989 when guards whisked her into Athens to appear again before Judge Holland. He announced that he had set November 8, 1989, for her execution date.

As she stood before his bench, Holland said, "You are to be taken to a room at some hour before sunrise as provided by law to be injected with a lethal substance."

Handcuffed and pale, Betty quietly turned to her jailers to be taken back to Gatesville.

Her daughter Faye Lane said, "I feel sick. It seems like things are speeding up and it may happen sooner than we thought."

Frantic to stop her execution, Betty Beets agreed with her new attorney, Eden Harrington, when she suggested filing a writ of habeas corpus to postpone the execution date. This step would also elevate her case to the federal level. Betty resurrected the argument that the prosecution had made a deal with her son Robby, and daughter Shirley, in exchange for their testimony against her.

DA Bill Bandy vehemently denied Betty's claim, but Ms. Harrington said she would file the writ, ordering that the person placed in custody be brought before the court. The court had the burden of proving why Betty

Beets was being imprisoned. Beets insisted that she had a witness who overheard the deal being made with her children.

Judge Holland received a menu of complaints from Harrington: Betty's children had testified only to obtain their release, Betty was mentally incompetent to stand trial at the time of her conviction, the judge had erred in his instructions to the jury, and he refused to grant a trial delay as requested by the defense.

Judge Holland had no recourse but to postpone Betty's death sentence and grant her attorney until January 1990, to file papers on the writ of habeas corpus.

The merry-go-round continued to twirl with the time-buying efforts of the convicted killer and her attorney. Their latest plan bought them almost a year, but on December 6, 1990, the U.S. Supreme Court again refused to hear Betty's case. That decision made Betty eligible for a new death sentence.

Beets and her attorney had to come up with a whole new scenario.

A psychologist came in from Denver to perform elaborate tests on Betty Beets in January 1991, at the request of her appellate attorneys.

Betty received the Minnesota Multiphasic Personality Inventory—a widely used, objective personality test, and the Weschler Adult Intelligence Scale. The psychologists searched back and found Betty's school and divorce records, and also her mother's mental records. Then they talked with people who knew Betty at different points in her life.

According to a neurological examination, there was still evidence that Betty suffered organic brain damage and serious hearing loss dating back to her bout with measles. Because Betty had achieved her GED since she had been incarcerated, the psychotherapists held she had received extra help in order to accomplish that feat.

Betty had many interviews with the psychologists. She told them, "My father beat me when I was a child, but he never sexually abused me."

The counselors wrote off her last response, insisting that Betty was in denial about her father, whom they considered a jealous man since he wouldn't let her attend school functions or date. They held that repressing her father's sexual abuse was consistent with Betty's personality pattern and subsequent relationships with men.

Beets continued telling them about her husbands. "It seemed like we had so many arguments and fought a lot. Maybe it was my migraine headaches, but whatever, I was too afraid to act.

"After my first husband ran off with a younger woman, I married Bill Lane because he'd provide a home for me and my children, and only a few days after we married, he began beating me. But what else could I do? I had all these children to care for."

Betty acknowledged having visual hallucinations and hearing a choir singing when no one was around. She also admitted being ashamed of working in bars, which the psychologists termed "indecent employment."

After hearing Betty's life story, the doctors determined that she was a battered wife with Post Traumatic Stress Syndrome. In early 1990, the psychologists readied a report for the court describing the syndrome as a situation where a murder isn't necessarily spontaneous with the abuse. A murder can occur when an abused person becomes stressed at a later time and then kills her abuser. The appeals attorneys were critical that no mental-health information or reports of abuse were presented at her initial murder trial.

The doctors concluded that Beets's physical and mental disabilities made her dependent on a man to help her pay her bills and provide emotional support. They also said, "Her drug and alcohol abuse was her attempt to self-medicate and reduce the intrusive thoughts and feelings of traumatic events. She exhibited strong dependency needs that caused her to be in relationships with men who abused her."

The sister of Bill Lane's first wife added credibility to Betty's claim. She told the doctors that, "Bill struck my sister on numerous occasions with violent force causing physical and emotional harm. He had a violent, ungovernable temper. He attacked her without provocation and used offensive language in the presence of others."

Bobby Branson signed a statement that when he was a small child he remembered Ronnie Threlkeld slapping Betty. On the statement, his signature closely resembled Betty's, with the same large, proud capital letters.

Bobby had lived with his mother longer than any of the other children and eagerly testified. He told her appeals attorneys, "I knew Wayne Barker real good. Every few days he'd hit Mama."

The claims became more elaborate and accusatory as family members heard of Betty's newly discovered memory and came forth with their own distant recollections, complete with colorful details.

Bobby remembered a time when Wayne Barker grabbed Betty by her hair. With the children present, "He stood in front of her with her hair in one hand, and hitting her with the other. She was all twisted up trying to get away, but couldn't. Wayne also used to threaten her all of the time. Mom bought a little tape recorder and held it to the phone for forty-five minutes. She said she planned to take it to court."

When quizzed about the tape, Bobby admitted, "I don't know what happened to it."

Even Faye Lane's husband got into the act of accusing Wayne Barker of beating Betty. He said, "I never saw

Wayne hit her because he was a coward—always hit her when no one was around to help. But I would see her afterwards, and I sure do remember her black eyes and bruised chins. Hell, there were even choke marks around her neck. I got so damn mad that I took pictures of her to use in court."

The eager appeals attorneys wanted to see the photographs. "Unfortunately," he told them, "I can't find any of them. Turned the house upside down, but couldn't find a one."

Betty Beets's attorney shopped around for an antideath-penalty judge. U.S. District Judge Robert Parker in Tyler, Texas, fit the description. He signed an order staying Betty's execution because her latest appeal characterized Mrs. Beets as being raped and tortured throughout her life. She also had been an alcoholic, and suffered brain damage because of the beatings.

In April 1991, after Judge Parker studied the appeal, he found that "ample evidence supported the original jury verdict." Also, he found no evidence that prosecutors offered leniency to Shirley and Robby in return for their testimony at their mother's trial.

However, he brought up a new wrinkle. He felt that Mrs. Beets's defense attorney, E. Ray Andrews, who had tried to collect the insurance benefits before the trial, "should have testified on her behalf rather than represent her at trial, because it related to an essential element of the State's charge of murder for remuneration. The court finds that counsel pursued a course of action inconsistent with his client's best interests."

Then after the judge criticized E. Ray, he said, "Andrews is well known to the court as a competent and tenacious criminal defense lawyer."

Bandy protested that any lawyer, after getting to know

all the details about his client, would invariably be a valuable witness in some phase of the trial.

Finally, the Fifth Circuit Court of Appeals in New Orleans came to E. Ray Andrews's aid by ruling he had no conflict of interest. But as with past appeals, the courts learned of new appeal points they wanted to examine. It became obvious that resolving Betty's case would take at least another three years.

THIRTY

District Attorney Billy Bandy had suffered from prostate cancer several years earlier, but it had been in remission. Now in 1992, the disease came roaring back with a vengeance. Cancer ate his body while chemotherapy burned away his thick curly hair. Bald and frail, he insisted on staying in his job, even when his associates had to help him to and from the courtroom. Sometimes Bandy would be forced to ask for a five-minute recess.

The courthouse staff knew about his current chemotherapy treatment, which made him nauseous, and his need to go to the bathroom and throw up. He died on May 19, 1992.

To fill Bandy's unexpired term, Texas Governor Ann Richards appointed lifelong Democrat, E. Ray Andrews. At first, E. Ray did a good job. His charismatic way of dealing with people proved effective, and he hired conscientious employees who proficiently performed their tasks.

When time came to elect a new Henderson County District Attorney, E. Ray ran for the position. His opponent took out newspaper space and tried to tell everyone how E. Ray, while in private practice, left some of his clients hanging in the wind without fulfilling his contractual agreements. He also reminded voters that E.

Ray had once been sanctioned and couldn't practice law for two months, had a DWI on his record, and frequently didn't pay his bills.

Andrews could not challenge his accuser, for he told the truth, but E. Ray promised to "clean up my act." He'd stop drinking and pay full attention to his position. Wanting to believe him, the electorate gave E. Ray forty-one more votes than his opponent.

The following year, a three-judge panel of the Fifth Circuit Court finally made its decision regarding E. Ray Andrews's failure to testify in Betty's case. The essence of the court's thirty-four-page report stated, "Our review of the record convinces us that Andrews's failure to testify did not, and could not have adversely affected Beets's defense."

It somewhat vindicated E. Ray's representation of Betty. The court also said, "Mrs. Beets apparently never gave Mr. Andrews reason to suspect she had physical or psychological problems." However, in a footnote it suggested, "The State Bar might look into Mr. Andrews's 'apparent breach of his ethical obligations.' "

Once again, a court had reinstated Betty's death sentence.

In 1994, Betty's youngest son and the love of her life, Bobby, was run over by a car while he strolled down the sidewalk. She was devastated.

At the hospital's emergency room, doctors found that he had no broken bones, but was brain dead. Her family generously arranged to donate his eyes, heart, lungs, liver, and kidneys. The tragedy moved Betty to begin writing poetry that expressed her sorrow, for she suffered more pain than if she had been given an execution date.

While serving as the DA, E. Ray Andrews began doing favors for his friends, such as forgiving speeding tickets. Then he left the scene of an accident after slamming his Oldsmobile into a closed gas station with an empty bottle of Wild Turkey in his car.

Two years after becoming DA, in July 1994, Andrews resigned. "I just don't want no more of the cheese," he said of his turbulent DA career. "I want out of the trap."

E. Ray must have seen the writing on the wall, for he had slipped out of office only one month before FBI agents hauled him off in handcuffs.

Athens buzzed with the news of E. Ray's arrest, a man they genuinely liked, but knew had a black side. They called him "a heck of a campaigner, a talented lawyer when sober, and a real witty and friendly guy who had a winning way about him." A fellow worker said E. Ray would come late to work; other days he'd leave early; and then sometimes he didn't show at all. Everyone agreed that his downhill slide was a self-inflicted tragedy.

E. Ray had talked a friend into approaching a Corsicana businessman who had been indicted for murdering his wife, and to tell him that DA Andrews would drop the indictment for $500,000.

Once the businessman heard of the bribe, he told his attorneys, who immediately reported it to the FBI. The suspected murderer and the FBI collaborated to trap Andrews. With the FBI listening and recording the phone conversation, the businessman negotiated a new price of $300,000 for Andrews's service. The next day, the man placed $100,000 in Andrews's safety-deposit box. Later, the court dismissed the businessman's murder indictment after his attorneys argued that the district attorney's conduct had tainted the proceedings.

In that same year, E. Ray's wife of thirty-two years divorced him, the bank foreclosed on his four-thousand-square-foot house on the peaceful shores of Lake Athens, and took away his Mercedes.

Andrews pleaded guilty to violating the federal Hobbs Act and was sentenced to forty-two months in a federal prison.

In 1995, Betty Beets used E. Ray's fall from grace as a new attempt to save her life. Arguing incompetent counsel, Betty had her attorney petition the Fifth U.S. Circuit Court of Appeals to say that E. Ray Andrews should have resigned as her defense attorney in order to testify on her behalf.

The court's decision came swiftly. It held that E. Ray's testimony would not have made much difference in Betty's defense, since another witness had testified that Betty was unaware of her husband's death benefits before she met with Mr. Andrews. The court had heeded the testimony of Chaplain Denny Burris at Betty's trial, recalling that Betty didn't know the amount of Jimmy Don's insurance.

Betty again pleaded to the Fifth U.S. Circuit Court of Appeals under the guise that twenty-three of her constitutional rights had been violated. Judge Hannah studied them, including her right to competent counsel, and denied each one. Now her case would return to Henderson County for Judge Holland to set another execution date.

That threat came much closer when the court set the execution date of Betty's friend, Karla Faye Tucker. On

February 4, 1998, Karla Faye, and not Betty, became the first woman in Texas to be executed since the Civil War. Thousands of people congregated outside the Walls Unit at Huntsville to protest her execution.

Up until then, the public thought the state didn't have the stomach for executing women. Tucker's death cast a pall over the women on death row. Not only had they lost a friend, but they could hear the bell tolling for their own deaths as well.

In the meantime, Attorney Joseph Margulies of Minneapolis took up Betty's fight. He returned her case to the Fifth Circuit Court of Appeals to rehear an earlier ruling by the district court. Unfortunately for Betty, the court only reaffirmed the earlier ruling that upheld her death sentence. With that, the judges closed the appeals process at the circuit court level.

Beets had but one recourse—the U.S. Supreme Court. Her team of attorneys stretched the ninety-day time limit to buy their client a few more weeks, then filed their petition during the first week of December, 1999.

THIRTY-ONE

The explosion of notoriety around Betty Beets's trial could be considered a teaspoonful compared to the clamor as her execution drew near.

As soon as the U.S. Supreme Court decided not to hear Betty's case, Judge Holland set February 24, 2000, as her new execution date. Everything moved much faster than expected. But in a way, it had taken an eternity—almost fifteen years of appeals.

Publicity-shy Betty became a sought-after celebrity. Reporters from the major television networks interviewed her on death row, and television's legal minds and guest attorneys discussed her case daily.

Betty became a champion of abused women and now professed that *all* of her husbands had abused her, in addition to her father. Once getting everyone's attention, she added that her mother and grandmother had been abused as well. As usual, she offered no proof, but that didn't matter. Her followers believed her anyway.

Now a notable on the Internet with a page for abused women, Betty wrote a three-part story of her life. She told how she had been raped and abused, dragged out in a field and strangled, then left for dead. She pushed her hearing impairment as the weakness that had made her so vulnerable.

When former DA investigator Michael O'Brien was asked about Betty's hearing, he said, "She didn't have hearing aids in when I told her I had a search warrant to go out to her yard and dig up bodies. She had no trouble hearing that."

Her stories had a religious tone and she professed that God worked a miracle for the nonbelievers, saying, "I am God's miracle." Her Internet web page displayed her address where fans could write. And write they did. Internet viewers gushed: "We're praying for you, Betty. You're a wonderful person. Your strength has changed my life."

Her hardworking attorney, Joe Margulies, filed petitions on February 5 with both the U.S. Supreme Court and the Fifth Circuit Court of Appeals for a restraining order to prevent the execution.

The author of *Dead Man Walking*, Pulitzer Prize–winner Sister Helen Prejean, visited Betty Beets on death row for two hours and found her very sincere. Then the nun toured the country making speeches on Beets's behalf, urging people to write Texas Governor George W. Bush and ask him to stay her execution. Jesse Jackson wrote the governor, asking him to demonstrate his "passionate conservatism" by staying Betty's execution.

A week before her scheduled injection, *Good Morning America* ran footage of their death-row interview with a sad-looking Betty Beets peering through her glass-enclosed visitor's booth. Their reporters caught Governor Bush that day as he campaigned for the Republican presidential nomination and asked him if he intended to give the great grandmother a thirty-day stay. However, the governor bought into Betty's more recent testimony that all of her actions stemmed from a lifetime of abuse, and called violence in the home "a terrible scourge" and insisted the courts deal more sternly with offenders.

A taped video of Betty's oldest daughter, Faye Lane, appeared almost hourly on television channels. She held a photograph of her mother with a bruised jaw and a black eye. The picture depicted a younger Betty, most likely from the 1970s when she had been married to Billy Lane. The family gave no proof that any abuse occurred at the hands of Robert Branson, Wayne Barker, or Jimmy Don Beets.

Burden of Proof with Greta Vansustern, picked the minds of Betty Beets's two appeal attorneys, in addition to a criminal defense lawyer. The one-sided argument overlooked the evidence. Beets's attorney stated that her purchasing the $10,000 J. C. Penney life insurance policy on Jimmy Don's life shouldn't have raised eyebrows, since she also bought one for herself, naming Jimmy Don as the beneficiary. Had he checked more thoroughly, he would have learned that Betty had bought a $5,000 policy for herself, but named her son Bobby as beneficiary.

Geraldo Rivera, on his television show *Rivera Live,* had one of the more balanced shows. He involved Attorney Marcia Clark of O. J. Simpson fame. Ms. Clark had taken the time to learn the facts of Beets's case. However, that was somewhat negated when she was caught on camera sticking out her tongue at another panelist, Lenore Walker, Ph.D., who had testified for O. J. at his trial. The architect of the "Battered Wife Syndrome," Dr. Walker purported that the malady causes abused women to become helpless to act.

CNN carried nightly countdowns, while every newspaper in the country printed a photo of a sobbing Betty Beets. The *New York Times* devoted a half page of picture and newsprint to her.

The day before Betty Beets's execution, reporters found Governor Bush on the campaign trail in California.

"I'll be back in Austin tomorrow to study the Beets's case with my staff," the governor told reporters.

"Here's what I'll be looking at," Bush said. "Is she guilty of the crime? Did the jury know all the circumstances? Did the appeals court have all the circumstances related to her case?"

The governor received over five hundred letters from anti-death-penalty protesters to grant Betty's stay, and only a handful asking for her execution, mostly from the families of the victims. He vowed to wait until the Texas Board of Pardons and Paroles met to decide Betty's fate.

On the day of her execution, Texas radio stations broadcast a minute-by-minute countdown to Beets's six P.M. date with death. Crowds began gathering outside the Walls Unit in Huntsville, an ancient three-story building on Twelfth Street and Avenue One. A huge clock, made of black metal numbers and hands, was bolted to the outside of the redbrick building and counted the last minutes of Betty's life.

Every major news media in the country crammed their disc-crowned vans into the parking lot. Betty had been transferred that morning from Gatesville to Huntsville, and spent the afternoon visiting with family and friends. Prison chaplain Gary Mayfield dropped by to pray with her.

The anti-death-penalty advocates arrived with placards showing the abused-Betty photo Faye Lane had exhibited on television.

Some of the posters were printed with a Texas Council on Family Violence quote: "Beets' life is a chronicle of virtually uninterrupted physical, sexual and emotional abuse. She was severely abused as a child and was battered by multiple husbands. Beets suffers from severe learning disabilities and a hearing impairment she has had since early childhood. She also suffers from organic brain damage caused by repeated blows at the hands of abusive men."

The protesters rallied around the Battered Wife Syndrome, to the point of excusing murder. Their posters read: DON'T KILL BATTERED WOMEN, and WHAT MY HUSBANDS STARTED, TEXAS WILL FINISH.

The media strolled through the crowd with microphones on extended poles. People visiting in small groups would suddenly look up to see a microphone dangling inches over their heads, not realizing their conversations were subjected to technical eavesdropping.

One woman, garbed in a long black dress, black hat, and wearing white makeup with white lipstick, wore a sign around her neck depicting a thorn-crowned, bleeding Jesus. The caption read: JESUS CHRIST—VICTIM OF THE DEATH PENALTY. Another described Governor Bush as a serial killer because he had signed the execution orders on 120 murderers since he took office. Others unfurled a cloth banner with a huge green injection needle on it.

At five P.M., Margulies announced that both the U.S. Supreme Court and the Fifth Circuit Court of Appeals had denied his petitions for restraining orders.

Shortly after that, the Texas Pardons and Parole Board voted down a stay. Then word came from the governor's mansion thirty minutes before Betty Beets's execution. Bush had decided to not extend Beets's life.

As the clock crept closer to six P.M., the crowd grew and the assembly took on a circus atmosphere. College students gathered for the experience, not particularly caring one way or another about Betty Beets, but treating the execution as a happening.

A few moments before six P.M., the witnesses to the execution marched silently and single file past grim-faced guards and Texas Rangers into the building that housed the death chamber. Betty had asked her family not to attend, for she wanted only her spiritual adviser, Paul Carlin, and attorney, Joe Margulies.

The same number of friends of the perpetrator were invited as the families of the victims. Even though no chairs were provided, there was not enough standing room for all of the victims' families who wanted to attend. Some of them were looking for closure. Jamie Beets, being more realistic, said he had forgiven Betty, and only wanted it all to end.

Five media representatives were invited, including the Associated Press and United Press International. One place was reserved for a reporter from the county in which the crime took place. Gary Bass, a young reporter for both the *Athens Daily Review* and the *Cedar Creek Pilot,* received the nod.

While the execution began inside, a handsome, young preacher stood outside and raised his hand to quiet the gathering near the Walls. "Dear, Father," he said. "We pray for mercy for those carrying out this heinous act. We ask that Betty finds peace . . ." To listen to him, the murderer was the victim, law enforcement the villain, and the public held the responsibility for ending the madness.

The minister urged everyone to work for a moratorium on the death penalty. Someone in the crowd muttered, "What about a moratorium on murder?"

Inside the death chamber, the reporters divided themselves between the two viewing rooms. Gary Bass followed behind Beets's minister and lawyer.

Bass stood before a large window that separated the viewers from Beets by only five feet.

The vivid green death chamber measured six by eight feet, just large enough for a white-covered gurney, plus a doctor and the warden of the Walls Unit. The executioner, a prison employee who would add the deadly poisons to Beets's intravenous solution, stayed hidden behind a partition.

Bass noticed a set of wooden steps under the gurney and wondered if Beets, looking small and frail, had to climb them to get onto her deathbed. He recalled interviewing her three weeks before on death row. She was friendly and could have passed for anyone's grandmother. Then he also remembered that her demeanor had changed when he pointed out the inconsistencies in her story about what had happened to her fourth and fifth husbands. The tears stopped, her eyes narrowed, her gaze grew a little colder, and she became more intense. At that moment he saw the cold-blooded killer—two sides of the same coin.

By the time onlookers had entered the viewing room, Betty Beets lay strapped to the gurney. One strap crossed her chest, others held down her wrists and ankles, as she lay there in white prison scrubs and blue canvas deck shoes. An IV had been inserted into each arm. Twice Beets glanced at the victims' families, but made eye contact with no one.

Then she turned to the room where Bass stood and he saw her cold blue eyes stare at him. As her gaze passed over him, he felt the hairs on the back of his neck stand up—and he knew he'd remember that fleeting moment for the rest of his life.

The warden asked Beets if she wanted to make a last statement. She calmly shook her head, seemingly resigned to her fate. By doing that, she denied the victims' families that one last concession, that one last olive branch of peace. There would be no last-second confessions, just stoic silence.

She gave her attorney a small, melancholy smile as he placed his hand on the window and mouthed, "It'll be all right."

As the lethal injection began flowing into her veins, Beets coughed twice and gasped. She sputtered as if something was caught in her throat. Then she closed her eyes and slipped into unconsciousness, appearing to be asleep. For a few moments, her chest continued to rise and fall; then it stopped and her complexion grew pale.

At that point, Carlin removed his glasses and sobbed briefly, his burly shoulders slumped in defeat. As he wiped his eyes, he softly said, "The Bible says to be absent from the body is to be present with the Lord."

In the other room, both families of the victims held hands, forming one large group during the entire ordeal.

A long, profound silence descended. Then at 6:18, the doctor beside Betty Beets placed a stethoscope on her chest. Seconds later, he nodded to the warden. "She's dead."

Quietly, the families filed out to an anteroom where they held a brief group hug before leaving the Walls Unit.

Afterward, the witnesses strolled somberly down the ramp, except for Rodney Barker, who felt the weight of a truckload of bricks leave his shoulders. The execution of Betty was a catharsis for him. She had withheld his father from him in his teenage years, then permanently took away the father he had loved. Rodney shot up his arms in a victory salute. For him, nineteen years of grief and misery had come to an end.

Then he and Jamie Beets went to the conglomeration of microphones and spotlights to tell the waiting reporters and the world what good men their fathers had been.

A reporter roamed the crowd of onlookers and antideath-penalty protesters as word leaked out that the execution had taken place. He noticed a young woman with tears running down her cheeks.

The reporter, who had researched the details of Betty Beets's case so he could write about her, walked over to the woman and whispered in her ear, "Don't cry for Betty. Cry for the families whose fathers she killed, and cry for her own children who she turned into accomplices to murder."

ACKNOWLEDGMENTS

Writing a true story of two murders that took place over fifteen years ago forced me to search out many people, asking them to recall minute points of their experiences with Betty Lou Beets. I found an outpouring of detailed information and a certainty that no one had forgotten her. The dialogue and scenes have been reconstructed from these interviews, in addition to the court transcripts and signed documents obtained by investigators for the District Attorney and Sheriff.

I am indebted to the following for their help.

Judge Jack H. Holland of the 173rd District Court generously opened all trial transcripts and court records to me, and I had the gracious cooperation of Jovanna Herrington and Kim Gabel from the district clerk's office.

The Dallas Fire Department, for whom Jimmy Don Beets was a captain, cooperated fully. Thanks to Chief Tanksley, Captain James Blackburn and his wife, JoAnn, Chaplain Denny Burris, and Stu Grant from the Dallas Firefighters Museum.

Without former Henderson County Sheriff's Chief Investigator Rick Rose, who broke this case, this book would have been an impossible task. Rick generously gave me his insight, along with detailed recollections of an investigation that lay for two years until he grasped the reins. His counterpart in the Henderson County District Attorney's Office, Michael O'Brien, continuously amazed me with his photographic memory. Mike was invaluable in explaining the legal ramifications and details of the case, as well as the investigation from the DA's perspective. Karen Warner Hewitt, also a former DA investigator, provided me with the emotional side of dealing with Betty Beets. Karen remembered how Betty's mere presence could decrease the temperature of a room.

Henderson County Sheriff's Deputy Ron Shields put me in contact with many important investigators in this case.

Suzy Beets Huffman spoke openly of her ex-husband, and gave me insights only she could provide. Ronnie C. Threlkeld, Betty's third husband, shared memories of his life with her. Rodney Barker and his wife, Carla, talked with me. Rodney's father, Doyle Wayne Barker, was Betty's first victim, and Rodney related his memories of a loving father.

Others deserving mention are Jerry Kuykendall, Jr., Dwayne Garner, Mansfield Police Chief Steve Noonkester, Ed Spencer with the Dallas County Sheriff's Department, and criminalist Michelle Pressley.

Many people shared their personal remembrances, but asked that their names not be used. However, I want them to know how much I appreciated their time.

Dallasite and Cedar Creek homeowner Peggy Baldwin was very helpful. Barbie and Mason Brown crossed over the line of friendship and frequently hosted me in their lovely lake home, giving me hours of information. Barbie is an expert on Cedar Creek Lake lore, weather, flora, and fauna.

Friend and historical-romance writer Julie Benson combed my manuscript, making many beneficial suggestions. Fellow true-crime writer Carlton Stowers shared invaluable resources.

While I stood outside the Walls at Huntsville, Texas, a talented journalist, Gary Bass, was inside witnessing Betty Beets's execution and related the emotional details to me. Gary, I am grateful.

Praise for my friends at Kensington: Editor in Chief Paul Dinas, and Consulting Editor Karen Haas. After three books, we have a comfortable relationship. And I always appreciate my creative agent, Janet Wilkens Manus.

BOOK YOUR PLACE ON OUR WEBSITE AND MAKE THE READING CONNECTION!

We've created a customized website just for our very special readers, where you can get the inside scoop on everything that's going on with Zebra, Pinnacle and Kensington books.

When you come online, you'll have the exciting opportunity to:

- View covers of upcoming books
- Read sample chapters
- Learn about our future publishing schedule (listed by publication month *and author*)
- Find out when your favorite authors will be visiting a city near you
- Search for and order backlist books from our online catalog
- Check out author bios and background information
- Send e-mail to your favorite authors
- Meet the Kensington staff online
- Join us in weekly chats with authors, readers and other guests
- Get writing guidelines
- AND MUCH MORE!

**Visit our website at
http://www.pinnaclebooks.com**